S. W. Felch.

1857.

# THE
# DIVINE LAW OF BENEFICENCE;

# ZACCHEUS,

OR

# THE SCRIPTURAL PLAN OF BENEVOLENCE;

AND

# THE MISSION OF THE CHURCH,

OR

# SYSTEMATIC BENEFICENCE.

# THE DIVINE

# LAW OF BENEFICENCE

BY REV. PARSONS COOKE,

LYNN, MASSACHUSETTS.

Remember the words of the Lord Jesus, how he said, It is more blessed to give than to receive.—ACTS 20 : 35.

PUBLISHED BY THE

AMERICAN TRACT SOCIETY,

150 NASSAU-STREET, NEW YORK.

# CONTENTS.

# THE DIVINE

# LAW OF BENEFICENCE.

## I. GOD'S DESIGN IN REQUIRING BENEFICENCE.

God is not dependent on us for the support of his poor. He could have so diffused the gifts of his providence as to have had no poor. Or he could so have fitted our frames to the world, and the world to them, that all the elements of human life and comfort would have been as abundant and free as air and water, so that, like the lilies of the field, the whole human race might meet every want without toil or spinning; and he might have published his gospel to every creature without our aid. He might have made his angels, in another sense, "ministering spirits, sent forth to minister to the heirs of salvation." Or he might have written out the whole on the face of the heavens, and made them in a higher sense "declare the glory of God;" and made it in a higher sense true, that "their line is gone out through all the earth." He does not ask us to do this work or that, because of any dependence on us. He says, "Every beast of the forest is mine, and the cattle upon a thousand hills. If I were hungry I would not tell thee, for the world is mine and the fulness thereof."

Whatever necessity there is of our agency he has purposely laid, in the present arrangement of things, *for our good*. His benevolence could have reached its object without our concurrence, if it had not made us also its object, and formed the design of blessing us in its course by enlisting us as coworkers. He knew that it was "more blessed to give than to receive." And when he put in motion the broad mechanism of his mercy, he put upon it laws of action and reäction, and made the work of heavenly charity, in all its branches, twice blessed—blessing him that gives, and him that takes. He laid on us a necessity of cultivating benevolent affections. If we could so arrange one's circumstances, and throw around him such influences, as to keep him habitually and constantly giving to the poor—if we could attach to him dependent relatives, or in some other way bring to act upon him a constant succession of calls that he would not resist, we should bring him under the best means of cultivating benevolent dispositions; and this is what God does with us, in laying on us this necessity of giving alms.

The fact that he could have published the gospel and fed his poor without us, while he could not, without our concurrence in giving, secure to us the blessedness which attaches to those that give, indicates that his main design in laying on us the necessity of giving, was *to give scope to our benevolent affections.* For this end he has ordained that we shall have the poor with us always, in so many forms of human distress besetting our path, pleading at the bar of our conscience for the forth-puttings of that charity which is the high excellence of our nature. Yea, he has placed all the interest which we have in evangelizing the world on such a footing, that it will advance no further than his redeemed people pour forth the means of its advance; that in that forth-pouring the church may take in those riches of grace in which the whole work of redemption has its termination. In other words, he will not have the evangelizing of the world advance faster than the sanctifying of his church; and will sustain a reciprocal action between the two, advancing together.

Nor do we exaggerate in presenting this as the *main* ground of what necessity there is for alms-giving; for all the ends of redemption accomplished upon man are comprehended in his renovation from a state of supreme selfishness to that of perfect benevolence; and if we should say that all these occasions for benevolent action were created for the sole purpose of furnishing means of exercising men to benevolence, we should not make the means disproportionate to the end. The whole work of Christ, his humiliation, ministry, death, resurrection, and mediatorial government, the whole work of his gospel and his Spirit, and all the enforcements of his providence look to this end. We speak therefore not without warrant, when we say that all the human suffering that now pleads for human charity, and all the heathen darkness that lingers upon the nations for human benevolence to enlighten, is suffered to exist, among other purposes, as a means of developing Christian character.

But let none imagine that *the necessity* for giving alms is on that account the less real. Divine wisdom has appointed it, and made it as unchangeable and imperious as if God himself were bound by it. The poor that God has cast upon the charity of men will inevitably suffer and die, if men do not feed them. The people that are perishing for lack of vision will continue to perish, until Christian men convey to them the light of life. God will not lay this work on men for wise reasons, and then send down his angels to take it out of their hands. It is by establishing such an order of things, and sustaining it after he has established it, that he gives reality and force to the motives to benevolence, and to the means of drawing out and strengthening benevolent affections. And all his purposes to secure the sanctification of his people and the whole ends of his redemption, will lead him to an inflexible support of this order of things.

The sum of the matter thus far is this, that God throws on us his poor, for the purpose of enriching us.

He sends the poor, as the representative of himself, and of the cause of his gospel, out to begging of us, and so, as it were, repeats the act of his humiliation, that the din of their solicitations ever sounding in our ears, and the sighs of a ruined world borne on every breeze, may draw forth from us those benevolent emotions and acts that shall more and more assimilate us to him "who, though he was rich, yet for our sakes became poor." God takes the place of man: in his poor he asks, and man bestows; that in bestowing, man may accumulate the true riches—more precious than gold, which perishes. It is God himself who asks; and our enriching with grace is the end for which he asks. He asks in the only way in which he could test and exercise our benevolence. For this purpose he must needs ask as a beggar, and not as a king. Should he come to us in regal splendor or heavenly glory, his asking would be a command, which we should not dare to disobey; but our giving would be no act of compassion or benevolence. But now he comes to us in the person of his poor—he comes as the king dethroned and dependent—banished from heaven, covered with rags, pining in want—he comes uttering the tale of misery and real suffering, unless we afford relief. And now what we give is given by the promptings of compassion, and from no sordid motives. Here is both a proof and exercise of benevolence. Yet, to enforce his calls, he gives us to know that it is He that speaks and pleads for compassion, through the open wounds and uttered agonies of dying men; and that every donation shall be acknowledged by him in person when he shall come in the glory of his Father, with all the holy angels, and say to every one who has exercised compassion on his poor, "Inasmuch as ye did it unto one of the least of these, ye did it unto me." It is not for his good but ours, that he thus beggars himself, and pleads as a beggar before us. "Our goodness extends not to him." A wise father often draws out the dispositions of his child by bestowing gifts and then soliciting a portion in return, or getting proxies to solicit for him, anxious to open the child's heart to an expansive generosity. So Christ clothes himself in rags and casts himself on our compassion, for no purpose so much as to give us the reflex benefit of our own benevolent acts.

And here we wish it to be specially remarked, that this design appears prominent in the manner in which the duty of alms-giving is inculcated in Scripture. Like the other graces, this charity seems to be insisted on *for its own sake*—not because there is so much suffering to be relieved, but because it is good and right for us to engage in its relief. God will have us give, not of necessity, but from the spontaneous flowings of the heart. "Every man *according as he purposeth in his heart*, so let him give: not grudgingly, or of necessity; for God loveth a cheerful giver." Almost in every instance, you will observe, the duty is enforced from higher grounds than the fact that here is so much suffering to be relieved. In one case we are exhorted to "do good and communicate, for with such sacrifices *God is well pleased.*" In another, we are prompted to remember "the grace of our Lord Jesus Christ, who, though he was rich, yet for our sakes became poor." In another, the parity of reason drawn from the other graces is urged · "Therefore as ye abound in every thing, in faith, and utterance, and knowledge, and in all diligence, and in your love to us, see that ye abound in this grace also." In another case it is, "Freely ye have received, freely give." In another, "Give alms of such things as ye have, and all things shall be clean unto you," as if charity were the centre in which all virtues meet. When the poor Christians at Jerusa lem were in great suffering, and the apostles went round to solicit relief of Gentile churches, their inspired letters, sent here and there, contained no rhetorical painting of the distresses to be relieved. In all that they said, there appears next to nothing adapted to draw upon the natural sympathies. In this work they seem to be laboring with a single eye to the sanctification of the Christians of whom they asked relief—as if no relief was wanted. The fact that God was to be glorified, and the hearts of men were to be sanctified, was their main argument. One of the most distinct references to the distress was this: "For the administration of this service not only supplieth *the want* of the saints, but is abundant through many *thanksgivings to God.*" And here the revenue of praise to God is the great consideration absorbing the other.

Now, for a right appreciation of the views which we are to present, this fact, that man's sanctification for the glory of God is the main design of the scriptural provisions for alms-giving, and the main thing aimed at in the methods in which the Scriptures inculcate the duty, should be kept well in view; for by overlooking it we have lost a principle that is the key to the understanding of this portion of the Scriptures.

## II. THE OLD TESTAMENT LAW OF CHARITY

From the foregoing remarks, it may appear that a habit of charitable giving holds a higher place in the divine method for saving a lost world, than most have realized; and the Christian who is wont to ask, "Lord, what wilt thou have me to do?" may be expected to go to the Scriptures, not to find there the vague doctrine that he ought to be occasionally generous, and generally charitable, but something that will inform him why, and how he shall do it. And he will find that, both in the Old Testament and in the New, it is made a matter of distinct command, not that we shall do occasional acts of benevolence, when the appeal is too strong to be resisted, or the public sentiment allows of no evasion, but that we shall enter upon *a series of periodical acts of self-denial for the good of others;* and thus sustain a system and fixed habits of giving Whatever diversity there may be between the Old Testament and the New, they agree in this, that both, by express precept, require habits of periodical appropriations from our income to sustain religion and feed the poor. And they require that the habit of doing this should be as much a part of the character of the children of God, as the habit of prayer. They require a man not simply to hold himself in a position to be as it were forced to give now and then for the relief of distress, but to enter on the formation of an active character of beneficence, by keeping in constant flow a stream of bounties, lesser or larger, in proportion to his means.

Alms-giving did not originate with the Mosaic economy. There appears to have been a standing custom of giving gifts for religious ends, as an act of homage to God and benevolence to man, long before the Mosaic system was framed. Abram gave tithes to Melchizedek, the priest of the most high God. The custom is fully recognized in the book of Job. Jacob at Bethel vowed to give a tenth. And the principle of giving gifts under religious obligation is doubtless as ancient as religion itself—coëval with that of sacrifices in the family of Adam. And this may account for the early and wide diffusion which it had among all heathen nations. And though neither the customs of the patriarchal ages, nor the institutions of Moses are binding on us, they may serve to illustrate God's general plan of dealing with his people. He having his chosen nation before him in the wilderness, and about to enter upon the land flowing with milk and honey, put them under such laws as might bind them, as far as laws could bind, to a periodical series of acts that would counterwork their selfishness, foster their sense of dependence, and cultivate their love to God and man. These laws are found inwoven with the Mosaic ritual; and in their general design they concur with the New Testament law of charity. They required gifts to be made at stated times, often recurring, to insure the formation of the habit, and not to let the heart, opened by one gift, have time to close up before it opened for the next.

As to the amount required, there was as much definiteness as was needful to guide to a generous result, and as much as consisted with the other ends of the requirement; while room was left for the heart and conscience to play between different degrees of generosity. The nature of an act of charity requires some liberty of determining when and how much to give. If our Lord, after the purchase of our redemption, had written and hung out upon the skies a tariff, adjusting each one's tax for charities to his income, so that he might see at a glance that his

Redeemer required him to give just so many dollars and cents, he would have brought the requirement down to bind the conscience. But he would have constructed a system of *taxation*, rather than of charity. That would have changed the whole nature of the duty, and its whole influence upon the heart.

Two things were required in the law of charity: the terms must be specific enough to guide us to a course of habitual and generous giving; and they must be indefinite enough to allow us to show our heart, and give exercise to our love to God and man in what we give. And these ends were provided for in the Hebrew economy. The lawgiver seemed to have designed to set God's mark on the most common articles of property; so that while employed in his fields and with his flocks, and in gathering his harvests, each one should be constantly reminded of God's claims, and of his own obligation and dependence.

In the first place, each one was required to give the first fruits both of his flocks and of his field. The first fruits of the harvest were by custom a sixtieth part of the whole. Then money was to be paid as the ransom of the first-born male child. Then in reaping, the corners of the field were to be left for the poor; here also custom defined the requirement to be a sixtieth of the whole. Then whatever fell from the reaper's hand belonged to the poor Then every seventh year all the fields were to be left untilled, to produce spontaneously for the poor. Then a tenth of all the products of the fields was to be given to the Levites. Then there were trespass-offerings, sin-offerings, and specified portions of most of the sacrificed animals devoted to the priesthood and Levites. Then every seventh year all debts must be remitted; and the three yearly journeys to Jerusalem, which were required of all the males, at the festivals, must have been no small tax. Added to these were the half shekels for the sanctuary, and abundant hospitalities and gifts for the poor. So that a conscientious Hebrew could hardly have spent less than one-third of his income in religious and charitable gifts.

Nor did this generous charity hinder the secular thrift of the people. It was so adapted to their welfare, spiritual and temporal, and so sustained in the providence of God, that the people were prosperous or straitened in proportion as they obeyed or disobeyed this law. When they honored the Lord with their substance, and the first fruits of all their increase, their barns were filled with plenty. When they robbed God in tithes and offerings, they soon found that they had robbed themselves. And both in giving such a law, and in its providential enforcement, God impressively taught that he would have his people respond to his gifts by large and systematic outlays from them. Call this law, if you please, one of the rigors of the Hebrew economy which Christ has set aside. It rigorously bound that people to that course for the attainment of their highest good. It was really no burden, except when their transgressions involved them in the penalties of the breach of it.

The specific provisions of the tithe system have now vanished with the whole fabric of Hebrew institutions; but the end for which it was framed has never for a moment departed from the mind of the Framer, and the general obligation to extend religion and feed the poor, by freewill offerings, was far from being set aside in the more full unfolding of the mercy of God in the gospel. In displacing the ancient ritual with a simpler and nobler economy, the gospel has given vastly higher enforcements to what was of moral and permanent obligation in the Hebrew religion; and this is preëminently true of the substance of the ancient law of charity. Before the frame of Judaism was reared, the requirement for man to love God with all his heart, and his neighbor as himself, was recorded on tables of stone, to stand unobliterated for all ages. Then came in Judaism, specifically defining in what forms that love should, under such institutions, have expression. But when Judaism passed away, the original law stood unimpaired, and the gospel came in, specifying other forms of expressing this love.

On the basis of the original law of love, the gospel

lays another specific law of alms-giving. The temple and its costly apparatus, its sacrifices and its army of priests are set aside, and with them many of the occasions for the gifts prescribed. But the provisions of the gospel bring in vaster occasions for the employment of the grateful offerings of redeemed sinners. The command to publish the gospel to every creature, and to feed the poor which we are to have with us always, brings upon the Christian world occasions as great and urgent as those of the old economy; nor is there any intimation or ground of inference that the gifts of pious men under the gospel were to be more stinted than before. If the principle announced by Christ, that to whom much is given, of him will much be required, is applicable, a much more generous charity is required of us. There were many things in Judaism adapted to narrow the range of charity. It confined the view to one small nation, as the field of all benevolent operations. It gave no hint of the conversion of the world as a present duty. And yet, if a good man's charity, confined to such narrow bounds, was expected to consume one-third of his income, can less be expected of us whose charity is bound to embrace the world? Not that the poorest of us are required to give as much; but taking men of all conditions, who shall say that our average ought not to be as great?

## III. THE NEW TESTAMENT LAW OF CHARITY.

Before we come to the direct inquiry, as to what is the specific law of the New Testament on this subject, it may be well to see how the law of gospel love, as written in the hearts of *the first Christians*, expressed itself in their conduct. In other words, we will notice the effects produced on the church, in this particular, by the setting aside of the Hebrew law; and watch the motions of the first converts to Christianity, and see if they understood the New Testament law of charity as requiring less than that of the Old. Charity, in the form of gifts to the needy, because it was a prime element of Christian character, was made one of the most prominent traits in those specimens of that character that were first given to the world. There was no result of the first outpouring of the Spirit, after Christ's ascension, which the historian records with more of zest and delight, than the remarkable spirit of individual sacrifice for the good of the whole. On no other trait of character does he so much expand his description. And after an interval of two chapters, he returns to it again, and gives us other particulars, as if here were one of the most surprising phenomena of the whole. But this was a specimen of Christian character in its first formation. And would any one gather from it, that the law of charity had contracted its compass in passing over from Judaism to the gospel; or that the spirit of love breathed less freely in the heart of a redeemed sinner under the clearer light and intenser quickening power of the new covenant?

But a common misconception here intervenes, and robs us of the practical instruction of this luminous portion of Christian history. Most Christians, in determining their own duty, are wont to lay this wholly out of view, in the conceit that it is an instance of the practice of *the community system*, and of course impracticable for them. And it may be worth the while to devote a few paragraphs in rescuing this instructive portion of history from this perversion. If, by the community system, we understand the relinquishment of all private property, and consolidating the goods of all in a common stock, nothing like that resulted from the pentecostal revival. This appears from the fact, that the sequel of the history speaks of these and other Christians as being *in possession of their private property* after these scenes had passed away, and it gives us no trace of the common stock, nor of its managers, nor of any community of people gathered around it. Afterwards, Christians are casually spoken of as having their own houses, here and there, like other people; as in the case of Mary the mother of John, Tabitha, Simon the tanner, and Lydia. Nor did Paul think of a community system when he said, "If any provide not for his own, and especially for those of his own house, he hath denied the faith, and is worse than an infidel."

We have, then, no reason to believe that there was here a melting down of all individual property into a common mass, to be controlled by managers of the common fund; but that in laying the foundations of Christian institutions in the mother church at Jerusalem, and in meeting the wants of multitudes of strangers detained there long beyond their expectations, those Christians who had property submitted it to the free use of the whole, *as far as the existing occasion required.* This limitation is expressly inserted. "Distribution was made unto every man *according as he had need;*" but there was not an alienation of property beyond the present need. There was no actual formation of a common stock; but, for a limited time, there was a subsistence of the strangers upon the freewill offerings of those at home in Jerusalem. Peter, after this mode of action had been in use, makes an express acknowledgment of each one's right of property, by saying to Ananias, "While it remained, was it not thine own; and after it was sold, was it not in thine own power?" The assertion that they "had all things common," had a parallel in this Pythagorean proverb, "With friends all things are common." But the Pythagoreans did not mean by this, that among friends each one had not his own wife, children, property, profession, and business. Nor does the community of those first

Christians exclude such distinctions. The historian says, "Neither was there any among them that lacked; for as many as were possessed of lands sold them, and brought the prices of the things that were sold, and laid them down at the apostles' feet;" but to show that the sale of possessions went no further than *the wants of those that "had need,"* and that it was not a general and entire alienation of property, one person is named who actually gave up all, and one who pretended to have done it. One would not have been thus named, if the same had been done by all.

It is not asserted, then, that all gave up all their property, but that all subjected their property to a free use, so far as the existing occasions required. This fully justifies the broad terms of the historian. In a like sense, the disciples were said to have left all and followed Christ. Yet they neither alienated their estates, nor dissolved their families. For after that, Christ went to Simon's house, and found his family, even to his wife's mother, in it. After that, he taught in Peter's ship, and committed his mother to John's adoption and support—an act unmeaning, if John had no separate family nor means of support. And, after his death, the disciples seem to have returned to fishing in their own ships. Indeed, neither here nor in any other scripture, can we find a shred of a warrant for a community of goods. Such a system would nullify the whole law of alms-giving;

for, how can they exercise themselves in giving alms who have no property to give?

That development of the spirit of Christian charity, which was one of the greatest wonders of the pentecostal scene, was then no abnormal condition of the church, no production of a peculiar and temporary policy, but the natural unfolding of the Christian spirit, under the quickening influence of the Holy Ghost. It was nothing more than what would be required of *all Christians, in the same circumstances.* It was alms-giving, occupying the due relative position among the other Christian graces. It seems wonderful to us, because so strange to our present habits, so above our low conceptions of the duty. It involves no principle which cannot be shown to be universally binding. And as we pass from Hebrew institutions over into the first practice of Christian alms, we not only come into the sphere of a more expanded charity—a charity well escaped from confinement to a single nation, and going forth to embrace the world—but also find ourselves in a centre of light as to the duty in question.

In the first place, this example, vindicated from misconception, shows by what tenure the Christian holds his property. While those Christians had possessions of property, they had them "*as though they possessed not.*" Each felt that he had no claim to his own which could bar the claim of Christ. And he let Christ fully into his houses, and lands, and possessions, as far as the need of his people would carry him. Here we have the germ of the all-pervading principle of Christian alms. That principle makes every holder of property a steward, not an original owner. That principle was here set up, in the first setting up of the Christian church, claiming deference as a fundamental law of Christ's kingdom, in the whole work of raising supplies for the sacra mental host of God's elect, in the conquest of the world. And if this principle could now fully reäs-sert its dominion in every Christian heart, both the church and the world would soon be transformed. New force would be given to the law of love in all its ramifications. Let professed Christians feel that they hold their property only as stewards, bound at any time to surrender it when the wants of the poor or of the church are such that the general good requires the surrender, and the church will speedily come in possession of the means for every conquest. Let all, then, who have perplexities and cases of conscience about the right use of property, come and solve all doubts, by adopting the simple principle ot those first Christians, and have "as though they possessed not."

Another point of instruction in the example of the early Christians is, that the exigencies *of the church, and of a spreading gospel,* are not second to those of suffering humanity in their claims on charity.

The occasion for the pentecostal contributions was chiefly religious. Those converts were no paupers, nor beggars, but rather learners of the gospel, for the instruction of the world. They had come up to the annual festival of ingathering, as usual, with sufficient provision for their return. But, having themselves been gathered in, they found unexpected occasions to protract their tarrying. It was needful that they should "continue steadfastly in the apostles' doctrine and fellowship, and in breaking of bread, and in prayers." Those were most busy and important days. For there were the germs of the church for a thousand cities and villages, sprinkled over the world. Jerusalem was the only centre of light where they could get the instruction and furniture of mind which they needed, to become radiating centres wherever they went. And the interests of the whole Christian cause required that these first Christians should tarry at Jerusalem long enough to get adequate instruction, and the baptism of the spirit of the gospel. For, at that time, all the Christianity in the world was there. Not a word of it had been written; not a preacher of it had gone anywhere else. And all these Christians must there abide, till they got an adequate idea of what they were to communicate to the world. These interests, in such hearts, being paramount to all others, extinguished, so far as any had need, all private claims to property. This first and sublime instance of alms-giving, in the organized Christian church, was an instance of alms given for religious ends—for the spread of the gospel.

This instance also shows what a high position religious charity holds *among other Christian duties* These men, after embracing religion in its transforming power, and then in its outward ordinances, are said to have attended to Christian instruction, prayer, and fellowship. And the next thing said of them is, that among these prime duties of the Christian life they exercised this remarkable liberality. This duty is not located out on some remote branch or twig of the system, where our habits have placed it, but in the very heart and centre. And it is dwelt upon, and repeated by the historian, as one of the most delightful and characteristic events of the whole. Surely the genius of Christianity, as there developed, has entered but poorly into our conceptions.

There is also instruction in the fact, that those Christians "*sold their possessions*" to raise money for the emergency. This is a hint to us, that the advantage of good investments of property must yield to the higher law of the necessities of Christ. Many cannot afford gifts proportionate to their means, because their property is so invested that they cannot command the ready money. And perhaps some unconsciously felicitate themselves that they have their funds hid away from Christ, and dream not of any obligation to change investments of funds that are yielding good incomes, for any emergencies of charity. Yet here we see, that in the spring-time and primitive development of Christianity, men were of another mind.

You will next observe, that these gifts were all *free-will offerings.* Each one's right of property was respected; no law imposed a fixed rate of contribution, and none required the whole of any one's property. One, prompted by his glowing love for the cause, judged it to be his duty in his circumstances to surrender the whole. Here operated that principle which we have already noticed, leaving individual hearts to spontaneous action, and yet securing a generous action. So much for the Christian law of alms, as it appears on the first page of Christian history.

## IV. LAW OF PERIODICAL ALMS-GIVING.

God's plan, in making the wants of the church and of the poor a lever to bring the hearts of Christians up to higher elevations and habits of benevolence, appears on every page of the gospel, but our purpose confines us to those passages wherein the Christian rule of alms-giving is presented in its direct and specific form. We need not a law of charity which is every thing in general and nothing in particular. We need that which comes as near to regulating the proportion of each one's income, as the design of alms-giving will allow. And this we have in 1 Cor., 16 : 1. 2.

"Now concerning the collection for the saints, as I have given order to the churches of Galatia, even so do ye. Upon the first day of the week, let every one of you lay by him in store, as God has prospered him, that there be no gatherings when I come."

We have here, as we propose to show, a rule which binds all to the principle of setting apart, *every Sabbath, or at least statedly, a portion of their income or their means of living, as God shall prosper them, for charitable uses:* it being understood, that this, like all other rules of its class, binds in its general principle and intent, but is subject to modifications in its details, when brought to individual application. Even the law of the Sabbath, uttered in the broadest terms, bends in adjustment to cases of needful mercy. And though the rule here given is as universal in its terms, it does not of course bind those who have no income to set apart a portion of income. Nor does it bind the man whose salary or means of living is received annually or quarterly, or the merchant engaged in large adventures, or any one who cannot know at every week's end what his income has been, actually to set apart a weekly proportion of income. But it would seem to require that every one should have his stated seasons for a conscientious apportionment to his charity fund, either in cash or by entry on a benevolent account, according to his circumstances, and in such a mode as he shall see fit to adopt. The intent of the rule cannot be answered without *some form of stated, systematic action.* Each one is required to adopt some regular system of charity which shall come within the spirit of the rule; and it seems to have been a prominent design of the Lawgiver to put each one upon the exercise of his own judgment and conscience, in the execution of the general provisions of his law.

For illustration, and for suggestion to those who cannot devise for themselves a better mode, we here state the method in which two persons, unknown to each other, and in circumstances widely different, have fulfilled their own idea of this rule, with benefit, as they believe, to themselves and to the cause of Christ.

One, every Sabbath evening at the hour of his private devotion, lays aside the sum which he thinks he ought to devote for that week to charitable purposes. If he has not the money, he charges the amount against himself in favor of his charity fund When there is a call for donations, he takes from this fund what he thinks he should give. If a call of special urgency comes, which what he has set apart will not fully meet, he overdraws the fund, and charges against it the balance, to be cancelled by future incomes. Thus in a very simple and easy way the work is reduced to a system, in connection with the spiritual exercises of the Sabbath.

The other is a prosperous merchant, who resolves that whatever his future profits shall be, he will devote a certain per cent. to charity, enlarging the percentage if his profits shall exceed a certain sum. On the first day of every month he takes an inventory, ascertains what have been his profits, and credits the percentage on his charity account. When calls are presented, he draws from this fund; and for some years he has been surprised to find that it is so productive. He meets calls with pleasure, and is a happy man in prayer and labor to obtain means, of which not a stinted portion is sacredly consecrated to God.

But to return to the passage before us: the first point of instruction here presented is, that *this rule is not given as mere advice*, which we are at liberty to disregard. Paul says, "I have given *order*" to this effect. Nor was it a rule framed for mere local and temporary use. He had imposed it before on the Galatian churches, and now lays it on the Corinthian church, whose circumstances were very different; and it was laid in imperative terms by an apostle speaking by inspiration.

The next point is, that it is not a mere exhortation to benevolence in general, *but a specific rule requiring action in a particular way, and binding alike on all.* True, it has, like the command to preach the gospel to every creature, been lost to the church for a thousana years. Yet man's neglect cannot annihilate God's command. That it was intended for all is fully apparent. The epistle is addressed not to the Corinthians alone, but "*to all that in every place call upon the name of Jesus Christ.*" This is not a mere unmeaning salutation. Paul could not have saluted all Christians in his epistle in such terms, unless he intended to address to them all, the instructions contained in it, so far as they were in nature and form applicable to all. And no part of his epistle is more capable of general application than this text. Nor does this rule here come out in a solitary instance in Paul's teaching. The same which he here gives to the Corinthians, he had given, in more than one instance, to other churches—"to the churches in Galatia."

It is the way of the Spirit of inspiration to speak to the whole church, or the whole world, through a small company of immediate hearers. How comes it that Paul's letter "to the church of God which is at Corinth," with all its details of instruction, reproof, and correction in righteousness administered to them, should have been put forth as God's book of inspiration for the regulation of our heart and life? Every thing in that epistle which contains this rule, has as much of a special direction to those Corinthians, as this rule itself has. For instance, this same epistle contains directions about the discipline of the church, which all churches acknowledge as binding on them: yet they were given about a single case then existing there. It contains exhortations to purity of life, with a reference to impurities existing there. It gives important principles touching the law of marriage, with reference to cases existing there. It gives the Corinthians rules requiring of them a support of their ministry, and instructions respecting the Lord's table—respecting the exercise of spiritual gifts, and the like. None have doubted that the instructions and rules given, on all these subjects, were as much intended for us as for the Corinthians; and a principle of interpretation that would set them aside from present use, would exclude all the epistles from the sacred canon, and indeed a greater part of the other scriptures, for the great body of scripture is written on the same principle; even the ten commandments, the eternal law of the universe, were uttered specially to one people, and grounded on the fact that God had brought them out of the land of Egypt, and out of the house of bondage. Scarcely one of the rules in this epistle is given out with as much formality as that before us; and such formal rules of conduct, given by inspired men claiming to speak as they were moved by the Holy Ghost, and to speak to the few for the instruction of the whole world, may be taken as meant for all, unless there be found in their structure, context, or occasions, some implied limitation. But no limitations are here implied.

There is another question: Did Paul require these weekly deposits to be made, and appoint that there should be no gatherings under the impulse of his eloquence when he should come, in expectation that he would in this way make *a larger collection for that time?* Evidently he was not providing for that single occasion, but for the permanent influence of an established rule. If for one occasion only, he would most naturally have ordered the gathering to take place after he had come and exerted the force of his eloquence upon them in setting forth the details of the distress which he asked them to relieve. Who that knows with what force Paul could speak—how he spoke on Mars-hill, before the assembled wisdom of Greece—how he thundered in the ear and conscience of the hardened Felix—what effect he wrought upon Agrippa—who can doubt, that for a single collection, he would have secured vastly more if he had said nothing of weekly deposits, and had relied upon an appeal to the Corinthians with the electric force of his eloquence, backed by the moral force of his apostolic character and presence? It is clear, at a glance, that his object in giving that order, could not have been to get the greatest amount of money for a single occasion; and if not, it follows that he was looking to *permanent results*—forming the general practice of alms-giving in that church; and if in that church, why not in all churches?

If, then, the rule given have an evident fitness for universal application—if the circumstances of those for whom it was first made, show no reason why it was more fit for them than for all—if, from reason and the nature of things, the rule appears to be as well adapted to all as to any, the case is clear that this utterance of the divine oracle is the voice of God to universal man.

And let it be well considered that all that is shown in this discussion, of the fitness of this rule for the cultivation of the divine life, and enlarging the streams of Christian beneficence, is so much in confirmation of its claims to be considered a law of God requiring your obedience; and if it be such a law, you are as much required to act according to it, as you are to keep the Sabbath. And those professing Christians on the continent of Europe, who ignore their obligation to remember the Sabbath-day and keep it holy, have no more occasion to review their theory touching that law, than you have yours respecting this. They are no more offenders against the one law of God, than you are against the other; and the Christian minister, or Christian teacher in any sphere, who neglects to inculcate this rule, as really neglects his duty, as the teacher who neglects to inculcate the law of the Sabbath.

The next point is, that *alms-giving is a work for every Sabbath.* "Upon the first day of the week, let every one of you lay by him in store." Here nothing is said for or against collections made in the church on the Sabbath. The command is, that as often as the Sabbath comes, we should take out of our means of living a portion, and devote it to charitable uses. And this, in its very terms, refutes one of the commonplaces of Christian penuriousness: that the handling of money is a desecration of the Sabbath, and the preaching about filthy lucre is a profanation of sacred things; for here is an express command of God, to handle money for one purpose on the first day of the week. It would seem that the first Christians had such a type of religion, that their handling of money was indispensable to Sabbath sanctification, and that their Sabbath prayers and praises could not ascend, but as accompanied with their alms.

Another penurious maxim is also set aside by this text, to wit, that calls for charity are *too frequent*. Enterprises of Christian philanthropy are so multiplied and various, that scarcely a month passes without a call from Christian pulpits for new donations, and this is quite an annoyance to those who have some conscience and less benevolence. Now this text points out a way in which this struggle between conscience and inclination can be forestalled. Let every one come into a habit of not waiting for any calls, but of setting apart every Sabbath, or at other stated periods, the portion which he ought to give, and he will experience no annoyance from the frequent calls of agents. Until he does this, he fails to come up to the apostolic rule as to the frequency of his alms. This is the way to "make up beforehand your bounty, that the same may be ready as a matter of bounty, and not as of covetousness."

It will naturally be asked, *Why this duty must needs be done on the Sabbath?* Whatever may have been the reason of this provision, it is a matter of fact, that the converted Jews had been accustomed to a like arrangement. Both Philo and Josephus inform us that the Jews were wont every Sabbath to make collections at their synagogues, of their tithes and spontaneous gifts, to be sent to the temple. This custom was adopted into the Christian church, with such modifications as the new dispensation required. The appropriation required to be made at home, irrespective of a church contribution, would secure a more universal compliance, than if it was to be made in the church from which some would be detained; and yet it did not hinder public collections, when convenience required them.

One of the reasons for connecting alms-giving with the Sabbath doubtless was, to secure *the periodical and constant action of the heart* in the work. To make this action sure, a particular day of the week is named when it should be done, and when it would be less liable to be crowded out of mind by other cares. And this order being obeyed, the habit of frequent giving is secured. The mind as often as the Sabbath comes round, is put upon reviewing the course of providence, and the prosperity experienced, and deciding in view of it how much ought to be given, and so is kept in the constant exercise of benevolence, and holding constant checks on avaricious aspirations. So this employment, while it secures its main end upon the heart of the giver, harmonizes with all the other employments of the Sabbath. For the sanctification of the soul in its Sabbath work, it is required, not only to bring the mind under the quickening influence of the gospel, read and preached and meditated upon, not only to engage it in acts of prayer and praise, but to enlist it in acts of love to man, and in conflict with selfishness. Our Sabbath religion must be not only a matter of thought and feeling, but of self-denying action. "It is lawful to do good on the Sabbath-day." This action, steadily and habitually sustained, plays upon the very citadel of our selfishness, which is the great enemy of our sanctification: our keeping up a sleepless warfare at this point, brings assistance to the other appropriate operations of the mind, and employs the whole mechanism of the soul in harmony with Sabbath engagements. And the constant repetition of small gifts does more towards a benevolent formation of heart, than the same amount given in larger sums at wider intervals.

Another reason is, that gifts so often repeated, most effectually *secure a large amount*. The rule, in its structure, bears an evident design to favor the poorer classes, and give them an effective share in the blessedness of benefaction. Living more from hand to mouth, they have not the means at hand, if they would, to make large donations, but by weekly additions to their charity-treasure, they may produce a rich result at the year's end ; and in all this process of laying aside the little that they can spare, they are making just as much sacrifice and cultivation of heart, and of course doing as much towards the prime purpose of giving, as their wealthy neighbors who give ten times as much. The little sums thus laid aside fall into their place in the ordinary calculation of expenses, and are provided for at the same time with our meat and drink ; and in thus sharing, as it were, our daily sustenance with the poor, and bringing the toil-worn missionary, as it were, to eat at our table, we come into a most affecting form of communion with Christ, and all who love his cause, while we are taking the best course to enable us to make the most of our contributions from a slender income. Without some plan like this, the constantly recurring calls for things needful and superfluous would absorb our income, and for the most part exclude our charities. But were all who acknowledge the obligation to give at all, including old and young, rich and poor, to come under this rule, a vast increase of charitable funds would be realized.

The first application of this rule in its definite form, which we have on record, was to the churches in Galatia, in which *the poor* abounded. And then it was found to be equally suitable to *the wealthier* Christians at Corinth, situated amidst temptations to luxury and extravagance. At any rate, it is at once adapted to operate kindly among the necessities of the humbler classes, and to hold salutary checks upon the extravagances of the rich. It brings each one, once a week, to a reckoning with himself as to his use of the gifts of Providence. Is there a Christian whose easily besetting sin is extravagance, who is spending more than a good conscience would dictate, in the matters of style, or in the elegances and superfluities of life, this rule would seem to have been made on purpose for him. It arraigns him once a week before his conscience and his God, to debate questions touching this very subject. Let him adopt the rule, and he is led at once to a course of mental exercises, in which he cannot retain both his peace of mind and his habits of extravagance. The Sabbath comes, and after engaging in the devotions of the day, both public and private, he sits down under the full impression of all he has heard and read of Christ and his salvation, and of all that he has himself uttered in his prayers and praises, and makes his decision as to how much the Lord has prospered him, and for what end, and what obligations that prosperity confers; and he must be slow to admit reproof if some of his superfluities are not soon lopped off. If he fail to take the hint at first, this debate in conscience is of course renewed once a week, and he is brought back to the subject in all varieties of circumstances and modes of feeling; and if any thing can cure a Christian's habitual extravagance, this must be the remedy. By imposing this rule, God, as it were, every Sabbath takes each Christian aside and puts to him the delicate question, how he has been prospered, and how much he can afford to give to Him from whom he receives all. And he does this at the time when the rational powers and spiritual affections may be supposed to be in the most vigorous exercise.

But there may be a more specific reason why this day, and not any other of the week, is set apart for this purpose. We may be invited to bring *our grateful offerings* to the Lord's treasury on this day, because the very design of the Sabbath makes it a day of thanksgiving and of grateful remembrance of the work of redemption. The Christian Sabbath celebrates a new creation as a subject of more elevated praise than that on which "the morning stars sang together." And it is fitting, that our grateful joy should have expression in substantial acts, as well as in words and songs. He who made the mind, and who best knows how to touch all its springs and cause us to make melody in our hearts to the Lord, knows that the giving of gifts is a natural expression of grateful joy, and that the incense connected with freewill offering, sweetly blends with our songs of praise for redeeming love.

Again, *the religious nature and obligations* of the duty of alms-giving, make the appointment of the Sabbath for the time of doing it, peculiarly proper.

The several Sabbath employments naturally aid each other. Prayer and praise quicken and elevate the mind for more effectual meditation on the word of God, and so all the fit employments of the Sabbath may tend to revive our sense of obligation, and our benevolent emotions, and thus serve as prompters to our acts of charity. The Christian mind as really communes with God, in the act of devoting to a charitable use a portion of the gifts of God, as in prayer and praise. God's authority binds the conscience, and the love of Christ constrains the heart to the act, and the mind moves responsive to the known will of Christ. Such acts are a proper expression of that charity of which Paul says, "Now abideth faith, hope, charity, these three, but the greatest of these is charity." This is, then, one of the graces of the Spirit, and as the design of the Sabbath is for the quickening of grace, this grace should be called into action on the Sabbath; and as this grace is in many minds one of the most difficult of exercise, the aids which other Sabbath exercises give should be called in, and our prayers and our alms should go up together as a memorial before God. The fitness of this connection of things has illustration in the experience of ministers, who, after the exercises of the Sabbath, find their minds vastly quickened in forming conceptions of divine truth, and in all spiritual exercises.

*God has established* this connection between our Sabbath employments, and set the duty of alms-giving high among them, doubtless with the design that it may have a more effective performance. A time has been chosen when the mind may be supposed to be in the most favorable posture, a time when we have retreated farthest from the world and its excitements to avarice, and are most susceptible of spiritual motives. If we wished to get a large donation from one, for some benevolent object, we should choose our time to approach him, and especially the time when the realizings of eternity were most upon him. Thus God does, and comes to us for our gift in the midst of our Sabbath devotions—in the midst of our professions of gratitude and love. He comes in and takes us at our word. We have perhaps been singing,

"All that I am, and all I have,
Shall be for ever thine;
Whate'er my duty bids me give,
My cheerful hands resign."

He then comes in with an opportunity for us to give what our duty bids; hence the admirable fitness of the time. If there is to be a set time, who will not say that *this is the time?* If it had been a universal custom to do this work on one particular day of the week, and that not the Sabbath, and if now a transfer were to be made, and the work were to be brought within the Sabbath, a great advance in the amount given would doubtless be realized. Even the merchant, who monthly or at other stated times carries to a benevolent account the sum devoted to charity, may derive great advantage from setting apart on the Sabbath a little season for "grateful communion" with Christ in reference to the claims of the various departments of benevolence, and in prayer for direction and a blessing on his humble offerings.

Further, the duty is laid *on every one.* "Let *every one of you* lay by him in store." Though those who are themselves objects of charity and have nothing to give, would not come within the rule; and though those whose incomes do not admit of so detailed a distribution, would be allowed to answer the intent of the rule in the form which their circumstances require; yet, with such modifications, the rule is universal with rich and poor. If it be thought an objection that too much of religious charities must thus come from the gifts of the poor, we answer, it will not be so, provided they do not go beyond the measure of the prosperity which God has given them. Hitherto religious enterprises have been mainly sustained by the confluence of small streams, coming in from those in moderate conditions. Yea, it is one of the excellences of these enterprises, that they unite the hearts of rich and poor; and convey to the poor as much of the benefit of giving as to the rich. And will any count it treason to allow the poorest to share in the luxury of sending the gospel to the poor? Has not the gospel done enough for the poor to warrant such responses of gratitude from them? Has not God chosen the poor of this world rich in faith and heirs of the kingdom? And has he denied to these heirs of the kingdom all share in the work of advancing his kingdom? His order to the churches in Galatia, where the poor abounded, was, "Let every one of you lay by him in store."

Nor did he intend to impose a burden, but to confer a privilege. And he has so shaped the requirement, because unwilling to exclude the poor from a needful means of grace. He who was anointed to preach the gospel to the poor, would not so frame his system as to cut off the poor from the channels through which he conveys the riches of his grace; and most impressive is the assurance which he has given us of this, in the value which he stamped on the widow's farthing. While sitting in the temple and watching the people casting their gifts into the treasury, and after some had made princely donations, he saw a poor widow come and drop in two mites, which made a farthing. That went to his heart; and with solemn emphasis in the use of that "Verily," or Amen, which only *he* ever used in such a way, he asserted that the value of the widow's gift exceeded the sum total of all the rest; and why? Because there was more of sacrifice made, more of benevolent heart expended, and so a deeper and richer participation of sanctifying experience had, which is the ultimate end of all gifts.

Here is presented such a scale of valuation of our gifts as brings the rich and poor upon one level, and puts to flight all reasons that would exclude the poor. Whatever others may think, Christ makes the smallest gifts of the poor as indispensable, and of as much value, as the large donations of the rich. Ever watchful for fit incidents from which to flash forth instruction upon all ages, he here seized upon a case of the smallest donation made by extreme poverty, and held it forth as our warrant to value all gifts according to the sacrifice made, and so make the gifts of the poor, not only as acceptable to God, but as valuable towards the ultimate end of filling the world with the glory of God, as the proportionate gifts of the rich. And so when he said, "It is more blessed to give than to receive," he intended not to utter startling paradoxes, but to declare a plain matter of fact in that divine plan which in many ways betrays a generous partiality to the poor, in the distribution of spiritual favors; and to sustain this partiality, he must give the poor an equal share in the blessedness of giving, and this, and even more than this, they have ever had.

But if it be a general law of Christ's kingdom, that gifts in charity weigh in the balance of the sanctuary according to the amount of the sacrifice made, the concurrence of those of the smallest income is indispensable. Suppose you can give but a cent a week, that shall introduce you to all the soul-enriching influences of giving. As an instrument of communion with Christ, and of binding your soul to him, your copper coin is as effectual as the gold of others. And who can tell, that carrying a special blessing with it, and guided to its result by the partial regards of the Redeemer, it may not actually produce more than the larger gifts, made with less sacrifice and prayer? Cases are not wanting of the single penny-tract having originated trains of light and salvation, branching forth and extending beyond human computation. And who can tell that these small grains of mustard-seed, that have produced the great trees, have not come from those whose "deep poverty abounded to the riches of their liberality."

Make the small gifts of the poor a matter of indifference, and confine to the rich the obligation to give, and you would render the whole commandment a nullity. If God had left to *all but the poor* the command to give, this would have been a poverty-stricken world. To make it of any effect, it must run impartially from the highest to the lowest. It must hold the pence as carefully as the pounds.

Indeed, imperfectly as this rule has been understood, the greatest aggregate of gifts has come from those of more limited means. Never did charities more abound than in the primitive ages; never did evangelizing go forward with greater rapidity and power; yet, "not many wise men after the flesh, not many mighty, not many noble were called." It was the gifts of the humbler classes, flowing in countless minuter rills, which cut the channels to convey the riches of salvation over the civilized world. That broad and fertilizing shower that in the space of one generation made the wilderness bud and blossom as the rose, was composed of single drops. And so is every other shower. He who is the Father of the rain, and who begets the drops of the dew, finds it not beneath him to produce the single drops and the smallest drops, without which there can be no showers. Sometimes when the ground, under a scorching sun, is opening the seams on its bosom, imploring from heaven the mercy of a shower, a thin cloud comes over, dispensing a large drop here and there—a fair similitude of what the work of charity, confined to the rich, would be. The drops are large and generous in themselves; but they are too few, and do but mock the distress. It is the constant distilling of the small rain by which God gladdens the earth.

And this law of charity lays itself on men in all varieties of condition, with an admirable equality of pressure. It requires each to give *according to his means, and according to his own judgment, formed with an enlightened conscience and a benevolent heart.* It puts into the hands of each one a scale of duties, ascending and descending with the increase or decrease of his means. The poor man is expected to "labor, working with his hands, that he may have to give to him that needeth."

If this rule presses heavily anywhere, it is on those who have difficulty in meeting their urgent wants from week to week. But even they could make a cent a week sacred to the cause of benevolence, without any sensible increase of their burdens; and that for them might answer all the ends of the requirement, and make them equal co-part ners in the soul-enriching and world-enriching com merce of benevolence. But to an amount lesser or larger, each is bound to form the habit of giving a portion of his income—to act every week on the question of apportioning his gifts to his income. Among the duties of the Sabbath, comes that of dividing off a portion for alms. And this is a duty no more to be forgotten than that of prayer. The act involves an exercise of conscience and of heart—of love to God and man, in giving back a portion of God's gifts. The Sabbath's sun invites you anew to settle the question, how much you ought to deny yourself for Him who gave his life for your ransom.

The flexibility of this rule is one of its advantages. It *bends in perfect adjustment to each one's circumstances*, and to all changes of circumstances. It does not require, that one shall, at the beginning of a year, commit himself to give so much for the year, not knowing whether his present ability will continue through the year, or whether it may not be increased; he may determine on the proportion, or percentage of income which he will contribute, and that, if his income shall exceed a certain sum, he will give a larger percentage, "as God shall prosper him." It does not require each one to give just so great a proportion of his income; but it makes each one to judge for himself, in view of all his circumstances. There may be circumstances which would require one to give twice the percentage of his income which another gives. One may be under obligations to creditors, and bound to be just before he is generous; while the other, with the same income, is free from debt—though the man who early adopts and adheres to the scripture rule, will find it operating as a powerful dissuasive from contracting needless debts. There are a thousand other circumstances which may vary the proportion that different persons ought to give; and these are wisely committed to be judged of by each one's own conscience.

There is still another important point of instruction in this text: "*That there be no gatherings when I come.*" This detects a capital error in our present policy of benevolence; in that we are wont to wait to be lashed up to our duty by the periodical visits of the agents of the several benevolent societies. Paul was operating as an agent for gathering funds to relieve the distress of Christians at Jerusalem. But he did not tell the Corinthians, Wait till I come and lay before you the thrilling details of that distress, and by dint of eloquent appeals, move you to an amount of donations which you would not otherwise reach. He placed no reliance on such means. He preferred that all should be done without a word from him. He would have every dollar that was to be given, actually in the treasury before he came, "that there be no gatherings when I come." This uncovers a grand feature in the divine plan, and it may show us the error in our policy which makes it so hard to bring the churches up to this duty. We begin at the wrong end. We make the great reason why we should give to be, that somebody will suffer if we do not. And we depend on our agents to set forth that suffering, with an energy of eloquence which those only can command who give themselves wholly to a single branch of the work. And the result is, that the main spring appointed to move the soul to this work, is left untouched. The animal passions and natural sympathies are quickened, the understanding is convinced of the fitness of the work, and the justice of its claims upon us; in a secondary sense the religious affections are enlisted; but the whole energy of the heart is not roused, because we do not place the main reliance on the main motives. We wait for Paul to come first, and tell us all about the sufferings of the poor saints at Jerusalem; expecting by that communication of intelligence, to be led into the great and moving inducements to give.

But Paul just reversed this process. He relied on the intelligence of higher and more moving facts, which had already been communicated to them. He reminded them of their obligations to Christ, who had given himself for them—of the fact that they had already "given their own selves to the Lord," which gift involved all the donations that were needed from them; he reminded them that he was proving the sincerity of their love—that he was seeking the cultivation in them of one of the parent graces—that all their supplies came from God, who would cause them to reap bountifully from a bountiful sowing—and that the great end which he sought, was *the enriching of their souls "to all bountifulness."* These were the motives on which he relied. His great care was, not to stir their sympathies in view of the distresses of the needy, but to make those distresses an occasion of their exercising one of the Christian graces. And this he did by reminding them of their relations to God and Christ. His argument was purely evangelical—made out of the prime elements of the gospel. He was thus saved the necessity of descending to lower themes. He put the Corinthians upon the formation of habits of giving constantly and from principle, and so secured the gifts in actual preparation, when call should be made for them.

Now, so far as our present system has departed from this principle, we shall sooner or later be compelled to retrace our steps. There has long been with many, a desire to save the necessity of employing agents in the collection of funds; and yet, there has been a prevalent conviction, that in the present condition of the churches, they could not be safely dispensed with. Most experiments of dispensing with them have resulted unfavorably. And it is plain, that any change of the temper and habits of the public mind, that will warrant our dispensing with them, must have a gradual introduction. If we are not mistaken, that change, so much desired by all—and by none more than by our most efficient agents—can be secured by the restoration of this rule of alms-giving, and by our ministry returning to the scriptural method of inculcating the duty. If a display of facts and statistics, and the communication of intelligence respecting the particular charity for which the agent pleads, is to be the great lever to lift the church up to an apprehension of its duty, then we shall ever want agents to do the work. But if the more excellent way be found to be, to bring the obligations to bear on Christian hearts first and mainly for their own sanctification, then the regular ministry will be the best of all agencies And while we find it necessary to employ agents, they will find it for their advantage to take a standpoint nearer the heart and centre of the gospel, and make less reliance on their facts, statistics, and pathetic appeals. The nearer they come to the plan of Christ and his apostles in this matter, the more effective will be their command over the hearts of their hearers. Their main endeavor should be to dig broader and deeper fountains of benevolence in the heart of the church, and not to eke out the largest possible stream from the shallow fountains that now exist.

There is then great wisdom in that single stroke of the inspired pen, "*that there be no gatherings when I come.*" It tells us, that our gatherings have been so meagre, because not before prepared in habits of giving, and in affections of the soul previously cultivated under the application of motives more purely evangelical. And it reveals a capital error in our present mode of action, and shows the remedy for existing deficiencies. Let the work of charity be taken up, like that of repentance, to be done *because it is right,* because the wants of the soul require it, because it is due from us as homage to God, and in gratitude to Christ. Let the ministry urge it on these grounds *mainly*, and let the great themes of redemption come to bear on the heart in a way to enlarge its fountains of benevolent feeling, and the result will be most happy.

Thus have we endeavored to give the spirit of Paul's injunction, to engage in alms-giving every Sabbath. In this we show a definite rule, formed by divine wisdom, binding by divine authority, requiring us to sustain a constant habit of giving more or less according to our means, and independently of particular calls; and so as to be beforehand, and ready for them when they come. This rule we propound to every one, as claiming his obedience. It is as definite and authentic as any of the rules by which the revenues of the Hebrew church were gathered.

But you will perhaps plead, that it has become obsolete; and say, that it has for many centuries been unknown to the Christian world. And so have many other things, which are as clear as the sun when attention is effectually turned to them, been unknown to the Christian world. The great duty of evangelizing the world, which is in some sense the sum of all duties, has, till within a short time, been buried from the sight of the church. The command to "go into all the world and preach the gospel to every creature," stood plainly forth on the inspired page. It was "read and conned by rote" among the lessons of childhood. It was a theme for the pulpit and the commentary. But it was but yesterday when its true meaning, simple as it is, began first in modern times to flame forth, and awake the hearts of a slumbering church. And it is nothing more strange, that this other command, written by an apostle, clear as a sunbeam, has slumbered so long.

Facts compel us to open our Bibles with the impression, that the church is committing some great error somewhere, in her practical sense of her duty, as to furnishing the means of evangelizing. There must be something out of joint. Some principle to which God has committed a moving power, is dislocated and bereft of its power. And previous to examination, who can say that the oversight has not been committed on this very page? The language is plain, binding every one to make alms-giving a matter of business, of habit, and part of his Sabbath work. And the fact that all Christians have so strangely overlooked this duty, is by no means a solitary fact. Nor can the united vote or non-user of all Christendom, vacate such a Christian duty. Remembering what a new impulse was received when the church began to recover the meaning of the command to evangelize the world, let us seek to recover the force of the command which binds us to furnish the means of that evangelizing.

Such is the law of the New Testament, binding us to interweave with our Sabbath-keeping, a constant habit of consecrating to God a portion of our means of living. We pass now to some reasons for a compliance with this law.

## V. REASONS FOR COMPLIANCE WITH THE LAW.

### 1. IT IS ONE OF THE MOST IMPORTANT MEANS OF GRACE.

This we place first in order, because it is the first in importance. We have shown, that all other ends of alms-giving terminate in this; and that the duty, in Scripture, is enforced chiefly on the ground of its being a means of sanctification to the heart of the giver We have shown, that it is indispensable to the growth of Christian character, that Christian beneficence have exercise; that it has been appointed that we shall have the poor with us always, as the means of exercising us in those habits which will promote us to true riches. If God's poor suffer, or if God's cause suffer, it is to give scope for cultivating the graces of those who exercise compassion. So when the poor saints at Jerusalem were in distress, and claiming the compassion of gentile Christians, the apostles were with divine skill making their sufferings an occasion of growth in grace to others.

See how Paul uses the occasion with the Corinthians: "Therefore as ye abound in every thing, in faith, and utterance, and knowledge, and in all diligence, and in your love to us, see that ye abound *in this grace also.*" Here, this grace, which has exercise in alms, is set into one and the same family with faith, love, and Christian diligence. And the same reasons why we should abound in one, are made good reasons why we should abound in the other. This branch of benevolence is here recognized *as a grace.* And what is a grace, but one of those qualities of mind, gratuitously imparted by the Spirit of God in regeneration, and put forward in sanctification—one of those qualities which make out the Christian character? It is one of a sisterhood that is never separated from the rest. Those who think that they can be good Christians, and have nothing to do with charities—those who abound in verbal faith and orthodoxy, and in fluent prayers, while they are deaf to all calls to give for the love of Christ, are strangers to the power of godliness. The Spirit of God never committed such an oversight, as to regenerate a soul and then leave it under the power of covetousness complete. The product of the new birth is a new man, with all the members of a man developed; and not one mutilated and wanting in this or that limb. Every grace of the Spirit has a proportionate, though it may be a feeble development. And it would be no more absurd to speak of a Christian without faith, than of a Christian without beneficence. A Christian infidel is no more a contradiction in terms, than a Christian without charity.

True and healthy piety involves in itself an advance of the several graces in fit proportions, as the growth of the body advances in all its several limbs. And to say that such a one is an earnest Christian in every thing else, but that he will give nothing and sacrifice nothing for the cause of Christ, is an abuse of language. Of such a one the Scripture says, "How dwelleth the love of God in him?" When we see large developments of Christian character in other respects, connected with small developments of benevolence, the large must be taken with some allowance—keeping good the principle, that as ye abound in the other, ye will "abound in this grace also."

This grace has its root in our *self-consecration to God.* For the apostle in the same connection, enforcing this grace from the example of liberality in the churches of Macedonia, says, they "first gave their own selves to the Lord, and to us by the will of God." Here is the beginning of all charity. The man ceasing to live to himself, and beginning to live for God, asks himself, not how shall I most successfully rear a separate and selfish interest; but how shall I best employ my means, great or small, towards the true end for which I live? He has in his soul a propensity to acts of Christian generosity; and this propensity is the grace that is to be cultivated in harmony with the rest.

This propensity has its main impulse in the love of Christ. As Paul intimates in the same connection, it "knows the grace of our Lord Jesus Christ, who, though he was rich, yet for our sakes became poor, that we through his poverty might be rich." In every gift, the Christian, acting as a rational being, has a reason for his act. And though he may not have analyzed his feelings, so as to be conscious of it, his chief motive is, that he acts in harmony with the will and benevolent design of the Saviour, who embraced poverty to confer on the redeemed the riches of heaven. The loss which he is to incur by his gift, reminds him of the amazing loss by which Christ bestowed on him an unspeakable gift. When his selfishness begins to rally, and he is half resolved to withhold his reasonable share in any good work, the thought comes back, that He who was rich in all the wealth of heaven, emptied himself of all, and had not where to lay his head, that he might hereafter have a house of many mansions to open, and an inheritance incorruptible to make over to him. Seeing what Christ has done and lost for him, to confer the wealth of the eternal God as a free gift, and seeing that all he demands in return is the natural response of a grateful heart, he becomes ashamed of his best gifts, and says,

> "Were the whole realm of nature mine,
> That were a present far too small;
> Love so amazing, so divine,
> Demands my soul, my life, my all."

If such a thing could be, as a redeemed sinner inflamed with the love of Christ, and now and then lifted to rapturous elevations and well-nigh mingling with the white-robed harpers before the throne, in that song, "Worthy is the Lamb," and yet this same redeemed sinner with a heart of stone against every appeal to benevolent feeling, he would be a monster for which we have no name.

Thus the same motives which actuate every other grace, are the motives to this; and these may all be reduced to one, *the love of Christ constraining us.* It is as important that this love should have expression in this form, as in other appropriate forms. And this grace, like the rest, grows by exercise—by bringing the motives to bear, and calling it into frequent action. That the love of God may be called forth and cultivated to be a strong and permanent principle of character, it is made our duty to be much in acts of prayer and communion with him. So also, that our benevolent affections may have strength, it is made our duty to hold ourselves to constant repetitions of benevolent acts. For this reason, divine wisdom has appointed that each Christian shall enter upon a series of such acts, and hold himself to them while the weeks and years go round, that he may bring to bear upon his soul a divinely constructed mechanism, for its gradual transformation into the divine image. You have then the great reason for this rule of habitual and systematic charity, in that it is the will of God for your sanctification—in that it is among the most important means of grace.

And that it may still further appear to be such, let us contemplate it in the opposite view—in the antagonism which it presents to the native *covetousness of the heart.* That which most effectually promotes our benevolent affections, best counterworks our avarice ; for our evil affections are displaced only by bringing in their opposites. And these habits of constant giving are prominent among the means which God has appointed for our habitual resistance to that love of the world which is idolatry, and that lawless *will to be rich* which involves us in a " snare, and in many foolish and hurtful lusts, which drown men in destruction and perdition."

The purpose to accumulate money for its own

sake, or for the selfish gratifications which it ministers, when once admitted to rule the mind, *takes possession* and spreads and fortifies itself, and leaves no place in the heart for homage to God. Every power of the soul submits, as if smitten with a palsy. All motions are excluded that do not obey the impulse of this ruling passion: the understanding cannot entertain the thoughts of God, for it is tasked to its utmost in gainful contrivances; the memory is imbecile as to all remembrance of God, for its main power is exhausted upon other things. The affections are so occupied with treasures of earth, that they set no value on the pearl of great price. In short, this love of accumulation is the easily besetting sin of the world, and one of the most dangerous enemies of our salvation; and the strategy of our spiritual warfare needs to be specially directed against it.

Selfishness is the parent form and central element of all sin; and *the love of money* is one of the main branches of selfishness, "the root of all evil;" and upon this "root of all evil," this dangerous enemy of our salvation, the enginery of redemption is made effectually to play, in the formation and nurture of habits of benevolence. Aware that this was our great point of danger, Christ said to them that "trust in riches," that is, them that come under the power of this love of money, that it is easier for a camel to go through a needle's eye, than for them to enter heaven. And having given command to take heed and beware of this covetousness, he has also shown the way of resisting it, by bringing the benevolent affections into vigorous and constant play. The Christian law of alms-giving he has made to give a benevolent character and a sanctified direction to our necessary employments for gain.

He who, out of a principle of true benevolence, con secrates to a benevolent use whatever can be wisely spared from his income, and possesses the rest as though he possessed not, holding it as God's steward, does in fact write "*holiness to the Lord*" on all that he acquires. In all his labor of acquisition he is as much actuated by a benevolent design, as if he were laboring with the intent to give every cent of his gains to the poor; and in all his labors he is as much accepted of God, and is doing as much for the sanctification of his own heart, as if—his own and his family's support being provided in other ways—he was laboring exclusively for God's poor. Accordingly the apostle says, "Let him that stole, steal no more; but let him labor, working with his hands, *that he may have to give to him that needeth.*" Here, it is not labor to supply his wants, or support his family; but he must be actuated by a design which looks beyond these, while it embraces them both. The adoption of this principle of laying off the Lord's portion from our income, if done from right motives changes the whole direction of our labor for gains, and enables us to "do it heartily as unto the Lord," to make his glory the end of our ordinary employment; and this inverts the whole machinery of the mind, that had before labored to accumulate for selfish gratifications.

Most have need of the diligent pursuit of some methods of gain, as the means of living. They are put upon constant toil and care to keep up their supplies; and they make more or less acquaintance with anxious solicitudes about the future. This experience will operate to promote inordinate desires to be rich: the details of gathering cents and dollars by the hardest, for subsistence and for children's bread, tend to form habits of inordinately desiring riches; and these habits, with no counteracting force, would soon fearfully contract the heart.

Then the multiplicity of cares which come upon one devoted to worldly accumulations, and the keen solicitudes employed on money-adventures, are so exhausting to the benevolent affections, so adapted to fix an undue value on money, that we need, for our own safety, all possible *engagements of mind in opposite directions.* No apology for neglecting the soul is so much in use as that of the multiplicity of cares, the want of time occasioned by labors and enterprises for gain. Risks must be run; the issue of pending adventures must be anxiously waited; new plans must be framed; the eye must be out on all turns of times and shifts in the currents of business. Alternations of hope and fear, of success and disaster, must keep the mind upon a stretch. And here is the occasion for the action of some counteracting element; for this is the reason why the gospel, preached to anxious worldlings, is a precious seed thrown away among thorns. The cares of the world and the deceitfulness of riches choke the word; they follow a man like his shadow, engrossing his thoughts, absorbing his soul, even while his body is in the house of God.

Now the more one is exposed to this deluge of cares, all tending to put forward the growth of selfish affections, the more he needs that method of counteraction provided in the divine rule under consideration. The mind acting so much in one direction, needs to regain its health and balance by much action in the other; and God has interposed to bring relief to this point of danger, and laid on us the duty of combating our love of money by making sacrifices of money. In this way he engages us to put one of our greatest enemies to the torture, and crucify him till he dies. This is a main branch of that great duty of mortifying the flesh with its affections and lusts: we give our love of money a new wound as often as we make a sacrifice in a gift to the poor. It comports with the economy of grace, that our giant enemy shall not die by a single blow; his destruction must be the work of time, of our whole life; and the plan of warfare best suited to its design, and to our natures, is one which engages us to a constant repetition of wounds, under which he dies by inches.

We have often seen those who, when in comparative poverty, *were generous with their little, but who have become penurious in becoming rich.* While their means were small, their outgoes trod close upon their incomes; their habit of giving was exercised and strengthened in some proportion to that of receiving, and the passion for accumulating had not room to spread its roots. But when the gains began sensibly to advance beyond the outgoes, a habit was formed of calculating how long it would take to reach such and such a sum; and with no active principle of benevolence proportionally counterworking the growing passion for gains, every little increase served to feed the passion, and every call for charities was resisted, because it postponed the time of reaching the proposed amount to be laid in. Aware of this principle of human nature, divine wisdom has given the caution, "If riches increase, set not your heart upon them;" hinting to us that the "setting of the heart upon them" is a common result of increase.

How many thousands have said in their hearts, O if I were as rich as such a one, how would I multiply the streams of my bounty; I would do nothing else than employ my wealth in doing good. But all such talk is vain; the process of becoming so rich would expose you to the fiercer heats of temptation, consuming all benevolent affections. The process of increasing wealth, without the outgoes of benevolence, is a process of confirming a feeling of poverty, a grasping desire for more, which like the grave will be ever crying, Give, give. A case has been known of a man at the age of threescore and ten, with his hundred thousand dollars, free from debt, and well invested, and yet crying like a child in apprehension of a possible experience of poverty. And this state of feeling was induced by a most natural process, by a mind given up to the passion of accumulating, without the counter-process of distributing. This is an invariable result of human experience in like circumstances, and it shows the importance of some law of conduct to keep our benevolent activities in use. Our condition is like that of a leaky vessel, which needs the constant labor of the pump in throwing out, to prevent its being submerged.

This fact in human nature should be well considered by *the young*, who are just entering upon a course of business, and upon the formation of character. Here is a powerful element in the production of character, which one cannot overlook without great damage to himself. Whether the young person regards his happiness and usefulness for time or for eternity, it is immensely important that he adopt this divinely appointed method of enlarging his heart.

And the church as a whole, and each professed Christian, has a special interest in this matter, because *covetousness is more especially the sin of the visible church.* It is so, because it is of such a nature that it can better conceal itself under a Christian profession. Spurious conversions more often consist of a change of the dominion of one lust for that of another; and as long as the heart remains unchanged, the lesser changes must consist in some substitution like this—an outward reformation must have its compensation in indulgences of inward lusts. It is no easy matter to be a drunkard, or profane, or dishonest, or licentious, and maintain a reputable standing among Christians; but one may indulge his supreme love of the world in the form of covetousness, and yet maintain a specious semblance of religion, and a fair standing in the church: indeed, the church is quite too charitable towards her uncharitable members, and that because her own standard of beneficence is too low, and her own perceptions of Christian obligation in this matter are dim. There is now and then in human society what is called a *miser*—a man of large means, whose selfishness is so extreme, as to defeat its own purpose and inflict misery on himself. Such a one is held in general abhorrence, as a violator of the primitive law of society. Living only for himself, and refusing to contribute to the pleasures and advantage of society, he is by the common consent of men degraded to a lower order of beings; men make themselves merry at his expense, and find amusement in discourse of his strange habits. But the man who, under more decent appearances, lives wholly to himself in the church of Christ, is even a more gross violator of the primitive law of that society, and his character deserves no more in dulgence. Yet, for the reasons which we have given, it finds a degree of indulgence; and worldly minds in the church can indulge their covetousness, when they could not other forms of sin as gross; and for the same reason, there are probably many in the church in supreme devotement to this form of sin, without being conscious of it. Hence, this sin should be the more guarded against in the church, by extending and confirming those habits of beneficence that counterwork it.

The grace of God first finds us in love of the world, inveterate, and supreme. It comes "teaching us, that denying ungodliness and worldly lusts, we should live soberly, righteously, and godly, in this present world." But its most effectual form of teaching this, is *by experience and active resistance.* It uses not only the word of instruction, but the power of action. All must be wrought into us, and wrought out by us. We cannot be put into the possession of a benevolent temper, and delivered from the tyranny of selfishness, by mere intellectual processes—by a mere presentation of reasons and inducements to benevolence. There is a work for the Holy Spirit; and, under that, there is occasion for all the processes of the human mind, by which the temper and habits are changed. And in the gospel law of alms, every Christian is bound to address himself to the cultivation of the benevolent affections, as one great end of life. Christ made it the duty of every one to pray, because his soul has need of all the quickening influences which prayer attracts ; and so he has made it the duty of every one to be constantly giving, because the heart has need of all these acts, for its own enlargement.

It is very possible, however, that some have never felt any want of the aid of such habits, and have never thought of giving as a means of crucifying the old man—just as many a prayerless man has never felt any need of those influences of the divine life which the good man secures by prayer. Of course, they have nothing in their own experience by which they can appreciate this Christian law of alms. They have no conflicts with the power of selfishness, because they have always been submissive to it. Such, however, would soon discover what is wanting, should they set this Christian rule before them, and endeavor to adopt it as the law of their conduct. Ye who have no need to cultivate a more benevolent heart, will of course find no reluctance to put in practice a rule of benevolence so reasonable. And if ye are reluctant, that reluctance is proof of your selfishness, and your need to enter a school of vigorous discipline. This reluctance is proof that you have need to exercise your heart to self-denials as constantly as the rule contemplates.

2. THIS SYSTEM OF BENEVOLENCE TENDS TO THRIFT.

Another reason why each one should enter upon these habits of systematic beneficence is, that God so attaches his blessing to them, that *even the temporal interests of the giver are usually promoted by them.* Out of the gifts of God to us, we bestow our gifts; and out of our gifts he brings the elements of our increase. There is here a circulation not unlike to that between the clouds and the earth watered by them. Suppose the clouds should withhold their gifts, and all the waters in the bottles of heaven should be hoarded there, for fear of exhaustion; the earth would soon become parched, and its lakes and rivers dry, and the supplies of rising vapor to fill the clouds would be diminished. But let the clouds freely dispense their treasures, and these treasures will have prompt returns.

In order to illustrate the principle that benevolence tends to thrift, let us now leave out of view every other purpose, and treat of the habit of giving simply as a means of benefiting ourselves. The Scriptures speak abundantly of this result. Take one example out of many, and one wherein temporal and spiritual benefit are intimately blended in the result. "He that soweth sparingly, shall reap also sparingly; and he that soweth bountifully, shall reap also bountifully. Every man, according as he purposeth in his heart, so let him give, not grudgingly, or of necessity, for the Lord loveth the cheerful giver; and God is able to make all grace abound towards you, that ye always, having all sufficiency in all things, may abound in every good work." The increase here promised is "all sufficiency in all things," to enable us to "abound in every good work." And as the giving of alms is one of the good works, a supply of the means for future gifts must here be included with the increase of grace which is promised. The imagery holds forth the idea of a rich soil, well prepared, and which requires only a generous dispensing of seed, in the shape of alms, to produce abundant increase of the seed sown. It tells us, that if we withhold the seed, we shall lose the advantage of a richly prepared soil; and if we dispense with a liberal hand, we shall have proportionately liberal returns. In other words, a wise and generous use of our property to charitable ends is, like the sowing of seed, a means of enriching ourselves, both spiritually and temporally.

That is, indeed, a narrow view which sees a reward in nothing but what terminates on ourselves. "None of us liveth to himself." The Christian blends his spiritual prosperity with that of the cause of his Redeemer. If he gives his money to carry and deposit the seed of the word in the most distant climes, and afterwards finds that that seed is bearing fruit sixty or a hundred-fold, he has his reward—that increase is a rich compensation for his money.

His own soul is enriched, both by sowing the seed and reaping the harvest. This is one of the most encouraging views of this work. By "dispersing abroad" and "giving to the poor," we "sow beside all waters," and deposit seeds which God watches over with delight. We have a wide and hopeful field on which to plant. And if the field be overgrown with briars and thorns, such agencies, under the divine economy, go along with the seed—such a powerful hand of a divine Cultivator prepares for it a place, that it will not return void.

"He that goeth forth bearing precious seed," goes in the strength of all the agencies that, in the economy of salvation, precede and enforce the word dispensed. And he that gives his alms to give wings to gospel truth, mingles his agencies with those of the Redeemer, labors in an enterprise which fills the heart of a God of mercy, which commands the ministry of angels, and which is sure to give glorious returns to all benevolent action. He casts his seed on a field where showers of grace are to fall, and over which the life-giving breath of the Spirit of God, like the winds of heaven, is to sweep. This is doing more than to give impulse to the most powerful human agencies. It is touching the springs of divine power, and securing results proportionate to that power. We also enter into the advantage of the precious nature of the seed sown. It is the living word of the living God, "the incorruptible seed, which liveth and abideth for ever," which lives by an ever-expansive life, shooting forth new roots and branches, and yielding seed for new plantings, long after the hand that planted is laid in the grave.

By contributing to convey the gospel into contact with the minds of men, whether through the pulpit or press, we are sowing seeds for a *glorious harvest.* We are applying heaven's remedy to the deadly wounds of a world. True, some of the seed will be devoured by the fowls, some will be choked with thorns, and yet, in the general result, the sower will not be disappointed. The purpose and promise of God insures him. Thus saith the Lord, "As the rain cometh down, and the snow from heaven, and returneth not thither, but watereth the earth and maketh it bring forth and bud, that it may give seed to the sower and bread to the eater, so shall my word be, that goeth forth out of my mouth. It shall not return unto me void. But it shall accomplish that which I please, and it shall prosper in the thing whereto I sent it." God has "magnified his word above all his name." The more it has been dishonored hitherto, by a world's rejecting it, the more is he pledged to magnify and vindicate it in time to come. And among the great events yet to transpire upon the face of this world, no event, or series of events, will compare with the lustre of that in which God will bring forth to view the power and glory of his own truth.

Into this work we enter when we contribute for the sowing of this seed. We not only cultivate our own benevolence, in acts of giving, but in the participation of the hopes, and prayers, and efforts for a world's conversion, we are holding our hearts in communion with God, and enriching them with all divine communications.

But, in a narrower sense, these habits of giving tend to thrift, and *promote our temporal interests* Jacob, in that crisis of his history when he was thrown out from his father's house, empty upon the world, with his whole fortune to make, made a vow, responsive to the heavenly vision which he had at Bethel, that of all that God should give him he would give a tenth. He adopted essentially the same rule which we here recommend—a rule which is within the reach of all. And how he prospered under it we are well informed. And, in the general result, it will be found that men will accumulate property faster under the rule of habitually giving a due proportion of their income, than they would without it. Nor does the fact that men often come into possession of property in disregard of this rule, show the contrary. For though men often acquire property without diligence, economy, or honesty, yet these virtues tend to thrift. So, all other things being equal, one may be said to be more sure to thrive with habits of beneficence than without them. Sometimes the reciprocity between the incomes and outgoes is sc manifest as to strike the most careless observer. Providence has a thousand ways of sustaining it.

Habits of giving favor the formation of other habits that tend to thrift. This rule operates as a law of conduct in the use of one's income, which excludes the waste made upon many frivolous, not to say hurtful gratifications. Most are wont to spend on needless things many small sums, whose aggregate is a large sum. But he who taxes his income to do good, soon finds in doing it a gratification greater than in all those little wasteful expenditures, and saves more than the amount of his charities. He has a better estimate of the value and use of money, and he feels a steadier impulse both to benevolence and to a wise economy. He has inserted into his mind a better regulator, and so saves what without it he would have wasted upon his vices. And not only his economy, but his industry, and indeed the whole sisterhood of thrifty virtues, are fostered by his habits of charity. Then these virtues, by a natural attraction, draw him into connections with others of like mind, and so secure him against temptations to wasteful expenditures.

This habit of benevolence also involves *a practical acknowledgment of God* and his blessing as the source of all thrift, which acknowledgment is a direct means of securing blessings. Then, as it is a general law of Providence that thrift shall follow diligence, so it is a general law that thrift shall follow benevolence. There is in this what may be called a secondary rule of retributions, having relations to human society somewhat similar to those which the retributions of the last day have to the kingdom of God. God, when higher interests do not interfere, sustains a providential retribution in the secular affairs of men, that they may learn from others' experience how to regulate their own conduct. These retributions are conducted according to general laws, which exist for reasons similar to those for which he sustains the constancy of nature's works. Nature in all her processes is unvarying, that we may use her best by knowing and obeying her laws, that we may know before we try it, that fire will burn, and water will drown. And for a like reason, God maintains a law that the benevolent shall thrive. It is written in the book of his providences as well as in that of his revelation, "Cast thy bread upon the waters, and thou shalt find it after many days." And there is nothing in human experience that gainsays it. There are indeed exceptions. For now and then God has some better and higher ends to answer, which require him in individual cases to suspend the rule.

That it is really a rule of divine Providence, is abundantly asserted in such scriptures as these: "Honor the Lord with thy substance, and the first fruits of all thine increase. So shall thy barns be filled with plenty, and thy presses shall burst out with new wine." "There is that scattereth and yet increaseth, and there is that withholdeth more than is meet, but it tendeth to poverty." "The liberal soul shall be made fat, and he that watereth shall be watered also himself." "He that hath pity on the poor, lendeth unto the Lord; and that which he hath given, will He pay him again." "He that hath a bountiful eye shall be blessed, for he giveth of his bread to the poor." "Bring ye all the tithes into the storehouse, and prove me now herewith, if I will not open you the windows of heaven, and pour you out a blessing, that there shall not be room enough to receive it." These scriptures have a meaning, and the meaning which they plainly express, and one which an observant eye will see verified in human experience. You hear God himself saying, "With what measure ye mete, it shall be measured to you again. Give, and it shall be given unto you; good measure, pressed down, shaken together, and running over." Thus is the liberality of men paid first in their own coin, and then paid again in the coin that goes current in heaven. While bad crops, bad debts, midnight fires, and the like disasters may soon consume what is gained by withholding more than is meet.

But you will ask, If this principle have been in operation, why is not the wealth of the world concentrated in the hands of the benevolent, or of the church? One reason is, that there has been with professed Christians a sad want of habits of testing the power of this principle. When the Jews were under a blight and curse for withholding their tithes, their poverty was no disproof of the principle. And the like to some extent may be said of us. But there is another view. Christianity usually begins to work on the lower strata of society, and thence works upward, with a steady elevating influence on all. Leaving the mountains of hoarded wealth, she comes to preside over the countless agencies that work for the elevation of the humbler classes. Her influence in this particular may be best seen as exerted on a whole community. For instance, the foundations of New England were laid by self-sacrificing men, whose "deep poverty abounded to the riches of their liberality." With smallest ability, they secured the best means of mental and spiritual culture then had in all the world. And they did it in a spirit of self-sacrifice for the honor of God. And all this was done in the rigors of a life in a newly opened forest. The gifts of gold and precious stones which they contributed to adorn their tabernacle of God, were gifts made while dwelling in the wilderness. And to that wise generosity every subsequent year has been bringing in returns in secular advantages. The present vigor of the New England character, and all that it has achieved for this country and the world, is traceable to that liberality.

And there are luminous illustrations of our principle wherever the descendants of the pilgrims are found.

But if any doubt the soundness of the principle, they have an easy and satisfactory way of resolving their doubts. Let them try it. Let them begin by giving a due proportion of their income for charities. and observing the result. There would be less of doubt if there were more experiments. But there have been some examples of those who, in some good degree, have lived not to themselves. Most of these, occupying humbler stations, have been little noticed; yet their record is on high. But some have stood forth conspicuous, both in wealth and liberality; and also as illustrations of the principle, that "he that watereth shall be watered also himself." Andrew Fuller says the poor people of Glasgow used to say, "David Dale gives his money by sho'elsful, and God Almighty sho'els it back again."

### 3. THE SUPERIOR EFFICIENCY OF THIS SYSTEM.

It belonged to divine wisdom to lay the plan for raising supplies for the wars of the cross—the plan for gathering from a people, few, scattered, and poor, as the first Christians were, the funds for the wide propagation of the gospel. And the plan which divine wisdom devised for this purpose is above the products of human wisdom in its measure, as much as is the plan of salvation by the cross. In its simplicity, there is a comprehensive and far-reaching skill. In its seeming foolishness, there is the wisdom of God and the power of God.

Let us contemplate this rule of beneficence given by Paul under the guidance of the Holy Spirit, as a part of the system employed to gather resources for the first propagation of the gospel. Here was, so to speak, a great and expensive war to be sustained. The little company of Christians were about to engage with the powers of darkness, entrenched in the strongholds of heathen Rome. Jehovah had summoned them to conquer the empire that had conquered the world; and he gave them a plan for raising the supplies, that was equal to the emergency. He saw that if all Christians, as fast as they became such, adopted this rule of Sabbath-gifts, the war would be self-supporting in its progress and cumulative in its energy. Look then at the merits of this rule, considered simply as a part of a system of finance for such a vast enterprise.

And let not *its great simplicity* conceal its merits; for this itself is one of its great advantages, betokening its divine origin. All that comes from God unites simplicity with comprehensive utility and grandeur. And this, unlike the complex systems of national finance, requires not the profound skill of the statesman to execute it. Its simplicity puts it into the hand of the merest child; it makes each person a treasurer for the Lord, and appoints his conscience a collector of the weekly dues, and disbursing agent to meet all demands upon the treasury. The great wisdom of the plan consists much in this, that so many and great ends are secured by a provision so simple, so easily and universally applicable.

Nearly allied to this feature is that of its great *economy*. Most systems of finance consume a large percentage of the funds in the expense of collecting; and the same is true of our benevolent agencies. But the universal adoption of this rule will, as we have seen, save what is now a great loss, which we suffer as the penalty of our neglect of the heaven-taught plan. We may, if we will, retain our old habit of passive giving under casual appeals, and pay for working the machinery that gives the impulses; but if one and all should adopt the system which makes each a vigilant and conscientious treasurer for the Lord, there would be, through the length and breadth of Zion, an omnipresent and spontaneous inflow, every cent of which would be available to the main purpose.

Then this rule *secures us against ruinous burdens.* Our revolutionary statesmen were often at their wit's end to find how to get adequate supplies for so exhausting a war without absorbing the means and alienating the hearts of the people. But in this war of the cross, the wealth of the people from whom the supplies must come is in still less proportion to the wants; yet here is a rule of finance which, if fully adopted, would fill the treasury, and leave every contributor none the poorer and more attached to the cause; for its whole tendency is to nourish and cultivate our love to the cause, to widen and deepen the fountains of our benevolent feeling, while it guards against laying heavy burdens, by leaving each to judge of his own obligations.

The *equity* of the rule is another advantage of it in a financial view. Paul says, "I mean not that other men be eased, and ye burdened; but by an equality, that now at this time your abundance may be a supply for their want, that their abundance also may be a supply for your want: that there may be equality." In respect to the equality of the pressure of the burdens, the universal adoption of this rule would effect a great change. Now the main burden is borne by a part of those whom it concerns. Probably one half of professing Christians contribute nothing. And it deserves to be considered, whether their neglect has not, at least in part, come from our neglect of the scriptural mode of laying the demands upon them—from our neglect to convince them that there is such a specific and universal law of benevolence binding upon them. But if this rule of Christian finance could be restored, and set in the place where the Holy Spirit has put it, every Christian's conscience might be reached. Let those who are now in a habit of giving, contribute by their example to make it a common law of Christian life that each shall keep his treasury for Christ, and the time will soon come, when it will not be easy to hold a fair repute among Christians while avoiding every pecuniary burden of the Christian cause. Why is it a matter of common law in the church, that all professing Christians shall habitually partake of the communion? That is not more expressly and repeatedly enjoined in the Bible than this duty. But there is in the case of the Lord's supper a specific rule generally acknowledged. Let such a rule be generally acknowledged as to acts of beneficence, and it is easy to see how the restoration of this rule would tend to equalize the burden and work.

But the inculcation of this rule is desirable not so much for the purpose of equalizing the burdens, as for *multiplying the bearers* of them. If it be true, that one-half of professing Christians, to say nothing of others, are practically disowning their obligations to give alms of such things as they have for evangelizing the world, some means not now in use are requisite to awake the public conscience where it slumbers. What is wanted, in order that the work should advance with the requisite rapidity and all-pervading energy, is, that *every individual* of the church should be an actual coworker in it—that every church, lesser or larger; that every family, rich or poor; that every individual Christian; yea, every one who means to maintain a practical sense of allegiance to Christ, shall become a regular source of supply. And it is natural to ask, In what way shall this result be secured? The present mode of presenting the claims of Christ upon his church, has, for the last quarter of a century, made little progress in this direction. The proportion of persons in the church who contribute next to nothing, has scarcely diminished in that time. It is hence plain that some different mode of reaching the public conscience is requisite. And who will say that this requisite lies not in a restoration of this apostolic rule? If those who now sustain habits of beneficence were to adopt the rule, and in their practice to commend it to the public mind as an acknowledged law of Christian life, it would soon acquire a living, moral force upon the public conscience, such as it cannot have while it is treated with neglect, and such as it would not be easy to resist. For who does not see, that a requirement taking this specific and imperative form, and laying its grasp on "*every one*," would reach many that cannot be reached by a mere general exhortation to benevolence. Every one, indeed, thinks himself already benevolent, after some sort. Every one thinks he is in a degree complying with the spirit of the general requirements, even if he give not a cent a year. But ask him to do this thing *in this way*, and he will see that you require what he is not doing. Tell him that God requires him to do it in this way. Let him see that the church are practically regarding this rule as binding on each and all, and that in his neglect of it, he is as much setting aside a law of the divine life as he would be in the neglect of daily prayer, and you would reach his conscience with a force entirely new. So it strikes us, that here is the remedy for that wide-spread neglect of this branch of Christian obligation over which Zion mourns. Give to this specific rule of beneficence the binding force of a living command of God, addressed to every man; let it live and breathe and speak through the common practice of those who sustain the work of evangelizing, and very soon all professing Christians would either adopt the rule, or disburden the church of their connection with it.

It also gives omnipresence and ceaseless *activity to the collecting agencies.* It saves the expenses of itinerant agents by establishing a local agency in every man's mind, and so commanding the gratuitous services of a thousand agents where it dismisses one. It gives to each conscience an agent's commission, a pulpit to occupy, a sermon to preach, and a collection to take up every Sabbath. And as every Christian's conscience is supposed to be quickened and guided by the ever-present Spirit of God, these countless agents are supposed to act under the guidance and control of one central mind. So that the universal adoption of this rule would secure a countless host of collecting agents, all acting harmoniously under the omnipresent agency of the Spirit of Christ. Seen from this view, this system has a simplicity and grandeur unrivalled.

And then no odium attaches to these collecting agencies. Having learned the excellence of the work of gathering treasures for beneficence, we are in the best way to be reconciled to such agencies. If an appointed agent of some benevolent society were, like Paul, to come to receive the gatherings made before he came, we should receive him as an angel of mercy. Now, when an agent comes, some give him a cold reception, because they think he wants *their* money; but if they had first commenced acting under their appointment as the Lord's treasurers, having a portion of *his* funds in charge, they would welcome the agent as a convenient bearer of the Lord's funds to the point of their destination.

In some rare cases, this rule is needed as a check on those who, giving from casual impulse, give more than they ought. Some may perhaps do injustice to themselves and families, by an inconsiderate profusion of their gifts. One excellent minister's wife said, that she rejoiced that her husband had adopted this rule, because she was now sure that his gifts would be regulated by his deliberate judgment, and not exceed his ability. And if the reader has a like amiable weakness, here is his protection. Let all your gifts go first into the Lord's treasury, kept in your own house; then, when a case of want appeals to you, the simple question will be, how much of that portion of the Lord's money under your hand you ought to appropriate to that case. And when demands are made for undeserving objects, or when you are tempted to give, as the easiest way to dispose of a troublesome applicant, the question will be, Shall I take this portion of my Lord's money, which is sacred to his uses, and thus throw it away?

This rule also aids to a discrimination between what are, and what are not objects of charity. There is such a gradual shading off between gifts in charity and gifts for other purposes, that we are likely to credit ourselves too much on the score of charity, unless we have first made it a rule to take every gift in charity out of a fund already distinctly appropriated to the Lord. In that case, we should avoid underrating our obligations through our overestimate of our actual gifts.

This financial rule works admirably, in producing *large results from small means*, in that it both generates wealth where it gathers it, and makes massive ingots out of the carefully-garnered grains and dust of gold. A financier for a nation plans to gather into the public treasury the needed percentage of the existing wealth of the people. But Paul's plan of finance was laid to work where wealth was not—among those required to labor, working with their hands, that they might have to give to him that needeth. God has not set in progress a kingdom of poor men, and put it upon a work that involves great expenses, without putting it upon a course of action that will furnish the supplies. This is done by graduating the value of the gift of each by the ability and sacrifice of the giver—by putting the widow's farthing as high as the rich man's pound; thus making sure of the small grains, that will grow into the mass of a mountain. As it is not the dash of a single water-spout here and there that fertilizes the broad bosom of the earth, but the countless little drops falling thick and fast over the whole surface, so it is with the accumulations of evangelical finance. The wonderful capacity of that system lies in its power of generating and gathering up the minute grains, till they produce effective funds; and the secret of the power which brings forth even the smallest gifts, lies in the consideration given to the smallest gifts proceeding from the love of Christ The plan which puts the poor man's cent on a par with the rich man's dollar, generates funds where there are none, gathers the thick and pregnant cloud from accumulations of vapor too thin to be visible. It enables the poor to join in making many rich.

But we have not the whole of this idea, till we have seen how this system *increases the giver's ability*. Other systems only transfer a portion of the people's wealth to the public treasury; but this goes in among the contributors, and disciplines them to economy, diligence, temperance, and all the virtues that tend to thrift, and so generates more wealth than it gathers. If the poor man wishes to enter upon a thrifty course, he does well to begin where Jacob did, when, an exile and a penniless wanderer, he lodged in Bethel, with a rock for his pillow and heaven for his canopy, and when he made that vow, "Of all that thou shalt give me, I will surely give the tenth unto thee." It is no miracle, but the ordinary process of providence, that makes this habit of returning a portion of God's gifts contribute to our wealth. And this process of providence challenges our observation as much as the miracle by which the widow's handful of meal and cruse of oil wasted not, according to the word of the Lord.

A special beauty of this system is, that whatever it brings into the Lord's treasury, it brings by means most purely *voluntary*. There is not even the compulsion of eloquent appeals to sympathy. The Lord loves a cheerful giver, and will have his conquests made with no forced supplies. He will have the energy of his cause sustained by the concurrence of willing hearts. For this reason, he frowns on all attempts to sustain his gospel in its purity by compulsory means. Those battles of the warrior which are with confused noise and garments rolled in blood, may well be sustained by supplies raised by force. Before them is the garden of Eden, and behind them a wilderness. But Zion's King seeks this as his especial honor, that when his conquests shall be complete, and the world shall have welcomed his sceptre, it may be seen that all the supplies of his armies have come from the spontaneous gifts and the loyal hearts of his people. He has a right, indeed, to make forced loans; for in them he would only be drawing upon his own funds, since the silver and the gold, and the cattle upon a thousand hills, are his. And he does in many ways force an unwilling service from hearts and hands that intend it not. Yet his wisdom has appointed, respecting the carrying forth of the gospel to the benighted, that through your mercy they shall obtain mercy—that thus faith shall come by hearing the preachers of your sending. He will have it appear in the grand result, that the very essence of his kingdom and its self-expansive power, consists in that love to God and man which has expression in gifts for the spread of salvation. And that mode of benevolent action most intimately harmonizes with his plans, which is most purely spontaneous on behalf of his people coworking with him.

Another desideratum in public finances is, that the supplies shall be *steady and reliable.* And were this plan generally adopted, there would be no need of the expenses of our evangelizing societies running beyond their income—no need for extra and spasmodic efforts to throw off a crushing debt; for the income would be a steady stream, supplied by countless everflowing springs.

Another advantage of the rule is, that it has that

in its own structure and use which *disarms objections.* If one absolutely refuses tribute to Christ, and denies that he has any money-account to keep with him, he has indeed no use for it; but let any one admit his obligation to give alms of such things as he has, and he can give no valid reason why he should not do it in the way which this rule describes. If alms-giving be no part of your religion—if you think that your having been "bought with a price" confers no pecuniary obligations, you must be left to settle your accounts with the Redeemer at the final reckoning. But those who think alms-giving as much a duty as prayer or honesty, have here a rule which God has given for its performance. It claims their adoption by divine authority, and by reason of its intrinsic excellence and manifold advantages. And any one who refuses to adopt it, may be asked to bring against it a reasonable objection. Is it, that it would bind you to do more than you are able? The terms of the rule show the contrary. Is it, that your ability is small, and your gifts would be inconsiderable? It was for just such cases that the rule was more especially made. Is it, that you cannot always be sure of having the money in hand at the time? That is not needful. Is it, that you cannot so often judge of your ability? You *do* as often judge of your ability, in graduating your ordinary expenditures. Do you say that many have gone well through life without such a rule? Now, a command of God which has slumbered for a thousand years is coming to life, and you will do well to heed it.

Furthermore, this plan of finance exceeds all others *in its enforcements.* In these the great Contriver employs his infinite wisdom, and shows his control of the springs of our minds. He proposes an end to be accomplished *upon ourselves* by what we give to him; and he asks our gifts, not so much because he or his cause needs them, as that he may have them as proofs of our self-devotement to him. He comes, not so much to awaken our sympathies for the suffering, as to constrain us by the love of Christ. When he calls us to beneficence, he speaks not so much of the sufferings of man, as of the mercies of Christ. He says, "Ye know the grace of our Lord Jesus Christ, that, though he was rich, yet for your sakes he became poor." And by a substitution, warranted by his having stood as surety for a dying world—his having come to seek and save the lost, and his having made the lost his own—he says, "Inasmuch as ye have done it unto one of the least of these, ye have done it unto me." So he causes the wants of the world to plead with us out of his own mouth, and to plead all that he has done for us, and all the claims which he has upon us. And the whole is backed by eternal sanctions. He does not bind this law upon us with civil pains and penalties. If men prefer to set aside his claims, and snatch and hoard all that he gives them, he holds his peace for the time. It may be, he lets the stream of his bounty flow on, and lets them pass with credit among men, and without censure in the church. But in a coming day he will say, "Inasmuch as ye did it not to one of the least of these, ye did it not to me."

This rule then commends itself to our adoption by its superior efficiency as a mode of financial action. It was evidently appointed by divine wisdom, not only because of its being best adapted to cultivate a benevolent character, but because best adapted to increase the amount given in charity.

It opens a way in which the poor can contribute a considerable amount. Indeed, there is no other way for a large class of Christians, many of whom are the excellent of the earth, the true nobility, to bear any considerable part in the most excellent of all enterprises. The amount which they can give at any one time, without the previous process of laying aside a little now and a little then, is so small, that they would be discouraged from attempting any thing. But let this rule be adopted in the church, and restored to its proper place, and secure a general concurrence in it, and you will vastly multiply the hearts and hands engaged to swell the general amount. The single deposits of each will be small; but even the poorest at the year's end will bring you a handsome donation. And the aggregate donations of the poor will surpass all previous expectations. Of those whose means are smallest, there are some who, taught by an instinctive benevolence and sagacity, have adopted *the substance* of this rule as their only means of procuring their share in the luxury of beneficence, and are now actually laying aside their penny at a time, to nurse it up to the pound, to be devoted to the cause of Christ. But while this is true of some, the greater part are discouraged and excluded, in our exclusion of God's appointed rule, which is their deed of partnership in the enterprise. A restoration of this rule would then bring at once a strong reinforcement to the army for subduing this world to Christ.

But the reinforcements would come not alone from the poor. Let this rule be recovered from oblivion, and let it come to be a universally admitted truth, that every Christian is bound to obey it, as much as he is bound to keep the Sabbath, and the habits of a large portion of professed Christians will be revolutionized.

But the greatest increase will be from the operation of the rule on those who now sustain the burden of these enterprises. Let them come under a regular system, and from week to week set apart a portion "as God has prospered them," and they will soon find themselves giving more, with less of seeming sacrifice. They will come out at the year's end with much greater amounts deposited in the treasury of the Lord, and with their own funds not lessened by that increase. They will find their beneficence, as it has become a matter of more frequent recurrence, and more constant business, to have become also a matter of more substantial satisfaction; thus, more will be done with more pleasure, and with more ability for doing it.

Here then is a method by which, if the church is willing to obey a simple and plain command of her Lord, a vast increase may be secured to the means of evangelizing the world. And this fact pleads with unlimited power, when we reflect to what rich account all means can now be turned—when we reflect that the whole world is one inviting field of missionary labor—that Bibles will be received and used as fast as they can be made and given—that preachers will find a hearing in as great numbers as they can be sent—that colporteurs might advantageously be increased a hundred-fold, and that Christian presses might find employment in unlimited numbers. This is the time to sow abundantly beside all waters, and if there is any principle of action, that can put us in possession of ten-fold the present incomes of our evangelizing societies, we want it now.

### 4. EXAMPLE OF THE PRIMITIVE CHURCH.

The example of the primitive church may instruct us in this duty. The type of benevolence that appeared in the pentecostal revival, was nobly sustained in the church for several ages. The church first gathered at Jerusalem being scattered abroad, went everywhere preaching the word and kindling the fires of their own zeal and love; and apostles testified of the new churches reared in Gentile nations, that "their deep poverty abounded to the riches of their liberality," and that they extended their gifts even "beyond their power." Next to bringing their own minds into captivity to the obedience of Christ, their chief care was the conversion of others.

The history of the first two centuries of Christianity abounds with remarkable facts, showing with what zeal and entireness of soul, the church went into the work of converting the world. Those who perilled their lives and suffered the loss of all things *in preaching*, were not the only ones who made sacrifices for the spread of the gospel. Some spent all besides a bare support of themselves, to furnish the means of evangelizing others; those who had no property gave the avails of their labor; and it is recorded of one man that he sold himself as a slave to a heathen family, to get access to them for their conversion, and for years cheerfully endured the labor and condition of a slave till he succeeded with the whole family, and took his liberty from the gratitude of the converts. The same person, on a visit to Sparta, again entered himself as a slave in the family of the governor of Sparta and served two years, and again succeeded in his design. The fires of such a benevolence, burning wherever a company of Christians was gathered, could not fail soon to overspread the world, and in the space of one generation most of the nations then known to the civilized world, were more or less evangelized. And if such a tone of benevolent action could be now restored to the church, another generation would not pass before the earth would be "full of the knowledge and glory of God, as the waters cover the sea."

And *their kindness to the poor was boundless.* Christians felt as much bound to this as to prayer, or to the hearing of the gospel. Contributions and actual exertions for their relief, were made indispensable parts of Sabbath exercises. At the close of public worship, lists of the needy, the widows and orphans, were produced and considered, and additions were made from time to time as new cases occurred; and the wants of these were supplied from the funds gathered by free contributions. No heart-stirring appeals were needed to awake dormant sympathies. The spontaneous flowings of the fountains of their benevolence supplied every stream. There were no hospitals for the poor and sick except of their creating, and few of the heathen ever entered abodes of suffering on errands of mercy. The Christians supported not only their own needy, but bore the burden which hardness of heart in their heathen neighbors cast upon them; and the zeal with which they entered into every labor of love is well-nigh incredible. Ladies of highest rank acted as nurses for the sick, exposing themselves to contagions, and devoting their purse, their toil, their prayers, and their instructions, to pour consolation into the cells of extremest wretchedness. It was a day when scenes of wretchedness specially abounded—when the world was often visited by famines and pestilences, and the heathen had become shockingly corrupt in morals, and desperate and reckless under the fearful visitations of heaven; and the miracles of Christian benevolence shone brighter through the darkness, and contrasted strangely with the cold indifference of the heathen towards their nearest friends. For instance, in the time of Cyprian, the plague came upon Carthage with fearful and protracted visitations. The heathen abandoned their sick and dying. The highways were strewed with corpses which none dared to bury. But Christians faced every danger, and often sacrificed life in alleviating sufferings and burying the dead, whether of Christians or heathen. While, among the heathen, parents deserted their own children, and children trampled on unburied corpses of parents.

But one of the greatest taxes on primitive benevolence was laid by *persecution*, which now and then went through the church like a tempest. No sooner did the report go abroad that a fellow-Christian was in a dungeon, than crowds of Christians came around the prison-doors begging admission, meekly bearing the insults of surly guards, and using every means to procure the prisoner's release. Some would beset the prison-walls days and nights, praying for the deliverance, or the triumphant death of the imprisoned martyrs. When any were doomed to waste their lives in toil in distant and unwholesome mines, contributions were sent for their relief, by the hands of those who undertook long journeys to convey the sympathies and offerings of the church. To show the temper of the times, a party set out from Egypt in the depth of winter, to relieve some brethren in the mines of Cilicia. They came to Cesarea, and there the heathen seized a part of them, put out their eyes, and horribly mutilated them. But in spite of such dangers, such journeys were often performed. No floods of persecution could quench the desire to convey consolation to those suffering for Christ's sake. And those who lived to return and tell what they had seen of martyrs in the mines—how they toiled, and bore their chains, and honored their Redeemer, were loaded with many honors.

To supply resources for this great variety of pressing calls for charity, there was the Sabbath contribution, commenced by order of Paul, in which all, rich and poor, concurred. Then, in case of great public calamities, the people held fasts, and gave to the church what they saved by abstinence from food. In pressing emergencies, the plate which the church had acquired in more prosperous days was melted down and sold. Others bound themselves to set apart a certain portion of their income; others held periodical fasts, devoting the saving thereby to the church. Some wealthy individuals, when converted, sold their whole estates, and betook themselves to manual labor for their own support. Others managed their estates, devoting the whole income to the cause.

Indeed, so much did the first Christians excel in acts of charity, that these constituted their peculiar characteristic, and the wonder of the heathen world. If the church had any thing whereof to boast, it was this. This is illustrated by the well-known act of the deacon of the church at Rome, in the time of the emperor Decius. The tyrant demanded that the treasure of the church should be surrendered. The deacon required one day's time to gather it. In that time, he assembled all the blind, lame, sick, and poor, that were supported by the church, and then called in the emperor, and said, these are the treasures of the church! In the time of Chrysostom, the church under his care had on its catalogue of sick and poor, three thousand regular beneficiaries, besides extraordinary applications every day for assistance.

Indeed, so glorious and impressive was the robe of Christian charity worn by the primitive church, that Julian the apostate, seeking to effect in his day a resurrection of the prostrate heathen institutions endeavored to put this robe upon paganism, expecting that it would, like the bones of Elisha, give life to the dead. Here is the ever-memorable testimony of that crafty and politic emperor: "Let us consider that nothing has so much contributed to the progress of the superstition of Christians, as their charity to strangers. I think we ought to discharge this obligation ourselves. Establish hospitals in every place. For it would be a shame for us to abandon our poor, while the Jews have none, and the impious Galileans provide not only for their own poor, but also for ours."

## CONCLUSION.

Place, now, distinctly before the mind, what, if we have rightly read the New Testament, the Lord requires of you, be your property less or more. It is, that you shall now commence, if you have not already, a habit of *setting apart a portion of your income on the Sabbath, or at other stated times*, for charitable uses, regulating with a generous heart and a good conscience the amount appropriated by the ability which God shall give you. Knowing this to be a plain requirement of Christ, can you hesitate? If you can, you are not able to say, "The love of Christ constraineth us." Indeed, what right of choice have you in the case? "Ye are not your own: ye are bought with a price," and are bound to "glorify God," not only with your money, but with "your body and your spirit, which are his." "Ye are bought with a price"—"not with corruptible things, as silver and gold, but with the precious blood of Christ." Where Christ asks your silver, he has given his blood. Do you realize that he has borne the curse for you, and snatched you from the gates of hell? And yet, have you no generous emotions when he asks for these gifts, in token of your love? Do you forget the mercy of "our Lord Jesus Christ, who, though he was rich, yet for your sakes became poor, that ye through his poverty might be rich?" And now that through his poverty you are becoming rich, or think you are, now that the riches of his grace begins to flow in upon your soul, and God is endowing you with the wealth of the divine nature, and he comes to you in the person of his poor, and asks for a portion of his own gifts to be returned, have you a heart to deny him? After all your hopes and professions, is this the real temper of your mind? Look the thing in the face again. By becoming poor, he has made you rich; and in his poverty, which pleads in the mouth of his poor, he asks you to return enough of the gifts which he has put into your hand, to serve as a substantial token of your grateful love. And have you no heart to give it? We ask you, then, just to realize what is the state of your heart. We ask, how dwelleth the love of God in you? We ask you to realize with whom you are dealing, and to whom he will say, "Inasmuch as ye did it not to one of the least of these, ye did it not to me."

Furthermore, this mode of consecrating our prop

erty to Christ was included in the terms of our oath of allegiance, or surrender to him. That surrender included all that we are and have. Any thing short of this would not bring us into covenant with God. And if we have really covenanted with him, we stand pledged by oath to make such a use of our property. And as far as we are coming short of this, are we not keeping back a part when we had sworn to devote the whole? And how does this differ from the sin of Ananias and Sapphira?

But you say, perhaps, that the great body of professed Christians, and those of reputable standing have gone through life without any such rule of action, and why should more be required of you? "The times of this ignorance God winked at." A veil rested upon the minds of most respecting this matter; but the views of the Christian world are in the process of a great change. As new enterprises have been thrown upon our hands, new light has come into our minds. We now begin to see this thing as it is, and are now without the excuse which our fathers had. We are in a state of transition to positions of purer light and more scriptural benevolence; and soon the church will look upon neglect of this rule as we now look upon preceding ages, that for a thousand years gave scarcely a dollar for the conversion of heathen. We trust the time is not distant, when the professed Christian who has no habit and system of alms-giving, will be regarded in the church as the miser now is in society. This living to one's self, and withholding from Christ, will be as odious as is now the trade of the swindler.

But perhaps some will still say, that they admit the obligation to practise a generous charity, but they hold that the gospel leaves every one to decide for himself how much he ought to give; and why not let each one decide as to the mode of giving? Why insist so much on its being done in this particular way? You might say the same about the duty of Sabbath-keeping. You admit the obligation to preach and hear and pray and praise; but why insist on its being done on that particular day? We could in both cases give many reasons. But this is enough, that God has commanded it; and the command to do this work of charity on the Sabbath, or at other stated times, is as explicit as the command to keep the Sabbath. Some individuals might devote as many hours to spiritual exercises, if there were no Sabbath; and some individual might give as much in charity, if there were no law requiring this stated appropriation of portions of income. But to make the matter sure with all, divine wisdom has made this appointment, and who are we, that we set it aside?

# ZACCHEUS;

OR,

# THE SCRIPTURAL PLAN

OF

# BENEVOLENCE.

BY REV. SAMUEL HARRIS,

CONWAY, MASS.

And Zaccheus stood and said unto the Lord, Behold, Lord, the half of my goods I give to the poor.—LUKE 19:8.

PUBLISHED BY THE

AMERICAN TRACT SOCIETY,

150 NASSAU-STREET, NEW YORK.

# CONTENTS.

# SCRIPTURAL

# PLAN OF BENEVOLENCE.

## CHAPTER I.

### PLAN PRESCRIBED IN THE BIBLE.

THOUGHTFUL readers cannot but observe the importance ascribed in the Bible to acts of charity; the boldness with which the inquirer for salvation is commanded, "Sell that thou hast, and give to the poor;" the preëminence in deadliness assigned to the love of money as "the root of all evil;" the earnestness and frequency with which men are warned of its perils, and of the absolute incompatibility of serving God and mammon; the elevation given to the standard of benevolence, "Let this mind be in you, which was also in Christ Jesus;" and the vital connection everywhere implied between alms-giving and the highest attainments of piety, of spiritual power, and spiritual joy. They cannot but be startled, sometimes, with the apprehension that there is a strange contrast here between the Bible and the church; that the faithful applying of scriptural truth on this point, might make many a professed disciple go away, like the young ruler, sorrowful, or cry, as they did of old when Christ had been preaching on this very subject, "Who then can be saved?" And they cannot but be justified in inferring that this very contrast between the church and the Bible is a prominent cause of embarrassment in our benevolent enterprises; of the prevailing worldliness of Christians; the limited success of efforts for the conversion of souls; the fewness of those who enter into the deepest experience of the spiritual life; and the absence of that rapidity of enlargement and energy of action which marked the apostolic church.

But the Bible not only teaches the importance of charity, it lays down principles systematizing it. To secure its divinely appointed prominence in advancing the enterprises, the piety, the power, and the blessedness of the church, it is necessary to understand and to practise the divinely appointed plan of SYSTEMATIC BENEVOLENCE.

"UPON THE FIRST DAY OF THE WEEK LET EVERY ONE OF YOU LAY BY HIM IN STORE, AS GOD HATH PROSPERED HIM."

This requires that charitable appropriations be *systematic.* It requires some plan, deliberately and prayerfully adopted, assessing on the income a determinate proportion for charitable purposes. It forbids giving merely from impulse, as under the excitement of an eloquent charity sermon, or the accidental sight of distress It forbids giving merely at random what happens to be convenient. It transfers the control of charity from the capriciousness of sensibility and the parsimony of convenience, to the decisions of reason and conscience. It regulates impulse by principle. It brings the whole subject into the closet, to be determined by prayer and deliberation, according to the rules of the Bible, in the fear of God, and the spirit of consecration to him. In carrying into effect the plan thus deliberately adopted, charitable appropriations will enter into the calculations as much as the necessary expenditures on the person, the family, or the business; they will be managed with as systematic exactness as any branch of business; they may with advantage be as regularly booked. A line written on a memorandum of his charities, kept by a systematic giver and found after his death, suggests an important reason for keeping such a record: "I keep this memorandum lest I should think I give more than I do."

They who obey the scriptural rule of benevolence, *do not wait to be solicited.* Like the impoverished but liberal Macedonians, they are "willing of themselves." If a way of conveying their gifts is not at hand, they seek one out, as Paul describes the Macedonians: "praying us with much entreaty that we would receive the gift, and take upon us the fellowship of the ministering to the saints." Thus, according to the inspired plan, the urgent solicitation is not on the part of the agent of benevolence to draw charity from the giver, but on the givers' part to find the agent to receive and disburse their charities. Let this system be adopted, and the funds of benevolent societies would flow in unsolicited, and the expense of collecting agencies would cease.

The scriptural rule requires *frequent and stated* appropriations. "On the first day of the week, let every one lay by him." If it is allowable sometimes to depart from the letter of this law, the spirit of it must be regarded. Having adopted his plan of giving, the giver is required at frequent and stated times to examine his income, assess on it the prescribed proportion, and set aside the amount sacred to benevolence. His appropriations must be *frequent*, to keep pace with his earnings and with the constant calls of benevolence; *stated*, that they may not be forgotten. This is inconsistent with giving a large sum, and then for a long time nothing, and with the intention of giving only or chiefly at death.

The text cited requires that charities be *proportionate to the income*. In the laws regulating the Jewish tithes and offerings, God prescribed precisely what proportion should be given. This was practicable in a system of laws for a single agricultural people, among whom every family was entitled to an inalienable inheritance in the soil; but the gospel, designed for all nations and ages, could not with equity fix the precise proportion. And it fits the entire character of the gospel—free grace from God, free love from man—to leave the decision of this point to the unconstrained love of those who have freely given all to Christ; for "God loveth a cheerful giver." But the principle by which the proportion to be given is determined, is most explicitly stated. "Let every one lay by him in store, *as God hath prospered him.*" Nothing can satisfy God's claim less than a consecration to benevolence of an amount proportioned to the prosperity God has given. Do you think yourself benevolent because you give something—much? If you give less than "according as God hath prospered you," yours is but the benevolence of Ananias and Sapphira.

This principle of proportionate benevolence is repeated in various forms in the Bible. "If any man minister, let him do it as of the ability that God giveth." "As every man hath received the gift, even so minister the same one to another, as good stewards of the manifold grace of God." "As we have opportunity, let us do good unto all men." "I am debtor" to put forth benevolent efforts "as much as in me is." "Honor the Lord with the first-fruits of all thine increase." There are three points in this requirement of benevolence proportioned to the income.

1. *All must give.* "Let *every one.*" The gospel does not release the poor from giving. The smallest income can pay a proportion. Nothing

short of the total cessation of God's gifts can exempt from the law, "As God hath prospered him." The Macedonian church were praised for giving in "their deep poverty." The story of the widow's two mites settles for ever the acceptableness to God of offerings from the poor. And one dollar thus given, has often a moral power greater than a thousand. The benevolence of Louisa Osborn the colored domestic, who, from the wages of one dollar a week, paid twenty dollars a year to educate a youth in Ceylon, as it has been brought to light by the missionary who witnessed the unusual benefits of her donation to the mission, has thrilled the hearts of American Christians. The widow's two mites, which were all her living, lifted to the gaze of the universe and illuminated by the Saviour's commendation, have exerted and will exert a power which no mine of gold can equal—as if a dew-drop, expending its whole being to refresh one tiny flower, had been transformed, as it exhaled to the skies, into a star, and fixed in the brightness of the firmament to bless the creation for ever.

2. Donations should *increase with the increase of ability to give.* "As God hath prospered him." This requires the rich to give proportionally to their increasing wealth, though, in order to do it, they must give thousands of dollars where they used to give one. And these great donations are not to be regarded as specially praiseworthy, more than small-

er gifts which cost as great sacrifice and are proportionally as much. In both cases the giver has but "done what it was his duty to do."

3. *The rich must give a larger proportion of their income than the poor.* A poor widow with a helpless family cannot give a tenth of her earnings without taking bread from her children. Will any imagine that a man who has wealth, or even a competency, is required to give no larger a proportion of his income than that widow? A poor laborer may be subjected to more inconvenience by giving five dollars, than a man of wealth by giving five thousand. Hence, the greater a man's wealth, the larger must be the proportion of income which he gives. Hence the propriety of a rule adopted by Mr. N. R. Cobb, a merchant of Boston: to give from the outset *one quarter* of the net profits of his business; should he ever be worth $20,000, to give *one half* of the net profits; if worth $30,000, to give *three quarters;* and if ever worth $50,000, to give *all* the profits. This resolution he kept till his death, at the age of 36, when he had already acquired $50,000, and was giving all his profits.

Different individuals, who have aimed at systematic benevolence, have come to different conclusions as to the proportion which they ought to give; and, perhaps, each one to a correct conclusion, in his particular circumstances. Zaccheus gave *half* of his goods to the poor, besides restoring fourfold his unjust gains. The first converts at Jerusalem, to meet their peculiar circumstances, sold their possessions and made distribution of the avails, as every man had need. Paul repeatedly intimates that he had suffered the loss of all things. Others have adopted plans similar, in the main, to that of Mr. Cobb, already cited. Others, after paying what has been needful for a most economical support, have given all their income. John Wesley is an example. "When his income was £30 a year, he lived on £28, and gave away £2; the next year his income was £60, and still living on £28, he had £32 to give. The fourth year raised his income to £120, and steadfast to his plan, the poor got £92." Others, again, have given a tenth of the gross amount of their receipts.

Such is the scheme of Christian beneficence devised in heaven and enjoined by inspired wisdom. Let every man consider that in neglecting it, he sets at naught the authority and the wisdom of God. Men may deride it; and so it is written of one of our Lord's many discourses on the right use of property, "The Pharisees, *who were covetous*, heard these things, and they derided him."

## CHAPTER II.

### PRINCIPLES WHICH GUIDE IN REDUCING THE SCRIPTURAL PLAN TO PRACTICE.

We now suppose that the child of God, convinced that the foregoing is the scriptural plan of beneficence, has retired to his closet solemnly to adopt this plan, and to determine the details of its application to himself. We direct his attention to three principles which should guide him.

1. *The aim of all business must be to glorify God.* This aim must give simplicity and unity to the entire life. Property is to be sought, not as the chief end, but as a means of doing good. The Christian is not to ask, "What part of my income shall I consecrate to God's service?" By the very act of becoming a Christian, he consecrated ALL to God's service in doing good. He has only to ask what part he must devote to this particular way of serving God—charitable gifts—in order that his whole property may accomplish most for God's glory. He is to remember, that the same principle is to regulate every step in the conduct of business, every new enterprise, every investment, every expenditure; that he is not at liberty to appropriate a dollar in any way, except as he can see that by so appropriating it he can do most to glorify God. He is not to think of setting aside a certain proportion for God, and do-

ing what he pleases with the rest; he is to devote all to God's service, and expend, invest, or give it, in such proportions as will effect most for that end.

The law of systematic benevolence, therefore, does not forbid spending money on ourselves, educating children, laying aside something for the future. It does not forbid acquiring property; we may make the five pounds, ten. We are even required so to do serving God in the act; "not slothful in business serving the Lord." But no act of acquiring or spending money can be justified, unless it appears that by it most can be accomplished for God's glory.

The Bible everywhere exhibits business as wholly subservient to this great end. "Whether ye eat, or drink, or whatsoever ye do, do all to the glory of God." "Seek ye *first* the kingdom of God." It teaches that Christians are stewards, having nothing but the talents which God has intrusted to them to be increased for him. The requirement, "Sell that ye have and give alms," the similar direction given by Christ to the young ruler, cannot mean less than that all worldly business and possessions are to be entirely subservient to doing good.

Benevolence, then, must be not only systematic, but systematizing, pervading and regulating the whole business How is it possible to be seeking first the kingdom of God, when, practically, the controlling aim of all the transactions of business is to make money; when giving to the treasury of the Lord is only occasional and secondary, seldom occupying the thoughts; called forth, perhaps, only by solicitation; trifling, it may be, in amount; and determined only by the impulse or convenience of the moment? It is as if the steward of an estate should devote its income to himself, making only an occasional and trifling gift to the family of the absent owner, nay, leaving its members to suffer without caring for their wants. It is reversing the sentiment of the humble suppliant, "The dogs eat of the crumbs which fall from their master's table," and giving the crumbs to the master, while the dogs eat at the table.

In view of this principle, let the Christian decide what part of his income the promotion of God's glory and the advancement of his cause require him to expend on himself and his family, what part to invest, what part to give.

2. The Christian will recognize the duty of *self-denial.* Does he say, "I give all that is convenient?" This language has widely different meanings on different lips. Some do not find it *convenient* to dispense with the most costly, or even the most hurtful luxuries. Some do not find it *convenient* to give half as much in a year as they spend on a single article of luxury, or in the indulgence of a single pernicious habit. The Bible does not say, "Do good as much as is convenient," but, "as much as in you is." The necessity of self-denial is too plainly revealed to allow the thought that the scriptural

law of benevolence can be obeyed without it. It is not only reiterated in direct commands, but is woven into all the inspired teachings respecting the Christian life. The spirit that breathed on the cross is presented as the spirit which must breathe through the whole church. If the church is "the body of Christ," Christ's heart beats within it, sending to the remotest limb the throbbings of its own love. He who is not thus "in Christ," and imbued with his self-sacrificing love, is none of his. The Christian, then, must make his appropriations to charity in the spirit which says, "What things were gain to me, those I counted loss for Christ."

Here, however, every Christian is left to the decision of his own mind, guided by the rules and animated by the love of Christ. The following fact shows Wesley's practice: "In 1775 the Accountant-General sent him a copy of the excise order for the return of plate: 'Rev. sir, as the commissioners cannot doubt but you have plate for which you have hitherto neglected to make entry, etc.'—to which he wrote this memorable answer: 'Sir, I have two silver tea-spoons at London, and two at Bristol. This is all the plate which I have at present, and I shall not buy any more while so many around me want bread.'" Normand Smith of Hartford, deeming his house too expensive to be consistent with his rules of Christian benevolence, determined to sell it. An account was published in the newspapers a few years since of a man who lived in a garret, on bread and water, that he might have the more to give. The writer knows a minister and his wife who lived without many of the comforts of life, for the same object. Admit that some have gone to an extreme. But is not this nobler and more acceptable to God, than to go to the extreme of indulging self, without any denial? And where one goes to an extreme in this direction, are there not thousands in the churches who have never learned by experience what self-denial is? And which is most like Him who had not where to lay his head? As to the extent to which self-denial must be carried, "let every man be fully persuaded in his own mind;" as to its necessity to full compliance with the scriptural rule of benevolence, let every one heed the Saviour's words, "If any man will come after me, let him deny himself." And it is to be supposed that the rich are not excused from the duty, nor debarred from the privilege, more than the poor.

3. The Christian will regard his charities, however great, as the *discharge of an obligation.* The right to give or withhold at pleasure belongs to God alone. To his creatures God says, "Ye are not your own;" and emphatically to his ransomed children, "Ye are not your own; ye are bought with a price." The very beginning of the religious life is an act of entire consecration to God. The Christian's profession is a constant proclamation to the world, that the

claim of Him who bought him with his blood, covers his estate, his faculties, his all. "What hast thou that thou didst not receive?" Therefore, ransomed sinner, whatever thou givest, thou dost but "render unto God the things that are God's." So Paul felt: "I am debtor both to the Greeks and to the barbarians." But why a debtor rather than a giver? Because he was not his own, but bought with a price. So are we all debtors to the ignorant, the wretched, and depraved of whatever nation; and when we pay into the Lord's treasury for their benefit, must say, "Oh Lord our God, all this store that we have prepared cometh of thine hand, and is all thine own." Hence the terrible declaration of God—not against those who gave nothing, but against those who gave what was of inferior value—"Ye have robbed God."

## CHAPTER III.

### DUTY OF SYSTEMATIC BENEVOLENCE INFERRED FROM THE NATURE AND MOTIVES OF PIETY.

PIETY begins with *a change of heart*. The greater part of life is usually occupied with the acquisition and use of property. A change of heart, if real, cannot leave this principal part of life unaffected. The subject of it must be expected to show that he has found a more valued treasure in heaven by his new aims in getting, his new principles in using the treasures of this world. If, in that chief part of life occupied with gaining and using property, the professed subject of a change consisting in placing the affections on things above, continue to show the same estimate of property as the great end to be sought, the same eagerness in getting, the same tenacity in holding, the same self-seeking in using it, need it be surprising that his worldly competitors doubt the reality of the change? Must not Christ repel such professors with his own searching question, "What do ye more than others?" There is nothing less than absurdity in the idea of a change, in which the man becomes "a new creature in Christ," in which "old things are passed away, behold, all things are become new," which yet does not carry a new spirit through the business and consecrate the property as well as the heart to God—in which the theory is all for the glory of God; the practice, all for making money.

*Religion is love.* And love is active. It is as natural for love to act beneficently, as for a fountain to flow, or a star to shine; and its action is ungrudging, unstinted, delighting in toil for the loved object. Witness, for instance, the toils of parental love. Can love to God and man be the very essence of the character, while beneficent efforts are left to hazard, crowded into the by-corners of life, supplied by chippings and remnants? Can love control the heart, and not control the action of the life?

*Christians are laborers together with God.* God is always giving: if we labor with him, we must labor in his work; we must give. God is love; if we labor with him, we must labor in the work of love. God would form us into his likeness; to this end, we are no sooner brought into his kingdom, than we are put to doing his work. In revealing his will by inspired men, in the conversion of every soul, in the whole work of spreading the gospel through the world, we discover this sublime partnership in labor between God and his children.

Behold, then, believer, your sublime position, working with God in delivering the world from ruin. To reclaim men to holiness is God's great work; to it he has moulded his plans, and for it ordered his providence, since time began. May you be a laborer with

God, and make that secondary which he regards as first; pursue without plan, energy, or steadfastness, the object which he seeks with a steadfastness which knows no abatement, a zeal which spares no sacrifice, an outpouring of treasure which arithmetic cannot calculate? A laborer with God, and yet that object to which with him the destiny of nations and the movements of heavenly hosts are subordinate, be with you secondary to money-getting, to furniture, equipage—a mere appendix to business? Let the great fact possess your soul with the fulness which its reality demands, that you are a laborer together with God, and you will lose sight of self in the greatness of man's salvation, and instead of beneficence being an appendix to business, business itself will become but a means of beneficence.

*The cross of Christ* urges to systematic benevolence. "Ye know the grace of our Lord Jesus Christ, that though he was rich, yet for your sakes he became poor, that ye through his poverty might be rich." This is one of the most touching appeals to Christ's sufferings. Yet Paul wrote it expressly as a motive for taking up a charitable collection at Corinth. This beautiful sentiment in such a connection may seem sadly out of place to those who are wont to regard a charitable collection as an annoyance; but it shows the apostolic view of the connection of this duty with all that is sublime and affecting in the cross of Christ.

The peculiar motive of Christianity is expressed in the affecting words so often on the lips of Jesus, "For my sake." "Blessed are ye when men shall revile you, and persecute you, for my sake"—"hated of all men for my sake"—"hath left houses and lands for my sake"—"loseth his life for my sake." He presents this motive as effectual to induce the greatest sacrifices, even of property and life. And it would seem that a sinner, pardoned through Christ's blood, could not, for very shame, lift his eye to meet the melting look of his dying Saviour, if he felt not the overcoming power of that appeal—if he could not, like the apostle, say, "I take pleasure in infirmities, in reproaches, in necessities, in persecutions, in distresses, for Christ's sake." "What things were gain to me, those I count loss for Christ."

In a world so intensely selfish, it was needful that the cross of the divine Redeemer, sacrificing himself to save transgressors, should stand in the centre of the plan of salvation: the first object which greets the eye of the convert, and the last which cheers the dying saint; the source of the Christian's hope and strength through all his warfare, his joy on earth, and the anticipated theme of his everlasting song—that the great lesson of self-denying, all-consecrating benevolence may always be before the view—that with every look at the bleeding Author of salvation, may fall on the soul, with an eloquence too deep for words, the admonition, "Forasmuch as Christ hath suffered for us in the flesh, arm yourselves likewise with the same mind;" "he that saith he abideth in Christ, ought himself also so to walk even as he walked."

If God himself were in our circumstances, how would he measure his efforts for the good of men? Receive the answer in the conduct of Christ, "God manifest in the flesh." He would sacrifice his riches and lay aside his glory; he would consume all the energies of his earthly existence; he would lay down his mortal life, to do them good. The first promise of the arch-deceiver was, "Ye shall be as gods"—ye shall become so by gratifying self. Christ has uttered the same promise, "Ye shall be partakers of the divine nature;" but ye shall become so by denying self. "Gratify self, get, and ye shall be as gods," is Satan's lie. "Deny self, give, and ye shall be partakers of the divine nature," is Christ's truth. Satan has blinded mankind by this lie, so that they look for bliss and exaltation only by getting; Christ overturns this whole scheme, and teaches to find godlike bliss and exaltation by giving. This is godlike in man, to sacrifice self for the good of others. That was the highest elevation of human nature when it was lifted on the cross in the blood of its own agony for man's redemption; then human nature was exalted to participate in the sublimest of all the displays of God's glory. And there is no elevation of man to the godlike, except as he is elevated to the spirit of the cross. Who then can imagine that he has been made by regeneration a partaker of the divine nature, if he does not systematically devote of his choicest treasures, as God hath prospered him, for the good of men. And how little even that gift appears in the light of the cross; how little in contrast with the offerings of many who have laid down their lives for Christ's sake!

Thus systematic benevolence, instead of being an isolated and uninteresting topic, is seen to be a duty based on the very nature of piety, and enforced by its most affecting motives.

## CHAPTER IV.

### SUPERIOR EFFICIENCY OF SYSTEMATIC BENEVOLENCE IN PROVIDING FUNDS FOR BENEVOLENT ENTERPRISES.

SYSTEM *always promotes efficiency.* What would become of a man's worldly business, if he managed it without system, never executing a plan or making an investment till solicited, and abandoning labor to the control of impulse or convenience? And can he hope for any better results from a like disregard of system as a steward of God? From such lack of order, what but embarrassment and failure can result to the enterprises of benevolence? And what shall we say of those professors of Christ's religion who show so thorough an understanding of the necessity of system in worldly business, so utter a neglect of it in their contributions to benevolence: who are full of forethought and anxious calculation to realize the utmost of worldly acquisition; deliberate and far-sighted in planning, cautious in executing, lynx-eyed to discern an opportunity of gain, exact to the last fraction in their accounts, but heedless and planless in all they do for charity? Verily, "the children of this world are wiser in their generation than the children of light;" but "the children of light" show no lack of that wisdom, till they come to use property for the benefit of others than themselves.

Systematic benevolence will usually *dispose the giver to increase his contributions.* If a man gives without system, he will commonly give too little. Under the hallowed influences of the closet, let him estimate the claims of a world lying in wickedness, and the means of benevolence with which God has blessed him; let him ponder what amount of charity would be acceptable to God and is demanded by the love of Christ; and it will be strange if he is not convinced that he ought to increase his donations.

It is *more convenient* to set apart money for charity in frequent instalments. He who neglects to provide for his charities until the call for them is made, may find it inconvenient or impossible to raise at tho time the one dollar, or the hundred dollars, or whatever sum it is his duty to give. But had he set apart a proportion from his earnings as they were received, he would not be incommoded by giving the sum required. Persons even in the most moderate circumstances, adopting the practice of systematic benevolence, are often surprised at the amount they can give without serious inconvenience.

System will enlarge the amount of money expended in beneficence *by being a barrier against the temptations of selfishness.* Many a man means to answer the calls of charity, but does not weekly or monthly set apart a specific sum as sacred to the Lord. Hence, when he sees some tempting article of luxury, having by him unappropriated the money which should have been the Lord's, he buys it; when some tempting, though perhaps hazardous investment presents, having the money by him unappropriated, he invests it. Thus, through lack of system, many sums in the purses even of the benevolent are turned aside from the Lord's treasury. Self-interest has the advantage in being beforehand and having constant access to our hearts. Systematic charity helps to put the interest of Christ's cause on an equal footing.

System *prevents yielding to second thoughts* and withholding a purposed charity. Many a man, under the influence of a charity sermon, or of the teachings of conscience, or of the sight of distress, purposes in his heart to give a certain amount. As the subject first strikes his unbiassed judgment, such an amount seems not too large for the urgency of the case and his own means. But selfishness steps in and argues the point; it presents to the man his various wants, and pretty soon convinces him that the purposed sum is quite too much; then, forgetting Paul's injunction, "Every man, according as he purposeth in his heart, so let him give," he gives little or nothing. But let a man have a fixed plan, in accordance with which he consecrates a fixed proportion to the Lord as regularly as he meets his notes when they fall due, or pays the expenses of his family, and the matter is settled. Here is a breastwork by God's grace impregnable against all the pleading of selfishness.

System increases the contributions *by making it more pleasant to give.* When a man has no system of charity, every call to give is unprovided for: if he comply, he must give from money which he was expecting to spend otherwise; it is so much taken from what he had reckoned his own; it seems so much dead loss. Hence, every donation chafes him; he is tempted to make it as small as possible; giving comes to be surrounded in his mind with unpleasant associations; he often looks back with regret, when he gives any thing, that he gave so much; and the call of charity becomes repulsive. But when he systematizes his charities and at stated times sets apart to benevolence a sum proportioned to his income, he no longer reckons that consecrated money as his own, or depends on it for the supply of any want When the call of charity is heard, he is not obliged to take from what he had reckoned his own, but from what was already consecrated to the Lord. He can give both largely and cheerfully, and with no drawback from the blessedness of doing good.

System *removes many common excuses of selfishness* for "withholding more than is meet:" "I have lately given to another cause;" "I give as much as convenient;" "I have so many expenses;" "I give as much as others."

System increases the amount of charities by *forming habits of benevolence.* From earliest life, habits of gaining and using money for self have been strengthening, and these consolidated habits have never been overcome. Even in the church the covetous use of property is too generally the habit, the benevolent use of it only an occasional act. And it is but dimly apprehended that the gospel requires it to be otherwise. Hence, the gifts of the church are exceedingly stinted. To remedy this evil, it is necessary to make the beneficent use of property the habit of the Christian's life, and thus turn to the advantage of Christ's cause that law of habit which has been all against it. To do this, there must be systematic benevolence. It were the extreme of folly to think of subduing these consolidated habits by desultory efforts—to send up now and then a platoon of light troops against these most massive and well-appointed fortifications of selfishness. We must approach them by well-concerted, persevering siege, till they fall into our hands and the guns are turned against the foe. Mere occasional, unsystematized donations scarcely make a perceptible impression in subduing selfish and forming benevolent habits. But when beneficence is systematized, the habit of doing good is formed, it moulds the whole life, it becomes second nature, and shows in all its results its efficacious vigor.

These considerations show the duty of Christian parents to train their children to the habit of systematically making a benevolent use of money.

One of the greatest difficulties in the way of obtaining an increase of funds, is found in another influence of this same law of habit. Of those who contribute regularly to particular causes, and thus have made an approach to system, a large portion are in the habit of giving from year to year about the same sum. The same twenty-five cents, the same dollar, or five dollars, stands from year to year against their names. The wants of benevolent enterprises increase, the property of the giver increases, but the contribution is stereotyped. The attempt to increase this amount breaks up their settled habits of thought and action. They have never thought that perhaps Christ requires a revision of their whole plan of benevolence. The adoption of the divine plan of frequent and proportionate appropriations would remove this difficulty.

It must be added, that systematic benevolence may be expected by God's blessing *to increase the giver's means of usefulness.* But this thought will be reserved for a more extended examination in another chapter.

In these various ways the scriptural system increases the funds of benevolence. Were it universally adopted by the churches, nothing but the experiment would show how immense would be the resulting increase. Without expense of collecting agencies, thousands in the churches who now give nothing, would begin to give; and a permanent and growing increase would be realized at once from those who have given occasionally. Then would the channels of benevolence be like "the river of God which is full of water," and the waters of life issuing from the sanctuary with their healing power, would flow as the prophet saw in vision, ever swelling to the ends of the earth.

The following facts confirm the argument of this chapter. In 1844, Rev. Dr. Baird received, in two payments, thirty-eight dollars for some benevolent cause, from "one of the poor disciples of Jesus;" in acknowledging which he says, "The donor of it commenced giving, in a strictly systematic manner, the tenth part of all the money which he earned from the time of his conversion, and through God's blessing he has been enabled to give sums from time to time, to many, if not all the great enterprises for building up the kingdom of our Lord, varying from five to twenty-five dollars."

There is a farmer in one of the retired mountain towns of Massachusetts, who began business on his farm in 1818, being six hundred dollars in debt. He began with the determination to pay the debt in six years, in equal instalments, and to give all his net income, if any remained, above those instalments. The income of the first year, however, was expended in purchasing stock and other necessaries for his farm. In the six next years he paid off the debt, and having abandoned the intention of ever being any richer, he has ever since given his entire income, after supporting his family and thoroughly educating his six children. During all this period he has lived with the strictest economy, and every thing pertaining to his house, table, dress, and equipage has been in the most simple style; and though he has twice been a member of the state senate, he conscientiously re tains this simplicity in his mode of life. The farm is rocky and remote from the village, and his whole property, real and personal, would not exceed in value three thousand dollars. Yet sometimes he has been enabled to give from $200 to $300 in a year.

Let it be further considered in this connection, that *some feasible plan of enlarging the funds of benevolence* must be adopted, in order to realize the hopes of the churches from their missionary enterprises. This is apparent from the difficulty of sustaining these enterprises on their present scale. This deficiency is not owing to a want of means in the church. There is money in profusion for railroads, manufactories, any enterprise which promises a return to self. But where is the money for the Lord? "The great current of Christian property isas yet undiverted from its worldly channel. The scanty rills of charity which at present water the garden of the Lord, and the ingenuity and effort employed to bring them there, compared with the almost undiminished tide of selfish expenditure which still holds on its original course, remind one of the slender rivulets which the inhabitants of the East raise from a river by mechanical force, to water their thirsty gardens; the mighty current meanwhile, without exhibiting any sensible diminution of its waters, sweeping on in its ample and ancient bed."

The aggregate of gifts from its members to the church was probably larger in the times of its great est corruption than now. When it was believed that salvation might be bought by charity, wealth from the poor and the rich was lavished on churches and monasteries. But as, in the advance of the Reformation, charities with this motive have ceased, the churches have failed adequately to bring in the gifts of gratitude and love in their stead. It should make the ears of him that heareth it to tingle, that in this boasted age of progress, this nineteenth century, less is probably bestowed in charity by the Protestant churches to spread the true gospel through the world, than was given in the darkest ages to heap up the treasures of the church of Rome—that the love of Christ constrains to less valuable gifts than the arts and deceptions of a corrupt priesthood.

But the church is aiming *at the conversion of the world.* It is plain as sunlight that the world cannot be supplied with the means of grace without an immense enlargement of these operations. It was this contrast between the greatness of the enterprise which Christians profess to prosecute, and the littleness of the means which they devote to it, that wrung from the godly Abeel the exclamation respecting our missionary work, "If the great God could despise his creatures, it would be despicable in his sight." There must be some way devised of realizing such enlargement, if the world is to be converted. Nor is the expectation of realizing it vain. The scriptural system of benevolence, generally adopted, would realize it without embarrassment to the church.

Let it also be considered, that when God *by his providence* proclaims, "Behold, I have set before you an open door," "he openeth, and no man shutteth" Then, if his church will enter, no obstacles or opposition can prevent her triumph. But if his people will not enter, presently the door is shut; and "he shutteth, and no man openeth." Ages may pass before, in the revolving cycles of his providence, he will open it again. And when thus shut, the costliest labors of his church are labors where God is not. One day God opens Canaan to the Israelites and urges them to go up, assuring them that the Anaks and the cities walled and great shall not retard them. They will not go. Next day they are all eagerness to go, but the door is shut; the pillar of cloud moves not—they go up only to perish before their foes. All history demonstrates this principle—demonstrates, that as we must follow God's movements in the circling seasons, would we reap in harvest; so, in the enterprises of benevolence, we must not fall behind the workings of his providence, would we achieve success. When God in his own spring-time drives the ploughshare through the nations, as with such startling energy he of late has done, then must his people cast in the seed of truth; lest, neglecting it, they be compelled to fruitless toil till another spring-time returns. And when the time is come to set the fore-front of liberty and Christianity face to face with the hoary forms of Asiatic despotism and idolatry—when God reveals from the bowels of the earth the treasure which he had kept hid for this very juncture, and calls a population together from every land, and a nation is born in a day—then must his church bind the new-born state with the sweet influences of religion, and guide it to the advancement of piety in the earth, or it will lift its young and giant energies to smite her. God's providence never stands still. His church must move with it, if she would move effectively—if even she would avoid disaster. Hence, the necessity of adopting some mode of increasing promptly and efficiently the contributions of the church, so as to improve at once the precious opportunities which God opens.

It only remains to add, that *the prophecies foretell* that, in accomplishing the renovation of the world, an increase of appropriations to God's treasury, like what has been urged, will take place. "The daughter of Tyre shall be there with a gift; the rich among the people shall entreat thy favor." "The wealth of all the heathen round about shall be gathered together, gold, and silver, and apparel, in great abundance. In that day shall there be upon the bells of the horses, HOLINESS TO THE LORD." "Surely the isles shall wait for me, and the ships of Tarshish first, to bring thy sons from far, their silver and their gold with them, to the Holy One of Israel." "I will shake all nations, and the Desire of all nations shall come. The silver is mine, and the gold is mine, saith the Lord." Psalm 45 : 12 ; Zechariah 14 : 14, 20 ; Isaiah 60 : 9 ; Haggai 2 : 7, 8.

Thus the necessities of benevolent societies, the claims of a ruined world, the indications of Providence, and the predictions of the Bible, unite in demanding a great increase of benevolent contributions. These contributions, as now usually conducted, warrant no hope of realizing this increase. But the general adoption of the scriptural plan of frequent, systematic, and proportionate charities, will easily meet the demand.

# CHAPTER V.

## TENDENCY OF SYSTEMATIC BENEVOLENCE TO SECURE GOD'S BLESSING ON BUSINESS, AND TO ENLARGE THE MEANS OF GIVING.

THIS is a subject of difficulty, yet of importance. There is danger of extravagant theories on the one hand, and on the other, of an unbelief which shuts God out of the daily business, and practically denies that "godliness has the promise of the life that now is."

It is not to be supposed that systematic benevolence will insure wealth. Wealth is, in God's judgment, too cheap a gift to be made the reward of his servants.

> "Wealth on the vilest often is bestowed,
> To show its vileness in the sight of God."

Multiplied as are God's warnings of the dangers attending wealth and the love of it, and his exhortations to set the affections above, it would be preposterous to suppose that he offers wealth as the reward of obedience—the gratification of cupidity as the reward for denying it. And he whose heart is on a better portion, whose longings for God and holiness forbid his finding satisfaction with any thing less than being with God and like him, would feel it the bitterest mockery to be turned off with the promise of riches as his reward.

But *there are various ways in which systematic*

*beneficence tends to promote prosperity.* It promotes *industry, energy, and enterprise.* The man has placed before himself a lofty object, suited to draw out all his energies. Henceforth he is no trifler, but an earnest man, sharing in the very sentiments of earth's purest and greatest ones. The grand idea of toiling to rescue the world from sin never mastered a man's soul without enlarging it, without stimulating all his faculties to unprecedented vigor, unfolding resources not imagined to be in him, and producing a concentration and perseverance of action, which cannot fail of realizing great results. An account was published some years ago of two shoemakers whose hearts had begun to glow with zeal for the salvation of men. The elder proposed to the younger to fit himself to preach, promising to support him by his labor. The proposal was accepted; the promise was kept. The sublime purpose which had mastered that man's soul, and which surrounded his humble shop with a grandeur that never ennobled worldly greatness, gave him an energy and industry which enabled him to educate his companion, and to sustain him as he went out to preach to the destitute. When Christendom shall be full of missionary merchants, farmers, and mechanics, plying their business with the sublime aim of saving mankind from sin, no doubt it will be full of energy and industry unsurpassed.

Nor does the practice of scriptural beneficence stimulate the active powers alone. It promotes *so briety and economy.* With an object so glorious in full possession of his soul, the man will have no time nor money for gratifying either vicious or luxurious desires. What others waste on dress, delicacies, equipage, and show, he will save for the Lord. He finds, in advancing the cause to which he is wedded, a gratification, compared with which the daintiest gratifications of selfishness are insipid.

Such a course *attracts the favor of the good,* wins their confidence, and if the man be poor, or a youthful beginner, their friendship gains him employment and otherwise promotes his interests. Besides, being thrown into company with such, he avoids the temptations of evil associates.

*The habits of fidelity to his trust, of watchfulness, system, and exactness,* which systematic benevolence forms, are the very habits to win for a young man respect, employment, and friends, and to lead to a judicious management of business through life.

Systematic benevolence tends to *restrain from hazardous adventures.* In prosperous times, when business is brisk and its returns speedy and large, men become discontented with slow and steady gains; they "make haste to be rich" and "fall into a snare;" they become inflated with a rash confidence; they rush into hazardous and ruinous adventures and speculations; or the ostentatious desire of displaying a large business, tempts to an enlargement beyond their means, and to consequent ruin. But when a man has consecrated his business and its gains to the Lord, according to the scriptural law of benevolence, the feverish haste to be rich abates, and he is less tempted to dangerous speculations. Accustomed to do business with a sense of constant dependence on God, he is not puffed up with rash confidence by temporary prosperity. Accustomed to determine every enterprise with prayerful seeking God's will, and to regard property as sacred to his service, he will not thoughtlessly risk the Lord's money in hazardous adventures. Absorbed with the grand desire of aiding Christ's cause, he will be in little danger of ostentatious but unsafe expansion. Thus, "he that considereth the poor, shall be blessed upon the earth;" but "he that hasteth to be rich, considereth not that poverty shall come upon him."

It may be added that benevolence, in an important sense, *identifies the giver with Christ's interests,* and therefore may naturally be expected to secure Christ's blessing. The Saviour says, "Inasmuch as ye have done it to one of the least of these my brethren, ye have done it unto me." He receives into his own bosom every favor to his church. Nor is there any surer ground of expecting the continued prosperity of an individual, a church, or a nation, than that by their abundant efforts for Christ's kingdom, they have identified themselves with his cause, and are likely to be carried on in its triumphs. The very beast of which it was said, "The Lord hath need of him," had his way strewed with palms and garments, as it bore the Saviour to Jerusalem. The individual or the community that gives abundantly to advance religion, is the humble instrument of bearing the Saviour onward in his triumph. Of such it may reverently be said, "The Lord hath need of them;" and it may reasonably be expected that their way will be made prosperous before them.

In these several ways compliance with the scriptural law of benevolence may tend to temporal prosperity. There may be other ways known only to Him who holds all the invisible lines of influence in his hand.

If now we open the Bible, *we find it full of promises of temporal blessings to the benevolent.* A few must serve as specimens of the many. "Thou shalt surely give thy poor brother, and thy heart shall not be grieved when thou givest unto him; because that for this thing the Lord thy God shall bless thee in all thy works, and in all that thou puttest thy hand unto." Deut. 15 : 10. "He that giveth to the poor shall not lack." Prov. 28 : 27. "Honor the Lord with thy substance, and with the first-fruits of all thine increase; so shall thy barns be filled with plenty, and thy presses shall burst out with new wine" Prov. 3 : 9. "The liberal soul shall be made fat; and he that watereth shall be watered also himself." Prov. 11 : 25. "Seek ye *first* the kingdom of God, and all these things shall be added unto you." Matt. 6 : 33. "Give, and it shall be given unto you; good measure, pressed down, and shaken together, and running over, shall men give into your bosom." Luke 6 : 38. And in urging the Corinthians to give, Paul said, "He which soweth sparingly, shall reap also sparingly; and he which soweth bountifully, shall reap also bountifully." 2 Cor. 9 : 6.* To these special promises the benevolent are entitled. Resting on them, they may give with the expectation that the Lord will follow them with his blessing and protection. They will not fear want while they can hear God saying, "Trust in the Lord and do good, and verily thou shalt be fed." The same Being who made the Bible, orders the events of providence; and by what he does in the latter, he will not contradict what he says in the former. The principles of the Bible fit into all the windings of providence, like a key to all the wards of a lock for which it was made. Hence, however obscure the plan of Providence, and however uncertain what shall be on the morrow, he that conducts his business in conformity to all the rules of the Bible, may be sure that he has found the track of God's goings in the world, and that, if he continue to follow it step by step, it will guide him in the way of the divine blessing.

* See also Matt. 6 : 3, 4; Psa. 37 : 3; Prov. 11 : 24; 19 : 17; 22 : 9; 25 : 21; 24 : 11, 12; 13 : 7; Psa. 41 : 1, 2, 3; 112 : 5, 6, 9; Eccl. 11 : 1; Isa. 32 : 8; 58 : 6–11; Mal. 3 : 9–12; Dan 4 : 27; 2 Cor. 9 : 6, 7, 8, 11.

It will be seen from the foregoing reasoning, that it is not pretended that God's servants will be uniformly led in the way to worldly prosperity, and sinners visited with adversity in this life. The Bible makes no such representation. It teaches, that in this probation temporal benefits are scattered on the good and the evil, and refers us to the other world for the solution of this seeming confusion of right and wrong. "When the wicked spring as the grass, and when all the workers of iniquity do flourish, it is that they shall be destroyed for ever." It teaches that wicked men are prospered, but "the prosperity of fools shall destroy them." It teaches that God sometimes gives men "their request, but sends leanness into their souls." Their selfish wishes are gratified; but the gift comes, like the quails to the longing Israelites, attended by God's curse. Their riches increase; but they wrap the soul in the flames of covetousness, and "eat as it were fire." Their riches increase, but their "portion" is "in this life, and in the labor that they take under the sun." They are rich as Dives; yet soon will they be impoverished to beg "a drop of water to cool their tongues." Thus, inspiration explains these inequalities, and teaches, that "a little which a righteous man hath, is better than the riches of many wicked;" that Elijah, fed by unclean birds, but receiving his portion with God's smile, has no need to envy Ahab, cursed in the riches of a palace; that Lazarus the beggar, with a home nowhere but in Abraham's bosom, is more blessed than Dives with a home nowhere but in his own luxurious palace. But at the same time it teaches, that he who humbly uses what God has given for the honor of the Giver, freely giving as he has freely received, may feel at peace in the thought, that all his business is blessed with his Father's smile.

Facts corroborate the foregoing sentiments. There are, indeed, comparatively few facts to furnish data for this argument. Yet the writer knows a considerable number of instances, in which a greater or less approach to scriptural benevolence, has been attended with unusual prosperity. Mr. Cobb, whose case has been mentioned, giving away a quarter, then half, and then three quarters of his income, not only became worth $50,000 before the age of thirty-six, but gave besides more than $40,000. Normand Smith, a saddler of Hartford, Connecticut, after practising for years an elevated system of benevolence, bequeathed in charity $30,000. An anonymous writer says of himself, that he commenced business and prosecuted it in the usual way, till he lost $900, which was all he was worth, and found himself in debt $1,100. Being led by his trials, through God's grace, to trust, as he hoped, in Christ, he, at the age of forty, determined to take God's word for his guide in his business, and consecrated his earnings to the Lord The first year he gave $12. For eighteen years, the amount has increased by about 25 per cent., and the last year he gave $850 ; and he says, he did it easier than, during the first year, he paid the $12. Besides, though with nothing but his hands to depend on when he began this course, he paid the whole debt of $1,100 with interest, though it took him nine years to do it. Jacob went out from his father's home "with his staff," a poor man ; but at Bethel he vowed to give to God the tenth of all that God should bestow on him. Commencing thus, God blessed him, and in twenty years he returned with great riches.

We may also refer to the history of communities, in confirmation of the argument. When God issued his laws to the Jewish nation, he required, besides other liberal offerings, the tenth of all their income. We are not to suppose that every specific regulation for the Jews is the best for all nations. But in his dealings with the Jews, God meant to illustrate the principles on which, as to worldly affairs, he deals with all ; and this is one reason why their history is so minutely recorded. Thus, we find the law of tithes and offerings incorporated into their system as an exemplification of a universal principle in God's dealings with men. Many have pitied their unhappy lot in being compelled to give so much ; infidels have delighted in the objection that the wretched Jews were taxed so terribly for the support of religion. But the All-wise knew best what regulations would harmonize with the course of his providence, and prescribed accordingly. And it ever proved that the nine tenths were worth more to them than the ten tenths. If ever, to increase their gains, they robbed God by hoarding the tenth, or by bringing the lame and the blind, disaster and loss were sure to follow. Say not this was all a miraculous interposition. Inspiration has only lifted the veil here from the workings of that providence which, unseen, untraced, is ever working in the affairs of men on the same principles and with the same aim. Say not, either, that the tithe was a positive institution. True; and as to its specific form it might, therefore, pass away, as it already has. But was there ever a positive institution of God not founded on something permanent, either in man's nature or God's scheme of providence and grace? Therefore was the law of the tithe founded on a principle as enduring as God's government on earth; and as the tithe was a blessing to the Jews, so regard to that principle will be always a blessing. We may find facts of the same import in modern times. Those churches which are most systematic and liberal in their contributions, are, without exception, the most prosperous. The same is true of nations. The history of New England is a striking instance. The first settlers were men who, in a great trial of affliction, and in deep poverty, abounded in the riches of their liberality, in sustaining schools, and ministers, and colleges, and in laying deep a foundation for Christ's kingdom in this new world. It is not so fitly said that they contributed much, as that they offered all to Christ. And it is admitted that New England is, and in all her history has been preëminent in contributions and efforts to sustain every benevolent institution and enterprise. And where is the state or the nation which has ever possessed more of all the elements of true prosperity?

But an appeal to facts in the history of churches and communities must rest on imperfect data; for where is there one in which the efficiency of the scriptural law of benevolence, in developing and enlarging the resources of benevolence, has been fully put to the test?

In closing the argument, the thought may be suggested, that business, conducted as it is on the maxims of selfishness, when viewed *as a system* in its management and results, presents a picture of any thing rather than of permanent and healthy prosperity. The number of business men who fail once or oftener in the course of life; the numbers doing business who, should they pay up the as yet unpaid debts of their past lives, would strip themselves of all or a large part of their present property; the small proportion of those commencing mercantile life in cities, who, in the final winding up of their affairs, possess a comfortable independence; the fact that the property of those who die rich so often proves a curse to their children, and that so many who are born rich, die poor; the periodical recurrence of a "*crash*" in the commercial world; the alternation of commercial prosperity and distress, which for generations has marked the history of business, realizing the inspired declaration, "He hath swallowed down riches, and shall vomit them up again;" all these facts indicate any thing rather than a system of business which, as a whole—whatever may be true of individuals—receives the smile and blessing of God; they present evidences of the divine displeasure such as might be expected to mark a selfish and ungodly system of business.

The discussion of this part of the subject will not have been in vain, if it help to remove the impression, that the rules of the gospel cannot be obeyed to the last jot and tittle in business, consistently with its successful management; to rebuke the practical atheism which shuts God out of the details of daily life; to make men's hearts alive to the thought that the hand of God is on their ships, their merchandise, their cattle, and their shops; that the claims of his law and the promises of his gospel are twined about all the acts and gettings of daily toil, not less than about their destiny for the life to come; and that there is a reality here on earth in God's smile on those who heed his claims, in his blight and curse on those who disregard them.

## CHAPTER VI.

### THE ANTIDOTE OF COVETOUSNESS.

Covetousness is *deadly in its influence.* "Covetousness is idolatry." It is inconsistent with piety. It is unmitigated rebellion against God. It is the object of God's abhorrence and curse. It is classed by inspiration with fornication, drunkenness, theft, and extortion. It is "a temptation and a snare." It is unsurpassed in its power to harden the heart and make it impervious to divine truth, to deaden all the religious sensibilities, and to resist the Spirit of God.

Covetousness is *prevalent.* The miser is one of the most universally abhorred of men. But plume not yourself that you are not covetous, because you are not a miser. Misers are the rarest specimens of this sin. Under other forms, it rankles everywhere. You are warned against a covetousness of a more respectable appearance. It may exist unsuspected. There may be covetousness in saving—parsimony under the "*alias*" of frugality, avarice, which never parts with money without a twinge. Oftener there is covetousness in getting—sometimes rapacity which scruples at no means if money may be gained; but much more generally the more respectable form of worldliness, keeping within the limits of honesty but swallowing all the energies in money-getting, deadening the benevolent susceptibilities, pinching and shrivelling the soul, living only to "buy and sell and get gain." Covetousness may be found even in connection with prodigality: greediness to acquire, to supply the extravagance of expense. It enslaves multitudes who are neither misers in hoarding, nor rapacious nor extortionate in getting. In its diversified forms it is one of the most prevalent of the vices, and often, under its various disguises, honored rather than condemned; as it is written, "The wicked blesseth the covetous, whom the Lord abhorreth."

And there is *a liability to become covetous and to grow in covetousness*, to the existence and dangers of which the most of men seem not to be awake. In the prosecution of business, the love of money is freezing deeper and harder into their souls, and sealing up the springs of benevolence, and they know it not. One remarkable feature in the Saviour's teaching, is the frequency and earnestness with which he rebuked this sin, and pointed out the dangers of wordly acquisitions. He exposed it in the mansions of wealth and the circles of devotion, in the temple and in the street, in amiable inquirers after salvation, in pharisaical professors and vicious publicans. His warning was, "*Take heed and beware* of covetousness. Ye cannot serve God and mammon." The frequency and earnestness of his warnings contrast strangely with the eagerness and security with which his professed followers make haste to be rich, and show that he saw a danger imminent and prevalent to which they are strangely blind. We do not vary from the spirit of his teachings in saying, that covetousness is the most common, the most insidious, and the most dangerous form of selfishness, the one which the most deadens the church, and is the most likely to crush it.

A little consideration will show the reality of this danger. "Money answereth all things." It is the representative of all commodities and the means of procuring them. It is natural that selfishness should fasten with peculiar strength on an acquisition which is the quintessence of all objects of desire. Besides, men are necessarily occupied during the most of their waking hours in earning money. To this end the thoughts must plan and the hands must toil. It is natural that what so occupies the man should gradually grow upon his mind; as a picture long gazed at intently, gradually fills the eye and enlarges to the dimensions of a real landscape. Especially must this result be expected, when the object which thus occupies the attention is one so pleasing to the selfish heart.

Besides, it is the nature of covetousness to grow by what it feeds on. Acquisitions increase its strength. In accordance with this well-known fact, the tendency of gainful business is to make the man more covetous.

These tendencies would be exceedingly strong, and

would need to be most diligently guarded against, under circumstances the most favorable to benevolence. But they are strengthened by outward circumstances.

There is a perverted public sentiment, a prevalent overvaluing of wealth, which silently sinks into the inmost soul—the scarcely acknowledged, yet controlling feeling, that wealth is the great good of human existence, which has incorporated itself into our very language; so that "to do well," "to be successful," "to accomplish much in life," are phrases synonymous with making much money; "gain" is equivalent in our language to "filthy lucre" in God's, and "goods" on our lips, is "the unrighteous mammon" on Christ's; and a late writer has suggested the idea, that we speak of a man as being "*worth* much," or "*worth* nothing," as if all worth centred in money.

Worldliness, too, is the general character of the community, and a man finds few examples of scriptural benevolence, to show him his own selfishness by contrast, and to stimulate him to beneficence.

It is also an important circumstance, that the man has been trained from childhood under worldly influences; he has seen, perhaps, that whatever their professions, the chief actual anxiety of his parents concerning him has been to have him making money, and that to get him "a good situation," and a "situation where he can make money," and to "give him a good start," and to "start him well in the career of acquiring property," mean in their minds about the same thing; and that in all his training for business, he is taught that "the main chance" is to make money, and in effect, that a man's life *does* consist in the abundance of the things that he possesseth. From childhood he has been indoctrinated by precept and example with the maxims of worldly policy, rather than the principles of benevolence—with the proverbs of "Poor Richard" respecting property, rather than the precepts of Jesus Christ.

All these circumstances tend to make wealth the central idea of the mind, to beget a materializing, deadening worldliness, to blight benevolence, and to make men as laborious and untiring in their business, and at the same time as callous to the interests of others, as so many iron steam-engines at their work. The pious and benevolent, who mingle constantly in business, know that the danger is imminent; they know that the maintenance of benevolence is opposed by silent but powerful influences, with which contact with the world every day surrounds them; and they tremble at their own liability to fall under the insidious but fatal power of covetousness. It is alarmingly easy for gold and silver to "canker," and the love of it to become an eating cancer on the soul. Hence, the multitudes whose benevolence never grows with their riches; who, when rich, give nothing like the proportion which they gave when poor; nay, who give no more—who give less than they gave then. Hence is explained the admitted fact, that the greater part of the funds of benevolent associations comes from those of moderate means. Hence arises the general necessity of agents for collecting funds, and of the most pungent appeals for contributions. Have you ever considered seriously your own danger, and taken measures to guard against it? If not, your very thoughtlessness is presumptive evidence that you are already consuming with the love of money.

We see, then, that the path of worldly business is fraught with constant danger of a deadly evil. He who sets out on that path must climb a snow-capped mountain, where every step is along icy precipices, where the air chills to the heart the spiritual life, where every touch is upon nipping frost, and where the cold is perpetually producing a sleepiness almost resistless, but which, if indulged, will be the sleep of death. It is, then, a question of spiritual life or death, "How shall I do my necessary business, and escape covetousness—benumbing, paralyzing, deadly covetousness?" Alas, that Christians so seldom ask this question—so little take the tremendous meaning of Christ's assertion, "Ye cannot serve God and mammon"—so little realize the danger which gives the thrilling emphasis to his warning, "TAKE HEED AND BEWARE of covetousness."

He who knows what is in man, *has provided a safeguard against this danger.* He has, indeed, so contrived the plan of salvation, that all the motives of the gospel, radiating as they do from the cross of the Son of God offering the stupendous sacrifice of himself, may bear directly against selfishness and tend to unfold self-sacrificing benevolence. But this is not all. He has enjoined systematic benevolence. This is God's remedy for covetousness. Infinite wisdom would not trust to unsystematized contributions, knowing that irregular efforts, sustained by no habit, no fixed time, no predetermined plan, giving way to every casual expenditure, would be but a slender barrier against a tendency so constant and powerful. God requires systematic and proportionate benevolence.

This plan is most beautifully fitted to this design. It accords with the laws of the human mind. There is no way of subduing one of our active propensities, but by refusing it indulgence, and so starving it to death. This the scheme of benevolence does to the sinful love of money. As fast as treasures are gained, it tears them from the gloating eye of covetousness to consecrate them to the Lord. It compels the man to give something from the wages of every day, from the profits of every enterprise and investment. Thus, drop by drop, it drains the lifeblood of that giant passion. And as the gains enlarge, God follows with his enlarging claims: should money come into the hands by thousands a year, there would be none left as food for covetousness, and the man would be necessitated to obey the command, "If riches increase, set not your heart upon them." And there is no way of strengthening our active propensities but by exercising them. Therefore God's rule requires appropriations to charity every week, that benevolence may be strengthening itself by frequent exercise, and the disposition to give be consolidated by habit; it requires appropriations from all the earnings, that benevolence may preside in every department, and the heart, kept always open, may have no opportunity to contract; and it requires appropriations proportionate to the means, that whereas covetousness naturally grows by increasing acquisitions, this advantage may be wrested from it and given to benevolence. Thus the practice of this scheme becomes, with God's grace, like a fire-proof coat, in which the wearer may walk collectedly in the fiercest furnace of worldliness, and "not the smell of fire pass on him." It is impossible, according to the laws of the mind, to practise on this plan without continually weakening covetousness and strengthening benevolence; nay, the wonted influence of worldly pursuits is reversed: by pouring treasures into the lap avarice is starved, while even by the toils of money-getting benevolence is exercised and strengthened. Thus, by the very processes of business the power of benevolence goes on enlarging, till she stands up in her godlike majesty, the queen of the soul, and crushes beneath her heel the tyrant that had enslaved it.

We must not leave this part of the subject without considering *its bearing on the community*, as we have already considered its bearing on the individual. Since the revival of commerce, the warlike spirit of chivalry, the love of martial glory and of conquest have been gradually giving place to the spirit of trade; this spirit has been gradually extending, till it has become, more than any other, the controlling influence in the world. This change constitutes an era in history, the causes, development, and effects of which are worthy of the most serious study. While it has produced many happy effects, as in mitigating the spirit of war, it is yet a problem what results it will finally work out—a problem which, alarming as already is the tendency of the public mind to covetousness, is one of the most momentous subjects now demanding the attention of philanthropists. There is an absorption of all interests and energies in money-getting, such as was never witnessed in the world before. Under this stimulus the country is filling with power-looms, steam-engines, and telegraphs, and energies and resources are employed in the prosecution of peaceful business, which would once have been more than enough to build the pyramids or to conquer the world. We acknowledge all the blessings of these inventions. But while every orator and every newspaper is dwelling on our commerce whitening every sea, our enterprise penetrating every country, on the miracle-working of the iron horse and the lightning messenger, on our boundless territory and exhaustless resources; and while a manufacturing city is laid out in an uninhabited spot, and built up in a year or two, as the early settlers would have built a frame house—we cannot blind ourselves to the alarming tendency in the public mind to regard these things as the sum total of all prosperity and the essentials of all blessedness; nor to the fact that the energies which are so effective in aiding the acquisition of wealth, are scarcely less effective in stimulating the love of it. We cannot blind ourselves to the danger that the love of money will become more and more the ruling influence, absorbing into itself even that powerful passion, ambition; swallowing up the love of office in the love of the salary; overshadowing the enterprises of religion by the gigantic and spirit-stirring achievements of business; drawing the church into the current of the world, and making its members undistinguishable in their pursuit of money from worldlings; nullifying the influence of the means of grace, choking the word and making it unfruitful, and finally overwhelming in worldliness the piety of the church—the danger that the spirit of trade, not checked as it should be, by a contrary example from the good, will engulf the nation in a Dead sea of cupidity and luxury, or degenerate into that mercenary spirit which, reckless of honor and virtue, unscrupulous, untrusty, rapacious, despicable, has no principle but the Judas question, "What will ye give me?" no measure of good and evil but the profit and loss of dollars and cents.

Systematic benevolence is God's appointed safeguard against this danger. Practised generally and from the heart, it will introduce a loftier end of existence than the acquisition of property; will ennoble the pursuit of business by the spirit of love; will hold up a spiritual and sublime principle in antagonism to the materializing tendencies of the spirit of trade; will make civilization centre no longer on wealth, but on "charity that seeketh not her own," and thus will form it into a civilization pure, generous, heavenly, expressing in every aspect the godlike purpose of doing good; a civilization uncursed by want, ignorance, and crime, unblighted by oppression, unclouded by irreligion, because wherever were misery and degradation, millions of hearts will throb in pity, millions of hands be extended and purses be opened to relieve; a civilization which we see only in bright glimpses revealed in the prophecies of God.

From all these views of the relations of the subject to covetousness, it is plain that, to the church, systematic benevolence is a first duty of self-preservation. She has no walls and battlements but her own active benevolence, no army with banners but her sons and her daughters toiling to do good. If the church do not bless the world, she must be buried in it. If the piety of the church, as it makes its way through this wilderness, do not, like a fertilizing stream, make all its banks "rejoice and blossom as the rose," it must be swallowed up in it like a river lost in the desert sands which it fails to make fruitful. But let the scriptural law of charitable appropriations be adopted, and thus let benevolence keep pace with advancing business, following it into every new path, and laying her gentle hand on all its unfolding resources, then will covetousness wither amid increasing enterprise, and benevolence will unfold with an energy rivalling the energies of business, and making them her ministers. Then the enterprises of religion, no longer cast into the shade by the achievements of worldliness, will encircle the earth with a vastness and a vigor more amazing than the triumphs of commerce and manufactures, and the miracles of modern art.

We must gratefully notice *the remarkable coincidence of God's providence* in calling his children to great enterprises, and in opening the world for unlimited effort, at the very time when, from the unprecedented pressure of worldliness, there is unprecedented need of such counteraction to covetousness. Let Christians understand that it is God's mercy which multiplies the calls to give, to save them from the multiplied assaults of covetousness. Let them know that they neglect these calls at their peril—the peril of perishing in covetousness, of drowning in the "destruction and perdition" of them "that *will* be rich."

## CHAPTER VII.

### SYSTEMATIC BENEVOLENCE ESSENTIAL TO THE HIGHEST SPIRITUAL ATTAINMENTS.

Alms-giving was thought so important in the ancient church, that it used to be called one of the wings of prayer; and the angel seems to have placed them side by side as means of access to God's favor, when he said to Cornelius, "Thy *prayers* and thine *alms* are come up for a memorial before God." So Christ said, "If ye have not been faithful in the unrighteous mammon, who will commit to your trust the true riches?" plainly declaring the intimate connection, now so little appreciated, between high spiritual attainments and the right use of property. In the duty of systematic benevolence, then, may be found an essential requisite, seldom thought of, for securing that elevated tone of piety, the want of which is so much lamented.

It produces a more vigorous and elevated tone of piety *by giving to love that exercise which is essential to its health and growth.* Love is the essence of piety; and it is as preposterous to expect it to thrive without the habitual exercise of beneficence, as to expect the body to be healthy in perpetual inaction. Piety cannot thrive as an ineffectual sensibility, exhausting itself on its own emotions in the heart; but from the spiritual affections of the inmost soul, it must issue, a transforming and controlling influence, pervading the whole life. It is a life-blood, which it is death to drive back on the heart; which as the only condition of health, must flow through the whole being, and throb with living power in the remotest and minutest acts. This condition of spiritual health systematic benevolence is indispensable to secure; and thus it is essential to meet one of the greatest wants of the churches, and to remove one of the greatest, though not one of the most noticed obstacles to higher attainments in the spiritual life.

It aids growth in grace *by promoting a constant intimacy with God.* It requires the will of God to be considered in every act of business, and links every expenditure with a regard to his glory. "The hand of God is recognized in our worldly affairs; his presence is invited, so to speak, into the very heart of our prosperity, whence the world is most anxious to exclude him, invited to audit the account of our gains." Thus it leads to "walk with God."

It awakens *a deeper earnestness for the salvation of men,* and of course, a greater fervor in prayer. It is a law of our natures, that doing kind deeds to others strengthens our love for them more than receiving kind deeds from them. We love most those for whom we do most. Hence, the more we do for the welfare of men, the more we shall feel and pray for them. Thus systematic charity keeps the spirit of prayer lively and the religious feelings tender and fresh. He who practises it will be likely to become an eminent Christian, entering with all his heart into every effort to do good, sympathizing in every feeling with the soul of Christ, and electric to every touch with his loving and self-sacrificing spirit.

It *concentrates the energies*, and thus favors spiritual growth. It prevents the division of purpose which is the great hinderance of success, fills, enlarges, and nerves the soul with the sublime purpose of doing good, and bending every power to that one object, enables us to say with Paul's earnestness, "This *one thing* we do."

But its most important influence in promoting the spiritual growth, is in *counteracting the deadening influences of worldly business*. It has already been considered as the antidote for covetousness. In thus grappling directly with this mother sin, it withers the strength of some of the most powerful temptations, and exerts a varied and extensive influence in unfolding the whole Christian character in its beauty. It extracts the poison from worldly pursuits; it counteracts their usual perniciousness; and not only so, it compels them to become actually helpers to growth in piety, as the exercise and discipline of heavenly affection; so that Christians may be

"Like ships in seas, while in, above the world,"

and all the agitations of busy life be but the bounding billows which bear them on their appointed course.

It is a common impression that the highest exercise of religion is incompatible with the highest activity and enterprise in worldly business; that as business increases, the activity of piety must decline; and that revivals are not to be looked for in those periods when business is peculiarly urgent. This impression is wholly unscriptural. The Bible requires us at the same time to be "not slothful in business, fervent in spirit, serving the Lord"—a requirement, plainly, that fervor and activity in God's service go hand in hand with fervor and activity in business. Nothing is plainer than that the whole system of precepts, promises, and warnings in the Bible is adapted to man amid the annoyances, temptations, and cares of every-day business. Should a man become a hermit for the better exercise of religion, he would find a large part of the Bible with no applicability to his circumstances. Besides, such a withdrawal is impossible, for necessity is on the most of men to spend their time in business. God requires them to be industrious in some useful calling. To suppose God requires a piety which it is impossible to exercise in its higher degrees in the midst of that business which his providence makes necessary and his law enjoins, is to charge God with unreasonable and inconsistent requirements.

But such an impression prevails. Not only so, but it is certain that business, as usually conducted, justifies it; for it has tendencies almost sure to check the growth of the Christian, so that the good feeling aroused in the closet or on the Sabbath is benumbed as by the shock of a torpedo, as soon as he takes his worldly affairs in hand; and it has tendencies to prevent the unconverted from attending to religion, and to harden them in hopeless inpenitence. Business occupies the time so that the prayer-meeting is neglected, and sometimes the family altar, the closet, and the word of God; so that the fatigue of excessive toil through the week causes slumber in the sanctuary, or is made an excuse for absence. Sometimes the pressure of business, or the fear that machinery will lose a few hours in the week, leads to flagrant, perhaps habitual profanation of God's day. Business occupies the thoughts, so that all the week long nothing else obtains a lodgment in the mind, and though the body be in God's house on the Sabbath, the thoughts are on the world; and thus, like one perishing in the water, the man of business scarcely gets his head above the worldliness which ingulfs him, to catch a breath of the pure air of heavenly life. And worse than all, his business seizes his heart; there is a fascination about it which draws to itself all his affections and energies. "He makes gold his hope, and says to the most fine gold, 'Thou art my confidence.'" In short, it is tending perpetually to make him at last a worldling, for whom the claims of benevolence and the schemes of philanthropy have lost their charm, who has no eye for the glories of heaven, no ear for the terrors of hell; who heeds his "piece of land," his "merchandise," his "five yoke of oxen," more than the invitations of mercy and the attractions of the cross; whose heart is in his purse, and his life circumscribed to his farm, his counting-room, or his shop; who as to spiritual life is dead and buried in worldliness, and his prosperity is but the magnificent monument of his soul's burial-place, on which all who weep his untimely ruin, may read with shuddering the inscription which God's finger has engraved: "Lo, this is the man that made not God his strength, but trusted in the abundance of his riches." "So is he that layeth up treasure *for himself, and is not rich toward God.*"

Systematic benevolence restrains this pernicious influence of business. But mere restraint is not all. It is not enough to ask how business is to be kept from injuring the church. Doing business is not necessarily serving mammon, therefore not necessarily the antagonist of serving God. It is dangerous for Christians to stand merely on the defensive here, and think merely to shield religion from the onslaught of worldliness. We must go further. The question must be, "How shall we bring business within the pale of religion, make it a part of religion, and an aid to its growth? How make it help in exercising and strengthening piety, as really as does prayer?" The Bible requires business to be thus identified with

God's service, and never will the church be saved from wasting worldliness and grow to her full stature in piety, till she carries the war into the enemy's territory, "overcomes the world," and makes it tributary to herself; and that, not merely by securing the silver and gold for her enterprises, but by securing in the very acts of worldly business a discipline of piety and an exercising and strengthening of grace. Business must occupy almost all the time of the most of God's children: how preposterous to expect them to make great attainments in piety if this business, like a poisoned atmosphere, is perpetually enfeebling their strength; if their religion is confined for its sources of nourishment to the Sabbath and the closet, and during almost their entire waking existence, is helplessly exposed to an ever-blighting agency from their own pursuits. They must bind their business on God's altar, or it will bind them on the altar of mammon.

The practical separation of business from religion, the belief that the former is necessarily antagonistical to the latter, and conducting it so as to make it so, are among the principal causes why the tone of piety is so low, and the mass of the church are but babes in Christ. Nor till this difficulty is removed have we a right to expect the church to "look forth as the morning, fair as the moon, clear as the sun, and terrible as an army with banners."

Systematic benevolence is a most important and

an indispensable agency in making business a helper and not a foe to the religious growth. When a man acts on this principle, his place of business becomes a Bethel; every transaction becomes like a renewal of his consecration to God; money and bills and labor are associated with his obligations to his Master, and fragrant with the memory of the cross; and like the attraction drawing every part of the earth and binding it to the sun, divine love fastens its attraction on every possession, on every toil, and every gain, and binds him with all that he has to God the centre of his whole life's orbit. Then he is intimate with God not less on the exchange or the farm, than in the closet. Then his whole course of life becomes a help and not a hinderance to his spiritual progress; and like a healthy child, he grows steadily and unconsciously amid the ceaseless activity of life.

Normand Smith, when roused to a more entire consecration to God, falling in with the common notion that a life of secular business is incompatible with a life of eminent usefulness and piety, seriously purposed to abandon it. But more scriptural views led him to continue in business, consecrating it to God. He put on record the "purpose to engage in my business, that I may serve God in it, and with the expectation of getting to give." His biographer says, "From that time it was observable by all who knew him, that he made rapid progress in religion. There was a fervor and engagedness of spirit, a purity and elevation of aim, that could not be misunderstood or concealed. He rose towards heaven like the lark of the morning." From that time "he found no tendency in his worldly engagements to chill his piety, or to enchain his affections to the earth. His business became to him a means of grace, and helped him forward in the divine life, just as truly as reading the Scriptures and prayer."

When a similar habit shall become general in the church, one of the most important steps will have been taken to secure that elevation of piety for which as yet we sigh in vain; and the law of love, now written in Christ's word, will be written on the hearts of his disciples and read by all the world in their lives.

Says President Edwards of alms-giving, "There is no external duty, by which persons will be so much in the way, not only of receiving temporal benefits, but also spiritual blessings, the influences of God's Spirit in the heart in divine discoveries and spiritual consolations." "That this is one likely means to obtain assurance, is evident from 1 John, 3 : 18, 19, 'My little children, let us not love in word, neither in tongue, but in deed and in truth. And hereby we know that we are of the truth, and shall assure our hearts before him.'" "If God's people in this land were once brought to abound in such deeds of love, nothing would have a greater tendency to bring the God of love down from heaven to earth; so amiable would be the sight in the eyes of our loving and exalted Redeemer, that it would soon as it were fetch him down from his throne in heaven, to set up his tabernacle with men on the earth and dwell with them." "The late remarkable revival of religion in Saxony, which began by the labors of the famous professor Franke, and has now been carried on for above thirty years, and has spread its happy influences into many parts of the world, was begun and has been carried on by a wonderful practice in this duty." Thoughts on the Revival, part 5, sect. 3.

## CHAPTER VIII.

### SYSTEMATIC BENEVOLENCE INCREASES THE SPIRITUAL POWER OF THE CHURCH.

THE increase of spiritual power will be the necessary consequence of the increase of piety. And by promoting an increase of piety, systematic benevolence imparts an efficacy to the prayers and teachings of the church, an influence to her character, a success to her enterprises, a mightiness through God to the pulling down of strong holds, such as money cannot bestow.

Here, also, we may consider principally its influence in counteracting worldliness. No argument is oftener urged against religion than that founded on the alleged inconsistencies of its professors. The chief foundation for this plea, so far as it has any, is the conformity of Christians to the world in all the aims, the maxims, and the manner of getting and spending money, so that too commonly, Christians, away from their devotions, can scarcely be distinguished from the better sort of worldlings. Let the scriptural law of benevolence be usually obeyed; let the world behold Christians actuated by the sublime desire to do good in all their gettings and their expenditures, and consecrating spontaneously to the Lord as he hath prospered them; let it be seen, when men become Christians, by the change in their pursuit of earthly treasure, that they have found a better portion, and now have their hearts and their treasure in heaven ; and the church will stand up before the world with a consistency and elevation of piety which will prove that gainsaying springs only from opposition to goodness—with a triumphant power which will compel the exclamation, "God is in the midst of her; she shall not be moved"—with a manifest and practical renunciation of the world, like that which in the apostles' days compelled both Jews and Gentiles to confess the reality and feel the power of religion, and which, reäppearing in the church, will go far towards restoring the like rapidity and glory to her conquests.

It would be ungrateful, indeed, not to acknowledge, among the striking characteristics of this age, the revival, in a degree, of the benevolent and missionary spirit of apostolic times. We hail it as an omen of good; we have marked already its happy results; we wait as "they that watch for the morning," for "the glory that should follow." But alas, how much in vain! For the icebergs and snowfields of the long winter still linger, and the piercing winds from them wither the plants of righteousness and keep back the buds of promise, and when we might be looking for the luxuriance of summer, behold the lingering, frost-bitten growth of a backward and chilling spring.

"Bring ye all the tithes into the storehouse, and

prove me now herewith, saith the Lord of hosts, if I will not open you the windows of heaven, and pour you out a blessing, that there shall not be room enough to receive it." We so constantly *spiritualize* this text, as to forget that its literal and proper application is to *contributions to the Lord's treasury*. Paying these fully is declared here to be the condition of God's great blessing. Let this challenge of the Most High be accepted. Let his sincerity in it be—as for generations past, by the church generally, it has not been—put to the test. Let his disciples "prove" him, by giving all that he requires, and see if, through its direct and indirect influence, it will not elevate the piety and enlarge the power and successes of the church—if spiritual stupidity will continue to be, for the larger portion of the time, the lamentation of the churches at home, and slow and limited success the history of benevolent operations abroad.

## CHAPTER IX.

### SYSTEMATIC BENEVOLENCE PROMOTES HAPPINESS.

It is a privilege to give, and a reason for thankfulness to have the opportunity and the means. Money given to the Lord leaves a sweetness like the perfume of the alabaster-box of precious ointment, filling the soul long after the offering has been poured out. Those who have given most regularly and in the largest proportion, remember with the most joyous gratitude what God has enabled them to do. When David and his people had contributed immense treasures "willingly" to build the temple, we read that "the people rejoiced, and David the king also rejoiced with great joy. And David said, Our God, we thank thee, and praise thy glorious name. But what am I, and what is my people, that we should be able to offer so willingly after this sort? for all things come of thee, and of thine own have we given thee." The first Christian converts, after "parting their goods to all men," "did eat their meat with gladness." Mr. Cobb said, "By the grace of God—*nothing else*—by the grace of God, I have been enabled to give more than $40,000. *How good the Lord has been to me!*" Said a man in moderate circumstances, who was giving his whole net income, "I could not feel happy to spend the money on myself, while so much is to be done for the needy and the perishing. I could not enjoy myself if I should do it." At another time, when necessary extra expenses greatly diminished his charities for a time, he said, "I find it one of my greatest trials, that I cannot do more for the heathen."

Systematic benevolence promotes happiness *by its influence in subduing covetousness and strengthening benevolence.*

As we have already seen covetousness to be a principal hinderance to *the spiritual growth* and *the spiritual power* of the church, so now we find it a hinderance to *spiritual enjoyment*—nay, to human happiness in the broadest sense. And that same divine scheme which we have already seen to be essential, chiefly by its influence in subduing covetousness, to the growth of the church's piety and the advancement of its triumphs, we now see to be essential, in the same way, to happiness. This combined view of these arguments may show us at once the far-reaching and appalling dangers of covetousness, and the simplicity, efficacy, and unfailing adaptedness of God's scheme of prevention.

*The covetous or selfish scheme of doing business is always tormenting.* It is accompanied by great anxiety. He who does business on this system is perpetually anxious and chafed, feverish with an excitement and perturbation, which are avoided by him who calmly does business for the Lord, and asks only what the Lord would have him do. "What shall I do for the hundred talents which I have given to the king of Israel?" is like the feverish questioning of the former. "The Lord is able to give thee much more than this," is like the trustful reply of the latter. Normand Smith incidentally shows what a preservative he had found for unruffled calmness amid the annoyances of business, by the following entry in his diary: "I have forgotten and broken my resolutions to conduct all to the glory of God. This has been manifested in my being fretted at what I deemed untimely calls for settlement and for debts." He seems to imply that so long as he adhered to his "resolutions," fretting at the annoyances of business was not a thing to be expected. A man who for years has been doing business in one of our cities on the scriptural plan of benevolence, but who had previously done business otherwise, says of himself, that "the anxiety, the feverish excitement, and the impatience to get the news and the results of sales, or the results of their own business operations, which merchants, speculators, and others are continually burdened with, and at times almost to distraction, and from which there seems to be little or no prospect of relief, all such perturbations of mind, common to others, were once common to his experience; but he *now* seldom feels any thing of the kind; for he has learned in his Bible to 'cast his burden on the Lord.'"

Besides, upon the covetous or selfish scheme of business, a man can never be satisfied. "He that loveth silver shall not be satisfied with silver, nor he that loveth abundance with increase." This sentiment has been in the mouths of the wise from Solomon's day till now. Its truth must for ever cut off the covetous man from solid contentment. The more he acquires, the more he wants; and in the midst of the greatest acquisitions, he remains the very realization of those lean and ill-favored kine which devoured all that was fair and thriving before them, only to remain as lean, as ill-favored, and as voracious as ever. There has appeared in the newspapers a horrible story about a man who had an enormous tape-worm in his stomach: however much the man ate, it was devoured by the ugly reptile within, nourishing itself to greater bulk and voracity thereby, while the wretched man was wasting in the torment of perpetual starvation. Whether the story be true or false, it is a lively picture of covetousness. That is a worm in the soul, nourishing itself to greater strength and voracity by every acquisition, and wasting the soul in the agony of perpetual want. Relief, sought in vain by trying to satisfy, can come only by killing the devouring desire—by killing it speedily, before it proves itself "the worm that never dies."

It is related in the history of ancient Rome, that an immense chasm once opened in the midst of the city. The superstitious Romans, to appease the god whose anger, they supposed, had opened the abyss, threw in the costliest garments and the richest treasures; but in vain. At last one of the most distinguished nobles put on his richest armor, and mounting his steed leaped into the abyss, and it closed. Covetousness, in its insatiability, realizes this fable. It is an abyss yawning in the covetous man's path. He gathers treasures and casts into it, but it closes not. He toils harder, he gathers more and richer treasures and casts into it, but it closes not—it closes not, till the wretched man himself sinks into the widening chasm, and it shuts on him in the gulf of perdition for ever.

*The very opposite is the result of love*, which the adoption of God's scheme of charity cherishes. There is "comfort in love." In every act of relieving the wretched which it requires, is a present bliss, which partakes more of heavenly than of earthly joy. It produces trustful peace amid annoyances, perplexities, and calamities. It leads to satisfaction, even with little. In peace of conscience, the consciousness of doing good and of receiving God's smile, it imparts blessedness which gold selfishly used can never buy. It gives a lasting joy. Spend money on self, and how quick the gratification is gone. But the joy of beneficence grows and brightens in the remembrance. To know that by foregoing a selfish gratification I have relieved the misery of a fellowman—that for my gifts and self-denial there is less ignorance, less vice, less wretchedness in the world; to know that I have helped to vindicate truth and right, and to establish the blessed reign of Jesus; to hope that, by God's blessing on my charities, even one dark soul has been made acquainted with the Saviour and led to everlasting bliss; what can thrill the soul with a richer, and more lasting joy? And at the bed of death, when all earthly treasures are slipping from the grasp, and the memory of selfish gratifications, now past for ever, but imbitters the spirit, these memories of charities and sacrifices, offered for Christ's sake and by his grace, will stand like angels of mercy, fanning the soul with airs of heaven, and cheering it with an undying joy in the agonies of dissolution.

No language oftener meets a pastor's ear, than the complaint, "I do not enjoy religion." The churches present a painful contrast with the habitual happiness of the apostles, whose writings, though written usually in the depths of distresses, more than any human compositions overflow with a deep and exultant joy. But there is little apprehension of what is a prevalent cause of this lack of spiritual joy—the withholding of charity, and the consequent increase of worldliness and the stagnation of holy love. Happiness cannot be poured into the soul from without, like water into a cistern; the water of life is not said to flow *into* a man, but to flow "*out of him.*" To regain lost enjoyment, the Christian must increase the exertions and self-denial of love. Let him fill life full of efforts and sacrifices to do good, and he will fill it full of bliss. He can be blessed only in accordance with that law of the entire moral universe expressed in the comprehensive words of Christ, "It is more blessed to give than to receive."

Consider, now, *the universality of this law.* God is love. So far as any addition to his blessedness is concerned, God never received any thing. If, as many imagine, every thing given is just so much taken from the comfort of the giver, God would have lost more happiness than all his creatures, for he is always giving. But he is the most blessed of beings; and he is so, not so much in spite of his ceaseless beneficence, as by means of it. His infinitude of bliss is an eternal expression of the law, "It is more blessed to give than to receive."

Angels toil for others, happy in what to selfish hearts would be the humiliating and self-denying service of ministering to those immeasurably their inferiors in character and rank; waiting upon the very "babes in Christ" in this nursery for heaven.

In hell is neither giving, nor blessedness. Selfishness reigns alone.

Thus the spirit of Christ's self-sacrificing love is the spirit of all heaven, and the essence of its bliss. The spirit of selfishness is the spirit of hell, and the source of its misery. The principle of the cross,

"*Give, give,*" carried out to all its results, makes heaven. The principle of the worldling's search for happiness, "*Get, get,*" carried out to all its results, makes hell.

The same law is discernible even in the confusion of probation on earth. The purest joy is found, not in halls of wealth, power, or gayety, nor yet in cottages where covetousness is always craving; but, whether in palace or hut, in the heart most completely filled, the life most completely controlled by self-sacrificing love. Even at the martyr's stake are witnessed scenes of most ecstatic bliss, because there selfishness is most effectually crushed, because there love enfolds the martyr's soul brighter and purer than the flames which enfold his body, and is the chariot of fire and horses of fire which bear him up to heaven.

Imagine a young lady surrounded with wealth and luxury, who, instead of living to strew around her blessings, is the spoiled child of indulgence, the victim of a selfishness that has always reigned unchecked. She passes her existence, full of fretfulness and discontent, in the vain attempt to satisfy desires which indulgence has made numerous and insatiable as an army of locusts, and which, in their devouring march through life, turn all the anticipations and opportunities of enjoyment opening invitingly before her, into unhappiness, and make the life of their victim to be always "like the garden of

Eden before them, and behind them a desolate wilderness."

Contrast with this imaginary case an historical personage. She was one of the first missionary band that left our shores, when every step was uncertain and hazardous, and war redoubled the dangers of the untried undertaking. Arrived in Asia, she is driven from the country, tossed again upon the ocean, and buffeted with discomfort, sickness, and difficulty, till she dies. But her life was blessedness, and her death was peace. For the former, all outward circumstances combine to produce happiness: but selfishness makes her miserable. For the latter, all outward circumstances combined to bring discomfort; by her own self-consecrating act she had rushed into the midst of trials; but all the floods of affliction could not quench the fire of her love, nor drown the flame of joy which ever mounted from the altar of her consecrated heart. The former will vapor life away and die, and she and the silks that clothed her will decay and be forgotten together; but the memory of HARRIET NEWELL will always refresh the earth, and hope, and love, and self-denial will spring ever with new freshness from her sea-girt grave. Yes; better is it, greater is it, that, in doing good, we be like the sweet incense burned before the Lord, consumed ourselves while spreading a sweet savor of beneficence about us—better that we be like the sacred oil of the seven-branched candlestick, consumed ourselves, while giving a holy light to others, than to gain for our own enjoyment all that selfishness ever won.

Paul and Silas, having "suffered the loss of all things," bloody with scourging, fastened painfully in the stocks in the inner prison, broke the silence of midnight with songs of joy. And love always sings: toiling, sacrificing, suffering, yet it sings. And in proportion as that love fills our hearts, controls our lives, subdues the tormenting covetings of selfishness, and makes it our "meat to do the will of Him that sent us," in that proportion will be the fulness and the continuity with which we shall join the song of love—that song which no prison walls nor stake of martyrdom can silence; which, ceaseless as the exhalations from the bosom of the earth, is going up everywhere from humble hearts toiling and suffering to do God's will—that irrepressible song, which, when death shall have broken down the bars of this mortality, shall burst into the shout of eternal and heavenly praise.

Thus has God made the universe according to that law, "It is more blessed to give than to receive." Let any intelligent being cease to seek the good of others, and he ceases to be blessed himself. Let the sun cease to pour his beams abroad, let him gather his rays only into his own bosom, and he will not only cease to shine on others, but will become black and unseen himself in the universal night. So, while any spirit that God has made lives not for itself, but for its Maker and its Maker's works, it shines above the brightness of the sun in glory. But when it begins to gather its efforts into itself and to pour its blessings only into its own bosom, that moment its glory goes out in night, and it becomes a part of "the blackness of darkness for ever."

In vain, then, do you look for happiness, while the business of life is not penetrated and controlled by benevolence. It were a contradiction and disordering of God's whole scheme of providence to permit it. And it were equally a contradiction of God's word; for as the word of God is true, they who "*will* be rich," and therefore neglect in their business the beneficence which God requires, must "pierce themselves through with many sorrows."

Hasten, then, thankfully to adopt God's plan for saving you from these many sorrows, and learn by your own experience that "it is more blessed to give than to receive."

Nor think that these sorrows are for this life only. God has lifted the veil from the awful future, and recorded the decision, "No covetous man hath any inheritance in the kingdom of Christ." "Be not deceived; neither thieves, nor covetous, nor drunkards shall inherit the kingdom of God." If there be one cause more effectual than any other in satisfying men with false hopes, or in turning the attention quite away from religion, hardening the heart in impenitence, and peopling the realms of woe, that cause is worldliness. If you value your immortal interests, if you have any just apprehension how many and powerful are the obstacles to your salvation, and how imminent your danger of being snared into a fatal negligence of your soul, it will be presumptuous trifling with your eternal welfare, if you adopt not the scriptural plan of subduing, by God's blessing, that worldliness which is the deadliest of all these opposing influences, and which the apostle so solemnly warns you is sure, if not subdued, to plunge you "into temptation and a snare, and into many foolish and hurtful lusts, which drown men in destruction and perdition."

Such are the motives to systematic benevolence; and such its vital and extensive connections with the Christian life and the prosperity of Christ's kingdom. And the force of these motives is enhanced by God's own revealed estimate of the importance of the duty of giving to relieve the wretched. There is something peculiarly interesting in the language of Christ, when guarding his disciples against selfish motives in alms-giving, and enjoining the precautions useful to secure an eye single to the glory of God. "Thy Father, which seeth in secret, himself shall reward thee openly." As if the Monarch of the universe felt a peculiar pleasure in the humble disciple whose aim is to honor him by his secret charities, and would bring him before the assembled universe and with his own royal hand encircle his brow with the incorruptible crown. And verily, one "Well done, good and faithful servant," from the lips of the King of heaven, may well outweigh all human applause, all selfish gains. And as if to show the intensity of his interest, and the particularity with which he notices and rewards what is given and what is withheld, God has revealed from heaven that even so insignificant a gift as "a cup of cold water only," given with right motives, shall not lose its reward; and has transmitted to all generations the solemn record of his approbation of the widow's farthing.

And the Saviour has invested the duty with an immeasurable sacredness, even with all the sacredness of love to him and regard to his sufferings; for he declares from the throne of judgment, that every gift, given with the pure desire to aid his church, he receives as given to aid himself; and every refusal to give, he regards as a refusal to minister to his own wants. He puts himself in the place of his church; he bares his bosom to receive every neglect of her in her necessities; he opens his heart to treasure up as a favor bestowed on himself, every favor bestowed on her. "Inasmuch as ye did it," or did it not, "to one of the least of these my brethren, ye did it," or did it not, "to me."

Having thus invested these objects of charity with the sacredness of his own person, and, as it were, linked the performance or neglect of the duty with every sensation of his own throbbing heart, he invests it with a new solemnity, and reveals in it a new importance, by declaring, that in the final judgment the duty of charity to the distressed will be selected as the key to the whole life and the test of the whole character. " Come, ye blessed of my Father, inherit the kingdom prepared for you from the foundation of the world; for I was a hungered, and ye gave me meat; I was thirsty, and ye gave me drink; I was a stranger, and ye took me in; naked, and ye clothed me; I was sick, and ye visited me; I was in prison, and ye came unto me." "Depart from me, ye cursed, into everlasting fire, prepared for the devil and his angels; for I was a hungered, and ye gave me no meat; I was thirsty, and ye gave me no drink; I was a stranger, and ye took me not in; naked, and ye clothed me not; sick, and in prison, and ye visited me not."

Behold, then, in God's own estimate of this duty, that we have not overrated its importance. Behold your hardihood, if you leave, unsystematized, to caprice and chance, a duty which is held so important in the solemn estimation of God, and is presented by the Judge himself, as the key and test of the character in the final decision. Behold with trembling your peril, lest, though you have even sat at Christ's table, you be found at last with those who have not ministered to Christ.

THE

# MISSION OF THE CHURCH;

OR,

# SYSTEMATIC BENEFICENCE.

BY REV. EDWARD A. LAWRENCE,

MARBLEHEAD, MASS.

Israel shall blossom and bud, and fill the face of the world with fruit.
ISAIAH 27 : 6.

PUBLISHED BY THE

AMERICAN TRACT SOCIETY,

150 NASSAU-STREET, NEW YORK.

13

# CONTENTS.

## CHAPTER I.

### THE SPIRIT OR ELEMENTARY PRINCIPLES OF BENEFICENCE.



## CHAPTER II.

### PROPORTION IN BENEFICENCE.

## CHAPTER III.

### SYSTEM IN BENEFICENCE.

I. *Provisions of system.*



II. *Tendencies and advantages of system.*

THE

# MISSION OF THE CHURCH.

---

## CHAPTER I.

### THE SPIRIT, OR ELEMENTARY PRINCIPLES OF BENEFICENCE.

THE mind that was in Christ, the spirit that moved him through the whole period of his earthly life, was a deep, ever-flowing spirit of *love.* It was an illimitable and inexhaustible benevolence. Every stage of his history, from the manger to the cross, is a peculiar expression of "good will towards men." By his life he became an example, and in his death he made atonement for sin; thus illustrating the spirit of Christianity, and opening a way whereby it might be infused into the hearts of his disciples. In its impulses and operations, both in the Head of the church and in its members, it is the *spirit of beneficence.* To be Christian, therefore, beneficence must be *prompted by the Christian spirit, and be in harmony with the great design of Christ in his redeeming work.* This gives it the fullest scope in the objects of the gospel, and the highest character in the spirit of the gospel. By the development of this spirit in the church, through the perfecting of the Christian life of its members, it finds its true mission in seeking the salvation of the race. It thus answers its fittest description—"the salt of the earth," "the light of the *world*."

The spirit of Christian beneficence is distinguished from mere human *kindness*, which is neither universal in its extent, uniform in its operations, noı Christian in its principle. It is distinguished from natural *pity*, in that this arises from spontaneous sympathy, and does not take into account the praise or blameworthiness of its objects. It differs from *generosity*, which is not scrupulous to abide by the rules of justice, and has no end in the honor of God, or the highest welfare of man. It is unlike that desire of *applause*, which in the spirit of Phariseeism often prompts to liberal donations, but only "to be seen of men." Its bestowments are dissimilar to the *grudging remittances* made to purchase relief from the wearying importunity of persevering applicants. It is distinguished from the *reluctant yielding* of the crumbs which fall from the table of abundance, in order to pacify a clamorous conscience, and procure exemption from its upbraidings. It is the antagonist of that alms-giving which is *relied on as the ground of justification* before God, thus making salvation by grace superfluous and impossible.

Between all these and that beneficence which is truly Christian, there is a wide difference. Christian beneficence neither disowns the constitutional principles or emotions, nor takes its character from them. Incorporating into itself all the elements of joy and sorrow, pity and sympathy, honor and generosity, it constitutes a complex principle, above and beyond any one or all of them. Jesus was kind, and sympathizing, and compassionate, and generous But he was something more than these. Purer motives urged him—a higher impulse moved him—a nobler spirit inspired him. It was the impulse of *love*, whose spontaneous outgushings made his life an example of the most sublime beneficence.

Among the peculiar and positive elements of beneficence, distinguishing it as Christian, is,

1. An *intelligent* spirit. Whosoever would discharge the duties of life, must first know what they are. In nothing is this more manifest than in efforts to do good. As all alms-giving is not from benevolence, so neither is it all beneficent. It is as essential to the latter, that it should be directed to a right end, as to the former that it should spring from a right principle. Nor does even a good motive in the donor necessarily secure to his deed the character of beneficence, unless it is well directed; the action may be praiseworthy in its purpose, while, from want of knowledge, it may be disastrous in its effects. Under the incubus of ignorance, well-meaning men may multiply the ills which they would remove. Through unacquaintance with the condition of those

whom they wish to benefit, or through ignorance of the proper remedial agencies or modes of applying them, they may diffuse the bane instead of the antidote, propagate darkness instead of disseminating light, and carry havoc and dismay where they intended only healing and consolation. And the more munificent is such ill-directed charity, the greater the waste—the more wide-spread the ruin.

Christian beneficence walks not forth blindfold amidst the world's mendicity and its mendacity, scattering alike to both. She wields not her full hands, as the Cyclops his huge limbs, at random. Her zeal is an enlightened ardor, never roaming in the dark, and never impatient of results that come only through the gradual operation of appropriate causes.

In this age of busy reform, all kinds of objects have their solicitors. Men who aspire to philanthropy even, must discriminate: much more does Christian beneficence demand a wise and careful circumspection. She wishes to know what the work is, and where it is, and how it is to be done. She sends out her pioneers to survey the ground and gauge the difficulties. She takes the altitude of mountains to be brought low, and the depth of valleys to be filled. She examines the crooked places to be made straight, and the rough places to be made smooth, and traverses "the wilderness and solitary place," which, by her culture, are to "bud and blossom as the rose."

By this pioneer service, in which such men as Howard and Buchanan and Martyn and Marshman have been most successful explorers, benevolent men are better enabled to adapt means to their ends. They obtain a quicker discernment of the various phases of wickedness and want, and of the avenues of access to them. The delusive fancies of sentimental philosophers concerning the virtues and happiness of the savage state, have been thus dispelled. The glowing eulogies pronounced upon the mythology of modern paganism, have, by the testimony of honest and indefatigable examiners, been thrown into entire discredit. The principles of evil, inherent in fallen humanity, are found to hold their woful empire over the comparatively mild inhabitants of Southern Asia, "with such an absoluteness of possessive power, and displaying this disposition in such wantonly versatile, extravagant, and monstrous effects, as to surpass all our previous imaginations and measures of possibility."

For those who desire information concerning these things, the means are at hand. Let them study the character and operations and claims of the various humane and benevolent associations, as exhibited in their lucid and condensed reports and other publications. Let them study the providences and prophecies and promises of God, in his works and word. His providence is casting clearer light upon the prophecies, and his Spirit is fulfilling the promises, to a degree that illumines the whole Christian world. The spirit of Christian beneficence, in her reformatory power, is entering the convict's cell, and is applying her benign and recovering agencies to the condition of the poor, the orphan, the sick, the insane, the deaf, the dumb, and the blind. She is penetrating the darkest nooks of heathenism, inspecting its habitations of cruelty, and scattering light concerning the wants and woes of the race. A goodly cluster of eleemosynary institutions—of almshouses, hospitals, and asylums, is diffusing an ameliorating and remedial influence throughout Christendom. A bright constellation of Bible, Missionary, Tract, and other kindred and affiliated societies, is pouring a flood of light upon the world, demolishing the temples of paganism, hastening the wane of the crescent, dissipating the delusions of Judaism, and discovering the hoary abominations of the man of sin. The Sun of righteousness begins to gild the hill-tops of India, Southern Africa, Syria, Persia, and Turkey, and has generated moral greenness and beauty in many of the islands of the sea. These things, all who wish to know, can know, and all who can know, should know.

2. The spirit of Christian beneficence is a *diffusive* spirit. The distinctions of home and foreign, far off and near, it knows only as different spheres for the occupancy of the same general agency, and for the achievement of the same lofty ends. Remoter guilt

and misery affect the heart of the benevolent, if not as sensibly, yet with as really a moving power, as do those more near. Moral wretchedness makes its appeal as urgently from India as from Ireland, from the Celestial empire as from Wisconsin. And yet, in his beneficent mission to the far distant, the benevolent man averts not his eye from sin and suffering at his own door. No one is more eagle-eyed to espy the mute signs of contiguous want, or more ready to respond to the calls of charity at home, than he who, overstepping such narrow limits, carries the blessings of his bounty to the farthest verge of sin and woe.

The plea of "charity at home" has passed into a proverb, the significance of which seems often to be, hoarding all one gets, and getting all he can. It is sometimes only the sanctimonious garb of parsimony, put on to cover the shame of its nakedness—the formulary by which covetousness seeks baptism at the hands of the Christian priesthood—a broad phylactery worn by one who "devours widows' houses." "Charity begins at home." True. And where else should she begin? She is born at home, and she begins to act where and when she receives her birth. This is the order of nature. All vital principles work from the centre outwards. It is the order of Providence also. But it is contrary both to nature and to Providence, for charity to seek only "her own," and allow her cultivated and fertile fields to do no more than "supply their own wants and replenish their own wastes."

He, therefore, who in Christian beneficence ends with the beginning, cannot be said to have begun at all. And he who bestows nothing to relieve the misery of which he only hears the description, will be likely to turn away from that of which his eye gives him the living picture. Or if perchance, by some sudden antagonistical impulse, his iron-nerved grasp be tremulously relaxed, it is but to let slip a pittance much nearer the mockery of woe than its mitigation. He who thus contravenes the order of nature, of Providence, and of the word of God, gives no equivocal proof of being tight bound in the chains of icy selfishness. Covetousness has cast him into her iron-cage, and crushing out of him all humane and generous feelings, has contracted his aims to the narrow circle of his own selfish involutions. Doing good to his fellow-men is not his mission. He has lost the primal dignity of man. He has set himself aside from the human brotherhood, and his ear is bored in servitude to mammon. He no less needs a mission of mercy from the abode of angels, to re-assert in him the power of conscience, and restore him to his lost human fellowship, than does the poor idolater who makes to himself a god of one piece of his wood, and warms himself at the fire kindled by the other. The one worships a god of wood—the other, a god of gold.

The spirit of Christian beneficence neither halts nor hesitates at geographical boundaries. Contiguity of guilt and misery has the advantage only as affording opportunity for speedier relief. Hence, the faintest sigh of want, and the softest wail of sorrow, from whatever source they come, touch a responsive chord in the soul of the benevolent man, and vibrate there as the voice of God.

Thus diffusive is the spirit of Christian beneficence. Her "field is the world." Her own nature allows her no narrower limits as the sphere of her action, and the circle of the globe no wider one. With "onward" for her motto, she shrinks from no region however rigorous, and from no clime however sultry or remote. No barbarism is too rude, and no forms of error too venerable, for her assailment. No human condition is so degraded and no misery so woful, no wretchedness is so appalling and no terror so intimidating, as to check her flowing sympathy or daunt her adventurous courage. The arm of power may be raised to protect or to repel her, yet, with her eye upturned to the throne of the Eternal, and her hand fast hold of the cross, she goes forth to her work. See the illustration of her diffusive energy in the propagation of primitive Christianity, which, in less than three centuries, she made the sole accredited religion of the civilized world. See her too, in this age, planting her standard amid the snows of Greenland, and on the burning sands of India. She is unfurling the banner of the cross in every quarter of the globe. She is climbing the snow-clad sides of the Himmaleh and the Andes, crossing the Rocky Mountains and ranging the coasts of the Pacific, bearing in one hand the torch of truth, and pointing with the other to the Lamb of God. Nor will she rest, till every son and daughter of Adam is blessed by the gospel, and the whole earth smiles with the beauty and verdure of heaven.

> "Breathe all thy minstrelsy, immortal harp,
> Breathe numbers warm with love, while I rehearse
> Thy praise, O *Charity;* thy labors most
> Divine, thy sympathy with sighs, and tears,
> And groans; thy great, thy godlike wish to heal
> All misery, all fortune's wounds, and make
> The soul of every living thing rejoice."

3. The spirit of Christian beneficence is an *equitable* spirit, recognizing the principles of *stewardship*. From just views of man's relations to his Maker arises the idea of right; and from the idea of right, comes the sense of moral obligation or duty. It is indeed essential to true beneficence, that it should be voluntary. "God loveth a cheerful giver." But it is also essential that respect should be had to a higher than human will, as the rule of duty. Thus then stands the case. Man is free to give, and free in giving. But he is also bound to give, and to give equitably.

Every man is *a steward* of God. All that he

possesses is committed to him in trust, with the injunction, "Occupy till I come." At a future day it will be said, "Give an account of thy stewardship." Of every one who hides his Lord's money by hoarding, or embezzles it by squandering, it shall be said, "Bind the unprofitable servant, and cast him into outer darkness." He, on the other hand, who employs it for the glory of his Master and the good of mankind, shall receive the faithful servant's approval, "Enter thou into the joy of thy Lord."

Give to this idea of stewardship a practical prevalence in the church, and it bars out covetousness, and raises multitudes of nominal professors from guilty worshippers of mammon, into honored coworkers with Christ in the world's redemption.

4. The spirit of Christian beneficence is a *benevolent* spirit. "Love thy neighbor as thyself," is the great philanthropic principle of the gospel. It annihilates selfishness, and brings men into the sweet bonds of one common brotherhood. It plucks from the heart the "root of all evil," and plants in its stead the seeds of a universal charity.

We love our children, in some sense, as we love ourselves; but this is not benevolence: our instincts prompt it. We make common cause upon some subjects, and on some occasions, with our kindred or friends; but this is not benevolence: self-interest dictates it. We join in civil compact, and pledge "our lives, our fortunes, and our sacred honor," and sometimes pour out our blood like water for the common weal; but this is not benevolence: call it patriotism, or what we will, it has no Christian element, and oftentimes conflicts with every gospel principle, and charitable feeling. Benevolence makes a man the denizen of the world. By its inherent tendency to "do good unto *all* men," it annihilates distance, and by sympathy brings remote evils near. It knows no demarcation lines of sect, or tribe, or color. Its boundaries are the limits of humanity. In its expansive schemes, it regards men as under one common condition of guilt and suffering; subjects of one common righteous government; liable to one common woe; and for whom there is provided one common divine dispensary—one Gilead of the world. The African is our "neighbor," and has fallen "among thieves;" benevolence calls for the appliance of our "oil and wine." The Hindoo is our brother, and is "sick;" it bids us bear to him the "balm" from "Gilead," and tell him of the "Physician there."

To what enlarged schemes of beneficence would the prevalence of this spirit prompt the church. What masses of wealth would it consecrate to the cause of humanity. What thousands of devoted men, glowing with the spirit of Mills and Martyn and Brainerd, panting to carry the light of truth to lands darkened by sin, would it bring into the educational processes, preparatory to such a work. What fleets would it give to the winds, taking their course towards the heathen world, laden with the printed word, and the living preacher. How sublime the spectacle—the whole Christian church moved by such a spirit of beneficence.

5. The spirit of Christian beneficence is a *self-denying* spirit. It is the nature of sin to exalt self to preëminence. This disorders our relations both to God and to our fellow-men. It subverts the law of love. It discards the divine will as the rule of action, and substitutes each man's own will. Its tendency is to convert the world into an arena of ceaseless and sanguinary conflict, for as many separate interests as there are individual combatants.

Now, the tendency of Christianity is directly the reverse of this. It casts down self and enthrones the Creator in the soul. It meets the selfish spirit in all its vicious cravings, with an imperative denial. The foundation of the Christian faith was laid in *a sacrifice,* "Jesus Christ himself being the chief corner-stone." And as each disciple is built on this foundation, he receives from it a subduing power, which imparts to him this self-denying spirit. The beneficent career of Jesus on earth was marked in every period by humiliation and suffering and sacrifice. And shall his followers have no fellowship with him in these? Is the vital sap of the branches unlike that which flows in the vine? Shall there be self-sacrifice in the head, and self-indulgence in the members? Self-denial is the condition of spiritual progress. "A despicable indulgence," says Henry Martyn, "gave me such a view of my character, that on my knees, I resolved to live a life of greater self-denial. The love and vigor of my mind rose rapidly, and all those duties from which I usually shrank, seemed recreations." Self-denial is the very condition of discipleship. "If any man will come after me, let him deny himself, and take up his cross daily, and follow me."

See this spirit burning in the bosom of the apostle to the Gentiles. With unsurpassed devotion, he lays his ease and learning and cherished hopes joyfully at the feet of his Saviour. He is "in perils of waters, in perils of robbers, in perils by his own countrymen, in perils by the heathen, in perils in the city, in perils in the wilderness, in perils in the sea, in perils among false brethren ; in weariness and painfulness, in watchings often, in hunger and thirst, in fastings often, in cold and nakedness." And does he complain that his labors and sacrifices are too wearisome, or too costly? Rather does he glory that to him is "this grace given," that he may "preach among the Gentiles the unsearchable riches of Christ." The same flame glowed in the breasts of the martyrs, and the same holy fire should be kindled in the bosoms of the whole company of the disciples, consuming selfishness, and converting their hearts into censers, whence should perpetually ascend sweet incense unto God.

6. The spirit of Christian beneficence is a spirit of

*grateful love.* The most concise definition of the Christian religion is *love.* "God is love," and "love is the fulfilling of the law." "Though I bestow all my goods to feed the poor, and give my body to be burned, and have not love, it profiteth me nothing." The love of Christ takes the deepest hold of all the principles of our being. It allows no rival. It admits no equal. It must reign supreme in the soul, controlling all its emotions, and directing all its energies. Under the influence of this love, benevolent impulses become permanent affections. Our strongest desires for the welfare of man and the glory of God, assume the character of *fixed principles.* Beholding the world as the scene of moral achievement, surveying its desolations, its poverty and misery, its hatreds and strifes, its malice and murders, how sublime appears the enterprise of its recovery. Ascending the mount of vision fast by the cross, and witnessing the vast funeral processions bearing annually on their biers to the world of woe, twenty-five millions of lost souls, how moving the spectacle, how imploring the scene! Yea, Christian, mounting up to the throne of the Eternal, see Him whom your soul loveth casting down his cross upon the golden pavements of the celestial city, and by all his agonies upon it, by the accumulated worth of six hundred millions of guilty human spirits, to whom the church has not these eighteen hundred years carried his saving gospel, see him interceding for that church, that it may be filled with his own spirit, that it may become more *self-denying*, that it may cease its strifes at home, and go on its mission abroad: see this, and if love does not burn like a fire in your bones, if apathy does not seem madness, and the consecration of all fit means to such an end but a poor return, the very least you can offer, thou hast not known the love of Christ.

When Dr. Doddridge, having procured a pardon for a condemned criminal, entered the prisoner's cell, the grateful man threw himself at his feet, exclaiming, "Every drop of my blood thanks you, for you have had mercy on every drop of it Wherever you go, *I will be yours.*" So entire is the devotion prompted by grateful love. But redeeming love! Oh, it is this which awakens all that is tender in affection, all that is generous and self-sacrificing in devotion, and which gives direction to all that is executive in energy for high moral achievement. It imparts to the meanest sacrifice a divine fragrance. It gives to "a cup of cold water" a preëminence on the catalogue of beneficent acts, not reached by the pharisaic donor of millions. It clothes the simplest prayer of the poorest disciple with a power for the world's conversion, to which the most skilfully adjusted moral machinery can make no approach. It is the divine alchymy, which transmutes in its crucible the baser metals into gold, and sets the smallest gift as a priceless jewel in the diadem of Him on whose head are "many crowns."

As Christ's mission was to the poor, these, whom we "have always" with us, should be regarded as his representatives. To each of his disciples, he says, "In these I am 'an hungered;' feed me: 'thirsty;' give me drink: I am 'sick' in the islands of the sea; minister to me there: I am a prisoner in Asia; procure my release: I am bound in Africa; seek my deliverance. 'Inasmuch as ye have done it unto one of the least of these, ye have done it unto me.'" And when you have laid all your possessions and yourself with them, at the foot of the cross, and viewed him suspended upon it, how insufficient seem all human energies and offerings as a requital of his love. You wish that gold had a million times more value, and you a million times more gold to devote to him; that your energies were augmented into superangelic powers, that in the consecration of them all, your grateful love might find more fit expression.

"Oh thou who keep'st the key of love,
Open thy fount, eternal Dove,
And overflow this heart of mine;
Enlarging, as it fills with thee,
Till, in one blaze of *charity*,
Care and remorse are lost, like motes in light divine.

"Till, as each moment wafts us higher,
By every gush of pure desire,
And high-breathed hope of joys above,
By every sacred sigh we heave,
Whole years of folly we outlive,
In His unerring sight who measures life by *love*."

7. The spirit of Christian beneficence is a spirit *of prayer*. It is this which distinguishes the enterprises of the church from all other schemes for ameliorating the condition, and relieving the wants and woes of the race. While it does not impair the feeling of responsibility, it impresses the sense of dependence. It impels the heart to look upward for wisdom to direct its efforts, and for power to render them efficacious. Plans of moral achievement which, on any other principle than that of the divine efficiency, would be Utopian, by this are rendered rational and hopeful. It clothes the most gigantic and daring moral heroism with the garments of humility, and elevates the simplest efforts of faith and love to the most honorable position of successful instrumentality. Recognizing the divine agency as the sole efficient cause of all beneficent human agency, his people lay their gifts upon the earthly altar, and in answer to prayer, the angel presents them as an accepted offering upon the golden altar before the throne. Without prayer, alms fall like lead to the ground. On the wings of prayer they seek the skies, and come up as an acceptable "memorial before God."

Even Jesus the Son of the Most High labored not to do good without prayer. His life was one fervent intercession, the ardor of which abated not when it had consumed him on the cross. It mounted up to heaven. It still breathes and burns in the ear of

God, with a prevalence that gives birth, in the mission of the Spirit, to all human prayer, and efficacy to all human instrumentality for the good of the world.

See too how the apostles prayed when entering upon their beneficent work. Returning from the mount from which they had seen their Master ascend, they retire to "an upper room," and continue with one accord in prayer and supplication, until their baptism by the Holy Ghost. They then go forth to their labors praying with the conviction that they can do nothing without prayer, and laboring as if they could accomplish all things without it. Behold the martyrs, kindling their ardor at the altar of prayer, and pouring out their blood on the altar of sacrifice. The period of the Reformation was a period of intense, concentrated prayer. And the efficient power of all beneficent enterprise is a power answering to the voice of prayer, going up from the heart of the church. Here is a field into which all may enter as reapers. The pathway to the throne of grace is barred to none, and none are more accepted laborers than those who, having nothing else to bestow, pour out their strongest desires and their richest affections upon the angel's "golden censer."

Here is the divine philosophy of Christian beneficence. The church lays down her offerings at the cross, and sends up her prayer to him who died upon it, and one angel descends into the Bethesda around which earth's "impotent" are gathered, and another "angel having the everlasting gospel," is seen flying through the earth, "to every nation, and kindred, and tongue, and people," and "great voices are heard, saying, The kingdoms of this world are become the kingdoms of our Lord and of his Christ, and he shall reign for ever and ever."

Such are the leading elements which give character to beneficence as a *Christian* work.

## CHAPTER II.

### PROPORTION IN BENEFICENCE.

EVERY man's charitable contributions should evidently be proportionate *to the vastness and importance of the objects sought; to the adequacy of the instrumentality; and to his pecuniary means and facilities for applying that instrumentality.*

#### FIRST GENERAL PROPOSITION.

EVERY MAN'S CHARITABLE CONTRIBUTIONS SHOULD BE PROPORTIONATE TO THE VASTNESS AND IMPORTANCE OF THE OBJECTS SOUGHT IN BENEFICENCE.

What, then, is *the object* or *end* which Christian Beneficence proposes to secure? Comprehensively, and in a word, it is, THE RECOVERY OF THE HUMAN RACE FROM SIN TO HOLINESS. "*The field is the world.*" Ascend some mount of vision and behold the spectacle—a world in ruins. Sin has entered and strode across it, and death follows, mercilessly sweeping its guilty generations into the unfathomable abyss.

1. Look at *Protestant Christendom*, and what do you see? In the most favored lands, where the governments are popular and the people free, where science is cherished and the arts flourish, where civilization smiles and the word of God has free course, how do ignorance of the divine law and defiance of

right join in unhallowed compact, and generate a race of giants in wickedness! How are such lands covered over with houses of correction, and jails, and dungeons, and filled with the insignia of depravity—the proofs as well as preventives of dishonesty, treachery, and crime. How are all remedial and sanative agencies despised or disregarded by multitudes of the people; while cupidity gloats on gain and ambition strives to supplant and trample on a rival, and lust reeks in her dens of infamy, or saunters forth in the guise of innocence to capture and destroy.

2. Inspect those portions of the earth's surface, designated as *Roman-catholic* Christendom. They are left to the occupancy of a religious system that incarcerates in dead languages the prophets and apostles, and dispenses its dry dogmas and uncommanded ordinances where the Saviour has appointed the nutritious bread of heaven and the healing waters of life—a system, in whose fiscal arrangements sin is set down as a marketable commodity, by traffic in which, the guilty may purchase indulgence to any amount, and with no penalty except the prescribed pecuniary one, may escape from Delilah's lap into Abraham's bosom—wherein prayers and pardons, births and burials, suspensions of the divine law and its satisfaction, every thing, in short, is paid for in gold, except the liberty to believe and to teach the pure gospel—wherein the living are laid

under tribute for the benefit of the dead, whom, not content with assessing while in the flesh, it consigns to purgatorial torments, release from which can be procured only by purchased Pater-nosters and Ave Marias: a system in which freedom is fettered, and conscience is bound, and the right of private judgment has fallen among thieves, and the priest passes by on the other side—in which the Redeemer of the world is displaced from his mediatorial office by the elevation of his virgin mother; and the holiness of the poor canonized saint, is made transferable for the benefit of the rich repenting sinner—in which "science and ignorance, refinement and barbarism, wisdom and stupidity, taste and animalism, mistaken zeal and malignant enmity, may sanctimoniously pour out their virulence against the gospel, and cry, 'Hosanna,' while they go forth to shed the blood, and wear out the patience of the saints of the Most High."[1]

And if in any thing the workings of this matchless machinery for deceiving the people and destroying its opponents, is less wasteful than formerly of human blood, as the means of giving prevalence to its dead but gigantic formalism, it is because its former plenary *power* has departed, and it is hemmed in by moral and political influences which render such means both impolitic and impracticable. It is not, we believe, from any essential improvement in the system. That is unchanged and unchangeable.

Reform in the spirit and principles of the church of Rome, would be its ruin. Let it but give an open Bible to the people, with liberty to read and think for themselves, and it bites the dust. Yet, to the baleful nurture of this "mother of harlots," more than one hundred millions of the dwellers on the globe are subject, displaying the full "effects of knowledge denied"—of "a famine of the words of the Lord."

3. Next, turn your eye to the followers of the *false Prophet*, of whom there are over one hundred millions more. Here, instead of the Bible, you find the Koran—instead of the cross, the crescent. If the tutelary genius of Mohammed complimented the patriarchs, it was to "beguile the Jew." If the Saviour of the world was admitted as among the prophets, it was as a lure to nominal Christians. And by holding out to the faithful the certainty of sensual gratification, it was seen that a more easy conquest would be secured over papists, pagans, and infidels. The moral maxims from the Bible incorporated into the system, were only sufficient to give plausibility to its claims, and durability to the compact. Strong and resolute in the ignorance which it inculcates, its darkness has "strangled the travelling lamp" of truth, and its pride beaten back even the precursors of knowledge. To make disciples was its first object. Its second, was to make them iron-nerved and ferocious. The third, was to *crush* all whom it could not lure or compel to the faith. Occupying

for centuries the fairest portions of the earth, it has converted them into a wilderness, and covered them with moral desolation. Thanks to an overruling Providence, Islamism is in its dotage. "The keepers of the house tremble, and the strong men bow themselves. The daughters of music are brought low; fears are in the way, and the grasshopper is a burden."

4. To complete the view of the field which beneficence seeks to occupy, cast the eye over lands shrouded in *Paganism*. Bereft of the idea of one all-perfect and controlling divinity; with no standard of truth and right—no guiding demonstration, leading to a comparison of the false with the true, the malignant with the good—the appetites and passions rising into supremacy and converting the enfeebled remains of moral sense into auxiliaries of debasement, what can Paganism be but one "mighty labor of human depravity to confirm its dominion?" Vedas and shasters, filled with interminable genealogies, and transmigrations of the human soul, and of male and female divinities, are its holy books, containing neither precept nor example of moral excellence. Brahma, Vishnoo, and Siva, the consecrated patrons of the vices, are its chief deities. Vain theorists, skilful impostors, and lascivious sorcerers are its only guides and intercessors. Parricide, infanticide, sutteeism, self-torture, laborious pilgrimages, and obscene rites are its most approved forms of religious service.

Caste, with its impassable walls, fixing unalterably the station of each individual, annihilates all motive to improvement in the lower classes, and gives to the higher free course in vice and crime, by securing them against deposition or disgrace. "The entire empire of polytheism," says Harris, "is a realm of diabolical dominion. It assembles its votaries only to blaspheme the name of God; erects its temples only to attract the lightning of the impending cloud on their devoted heads; calls them around its altars, only that, in the very act of supposed atonement, they may complete their guilt; and gives them a pretended revelation only that 'they should believe a lie.'"

And the worst feature of all is, that in the systems of Paganism, there is no element of *improvement*, no principle of progress, except in the road from bad to worse. Time only deepens the gloom, and legitimizes among them the processes of ruin. Even the moral sentiments that here and there shone out of ancient heathenism, like stars in deep night, and the skill and taste apparent in the temples and divinities of Greece and Rome, find no place in modern Paganism. It has no recuperative, but only a degrading and destructive power.

And does no Macedonian cry, coming up from such an Aceldama, make its appeal to Christian hearts for some more vigorous and sustained beneficent effort? Behold poor, abused, bleeding Africa, pillaged and plundered by lawless and inhuman marauders, yielding up her tawny, barbarous sons to still more barbarous strangers from Christian lands. See Asia, "wholly given to idolatry," her miserable poor crushed under the heel of an oppressive and polluted priesthood—Asia, the cradle of the race, torn by intestine feuds and foreign aggressions, pouring her dense population of wretched and guilty spirits into the abyss of woe—Asia, with no Bible and no Sabbath; with no Saviour but the Ganges and her countless idols; with no worship but that of demons, or reptiles, or monsters of vice; and with no morality except what hastens the desolating work, and hurries human souls to perdition—how does she lift up her imploring voice, and call on us for a deliverer.

"Oh, could I picture out the *full* effect
Of that soul-withering power, idolatry,
I'd write a page which, whoso dared to read,
His eye, instead of tears, in crimson drops should bleed.'

Now, it is the *object* of Christian beneficence to recover this guilty and lost world to the service and enjoyment of God. It is to purify the earth from all its vile abominations, and clothe it in the loveliness of moral beauty. It is not her work to admire the proportions of ancient architecture, or the stateliness of modern palaces; to imitate the great masters in statuary and painting, or to gather the results of modern science; it is not to adorn the galleries of art, or enrich the collections of antique curiosities;

not to decipher Egyptian hieroglyphics, or muse on the remains of ancient grandeur, laudable as all this may be; but it is her work to found hospitals, open dispensaries, and establish asylums, wherein the poor may be cared for, the sick visited, the blind be made to see, the deaf to hear, and the dumb to speak. For such beneficent institutions, there was no place among all the public edifices, or structures, or organizations of ancient heathenism, as for them there was no name in all their languages. We might say, it is the MISSION OF THE CHURCH to raise up debased and brutalized mind, oppressed and degraded almost to extinguishment, and impart to it vigor and fertility; to give exercise to the kindlier sympathies and more elevated sentiments of the heart, and to restore liberty and supremacy to conscience. She aims to bury every tomahawk, to "beat swords into ploughshares and spears into pruning-hooks," to bear the olive-branch into all climes, plant the tree of peace in every soil, and bring wandering, warlike tribes into a social, civil, and religious position, surpassing that of the happiest and most prosperous community on the globe. What objects of temporal good are comparable with these? What career more like the earthly mission of Him who went about doing good?

But beneficence has a still *higher* object than to bless men in this life. She carries her projects for consummation, across the boundary of time, into the vast and indescribable eternity beyond. In the accomplishment of her design, she seeks to open a moral Bethesda in every land, and to make the Bible, God's directory to heaven, the book of the world; to "preach the gospel to every creature," and to make it "the power of God unto salvation" in every heart. She aims to break the frightful coalition of ignorance and crime, formed by "the prince of the power of the air," and to transfer the wretched captives from the power of Satan unto God. She seeks to tear down the funeral pile of the miserably devoted widow, and to give her, in her affliction, to the benign influences of the heavenly Comforter; to detach from the blood-stained car of Juggernaut its murderous human propellers, to raise up from before its ponderous wheels the deluded human victims, and to send them to the shrine of a pure worship, and to the altar of the living God. She enters the precincts of the demon-temples, surveys the abominable, soul-destroying rites, weeps over the appalling spectacle, and wrests from "the ruler of the darkness of this world" the prostrate human spirits there trampled into the dust. She points them to the cross of Christ, and tells them that "God so loved the world, that he gave his only begotten Son, that whosoever believeth in him, might not perish, but have everlasting life." She stands by the Ganges, and assures the suicidal worshippers that the path to heaven is not through its turbid stream, opens to them Jesus as "the way," and bathes them in the pure waters of the river of life. Like a visitant from the bosom of love, she sits by the shrines of Brahma, Vishnoo, and Siva, and proclaims to the millions of eager votaries, that these "cannot answer, and save them out of trouble." She would bear the cross into the very heart of Mohammedan imposture, and plant it within the grand mosque at Mecca, sprinkling the multitudinous mass of deluded pilgrims with the blood which "cleanseth from all sin." She would pour the light of a pure Christianity upon the darkened domains of Romanism, and introduce "the power of godliness" to a region wherein is found little save its gorgeous but lifeless forms. She would dispel the dark and inveterate disbelief of the Jews, scattered and peeled and oppressed, and lead them, through their own prophets, to the acknowledgment of Jesus as the Messiah, and unite all the dwellers on the earth under his tranquil and happy reign.

And is it nothing to you, that a mission is proposed for the accomplishment of such an object? Are there found in such forms and fruits of sin any sufficient remedial agencies to justify apathy and inaction? And is it thus you would shield yourself from the urgency of appeal which the case presents, and baffle the beneficent design of Immanuel in giving his life a ransom for the world? Can you think that pollution is as good as purity; that idolatry is as likely to lead to heaven as the service of God; that blasphemy and defiance of divine command are as efficacious for salvation as faith in Jesus? Will the eternal law of truth and rectitude be repealed, in consideration of the prevalence of error, imposture, and crime? Will ablutions in the Ganges, or the declaration of pardon by a darkened and ambitious priesthood, make their robes white, as if washed in the blood of the Lamb? Will the flames of suttee-ism purify the guilty soul like the sprinkling of the clear waters of the gospel? Do the rumblings of Juggernaut's bloody car make sweet music in the ear of God, like the prayer and praise of redeemed spirits, uttering their thanksgiving and love? Oh, speak it not—think it not. "Without *faith* it is impossible to please God." "But how shall they *believe* on Him of whom they have not heard? And how shall they hear, without a preacher? And how shall they preach, except they be sent?" Such is the resistless logic of the apostle, which divinely demonstrates the necessity of a mission to the ignorant and guilty in every land; and which proclaims the gospel as the sovereign balm for all wounded spirits—the grand panacea for all human ills—the "pharos of a benighted world."

To carry this gospel to the guilty and miserable of earth's teeming population, is the appropriate MISSION OF THE CHURCH. It is to tell them of the amplitude of God's love to man, and raise them to him by the efficacy of that love. It is to efface the foul blot of sin from the polluted soul of man, to restore primeval paradise to earth's outcast inhabitants, to people heaven with redeemed and blissful dwellers, and to give back to God his revolted, dismembered kingdom, in sweet and peaceful subjection.

How lofty is this aim! How sublime the end! It is in agreement with the end of Jehovah in creating the race. It is promotive of the object for which Christ died. It is included in the grand sweep of God's providential plan for the government of the world. It is identical with the main design of Heaven in the constitution of the church, and the continuance of redeemed ones for a time, as pilgrims on the earth. All holy motives converge to this one point, the glory of God in the salvation of men. All moral arguments, in their loftiest bearings, strengthen and confirm this. All spiritual appliances, in their ultimate reference and highest utility, minister to this one comprehensive and sublime end, the healing of the nations by the gospel of Christ, "to the praise and glory of God's grace." Nor will the period arrive when it can be said of the work, "it is finished," till

> "The dwellers in the vales, and on the rocks
> Shout to each other, and the mountain-tops
> From distant mountains catch the flying joy—
> Till, nation after nation taught the strain,
> Earth rolls the rapturous Hosanna round."

Now, if we have succeeded in impressing the reader with the vastness and importance of the *objects* of Christian beneficence, he has probably been led to the following conclusion: if there is an adequate instrumentality for the accomplishment of this object, the question of expense is worthy to be considered only so far as to ascertain whether it is within the limits of possibility to meet that expense. He will say, the cost is nothing in comparison with the end to be gained. If the work is practicable, it *cannot* cost too much. He feels that it is paltry meanness, with such an object in view, to haggle about dollars and cents; that it is treason against humanity to withhold giving, where such motives urge to liberality. He sees that he may never have taken a just view of his own duty and responsibility in this matter, and he resolves that his rate of benevolent contribution, in time to come, shall be more proportionate to the value and importance of the end sought in beneficence. And he also determines that what is done, should be done *quickly*. "Roma deliberat, Saguntum perit"—While the church deliberates, the heathen perish.

### SECOND GENERAL PROPOSITION.

EVERY MAN'S CHARITABLE CONTRIBUTIONS SHOULD BE PROPORTIONATE TO THE ADEQUACY OF THE INSTRUMENTALITY TO BE APPLIED.

The fallen world—what can raise it up from its revolted and degenerate state, and give it back to God redeemed, and clothed in its primeval loveliness and beauty? What can make atonement for sin, and give satisfaction to the dishonored law of God, and repair the ruin wrought? What can penetrate the obdurate heart of man, and turn its selfishness into benevolence, and impel the tide of its sympathies, ever tending inward to the contracted centre, to flow outward to the circumference and upward towards its Maker? Is there an adequate redeeming power? Are there sufficient remedial agencies for a work so vast, so momentous? These are questions which press upon the spirit of every earnest inquirer concerning the means of man's redemption, and of the mission of the church to the world.

The great desideratum with Archimedes, for moving the world, was a place whereon to stand. This was his necessity. A similar necessity meets the Christian philanthropist in the scheme for bringing back the revolted world into the sunlight and favor of heaven. The philosopher could obtain no such stand-point. The Christian can. The one could find no place outside of, or above the world which he wished to move. The other takes his stand on the Gospel of Christ, which is "from heaven" and not "of men." This gives him a position and a power fully adequate to his most enlarged and comprehensive benevolence. *All other expedients for the conversion of the world* are cumbered by the same unremovable difficulty which met the Syracusan philosopher

Within the most costly temples of *Paganism*, no divine light illumines the benighted worshippers, and no celestial fire warms their devotion into life. In the very act of giving "the fruit of the body for the sin of the soul," they but enhance the evil which they would remove. Notwithstanding the smoke of their ten thousand sacrifices, ascending to blacken the heavens they would appease, the sting of conscience rankles in their guilty bosoms still. In all these things, "they feed on ashes." "Pass over the isles of Chittim and see, send unto Kedar and consider diligently, and see if there be such a thing. Hath a nation changed their gods, which are no gods?"

Nor is there more hope in the alleged recuperative power of *reason*, and the progress of *science*. For nearly six thousand years, there have been promulgators of the doctrine of human perfectibility, and dreamers of such a result through the devices of reason and the advance of science. And successive generations have been working out demonstrations of the futility of the doctrine, as decisive as they are humiliating. Human reason has no such recovering moral energy. It can never relieve itself from the dominancy of the passions, or rise from its subjection to the perverse will. It may *intimate*, in some things, the right, the true, and the good; but it cannot compel to their observance. Reason and science may polish the exterior into a degree of comeliness and decency, but they cannot successfully resist the on-workings of the law of sin. They cannot remove from the soul its appalling sense of guilt. They cannot lead man to "deny ungodliness and worldly lusts, and to live soberly, righteously, and godly in this present world." See their boasted triumphs in the reign of terror which swept across France at the close of the last century, deluging the land with blood, and leaving it in a state which forced from the republic the humbling confession, that their "children are without any idea of divinity, with out any notion of what is just or unjust."

And what are the claims alleged in favor of *civilization* as a remedial agency? It should be a sufficient answer to say, that civilization contemplates man only as an inhabitant of this terrestrial globe, and provides not for his weal beyond. And its most beneficent instrumentality is composed of the implements of agriculture, and of the mechanic arts. It sends to the savage tribes of the earth, as its best boon, the plough, the spindle, and the loom, whereby they may clothe themselves "in purple and fine linen, and fare sumptuously every day;" but it leaves the soul a prey to remorse, and under the frown of heaven. It excites no hope of future good; awakens no gratitude to the Father of mercies; points to no divine, atoning work; tells of no redeeming love, through which is seen,

"Up earth's dark glade,
The gate of heaven unclose."

The Bible, the Sabbath, and the cross constitute no elements of beneficent power, in all its boasted instrumentality. In its happiest influences, it leaves man as it finds him, guilty and miserable, in darkness and distress, where he most needs light and relief.

Nor can there be more reliance upon the enactment of *civil law.* This is only a defensive expedient, adopted by communities to prevent such overt crimes as are injurious to the social compact. But in preventing the criminal *act*, can it dictate to the *heart*, and sway a resistless sceptre over its stormy passions, and hush its wild discord into harmony and peace? Can it carry the force of truth into the dark caverns of the soul, combating and conquering iniquity, dethroning selfishness, purging away lust, casting out revenge, and turning the plottings of villany into plans of benevolence? Can it restore to the conscience its legitimate supremacy, and cast down pride, and introduce love and mercy and meekness? Can it break up "the fallow ground," and "scatter the good seed," and fructify the barren soil, and cause it to bring forth a rich harvest unto God? "Canst thou draw out leviathan with a *hook;* or bore his jaw through with a *thorn?*" Law is a *rule*, not a remedy. Its language to the guilty is of *punishment*, and not of pardon. "The letter killeth." It is the Spirit that giveth life. It is not the twelve tables and the Justinian code that man needs, but the four gospels and the twenty-one epistles.

*Literature* and its refinements are no more adequate to the ends of Christian beneficence, than is civilization or law. If we look to the periods of antiquity in which the arts were carried to the highest degree of refinement, and the muses were most successfully wooed; if we take our stand at Athens, the eye of ancient Greece, and muse on the banks of the Ilyssus with Socrates, or sit in the academy with Plato, or walk in the grove with the Stagyrite; or if we ascend Parnassus to Apollo and the muses, or sit by the Castalian fount, what do we see and hear? Poetry, the enchanting priestess of Nature, by her creative genius originating a popular, pantheistic mythology, breathing an ideal divinity into inanimate objects; singing of Elysian fields, and delighting and deluding the people by allegory, fable, and fiction—Sculpture, setting forth her matchless skill in the works of a Phidias and Praxiteles, to maintain, amid the perfection of physical development by gymnastic exercises, the endangered preëminence of the gods—Eloquence, with ease, with grace, with action, "pouring the persuasive strain," and stirring the soul to deeds of daring and of blood—and "Philosophy, flitting across the night of Paganism like the lantern-fly of the tropics, a light unto herself, but alas, no more than an ornament of the surrounding darkness."

In surveying the wide field of ancient literature, the Christian eye scarcely rests upon one spot of moral greenness and beauty. Rich in intellectual productions, abounding in the fruits of taste, acute in metaphysical discrimination, and sparkling sometimes with admirable moral precepts, the mass of ancient literature is nevertheless, in its moral influences, corrupt and corrupting.

Nor has the literature of modern times, when divorced from Christianity, accomplished any thing more beneficent for the world. The offspring of scepticism and sensuality, baptized by the priests of mammon, it has sold itself as the servile minister of selfishness, the base pander to lust, to pride and power. It is the arsenal of evil, rather than an auxiliary of good to mankind. The unsanctified literature, the prostituted press of the nineteenth century opposes one of the greatest obstructive forces to the progress of Christianity.

Almost equally imbecile has *a corrupted Christianity* been found, in the work of repairing the ruin of sin. When its doctrines are adulterated by the subtleties of the schoolmen, and its morality is displaced by the refinements of Jesuitical expediency; when the church, instead of transporting the word of God to the benighted abroad, locks it up in cloisters at home, practically teaching salvation through the efficacy of sacraments, rather than by the power of the cross; when priestcraft joins unholy alliance with kingcraft to pervert the pure gospel into an engine of state, fettering freedom and forging chains for conscience; when pride and power put on the sacerdotal garb, and ambition strides into the metropolitan chair, and wicked men lord it over God's heritage, and shut up the fountains of living waters from the thirsty people, and give the hungry children's bread to dogs—then Christianity is shorn of its mighty power, and grinds in the prison-house of its enemies. Such dreadful perversion blots out the sunlight of heaven, and leaves men to walk in darkness. It intercepts them in their approach to the inner court and the mercy-seat, and leaves them to wander around their heavenly Father's house as orphans or criminals. It bolts the windows of heaven, pushes back the hand reached down for human deliverance, and turns out of its appointed channels the current of divine life gushing forth for the cleansing of human souls. Oh, how has such corruption made the church, instead of light and life and salvation, a kind of pestilence and plague, the occasion of a more malignant development of the general disease, rather than of its cure! "If the light that is in" her "be darkness, how great is that darkness!"

From all such instrumentality, Christian beneficence studiously withholds herself. Instead of relying upon such means, it is her appropriate work to assail them, and by rectifying reason, sanctifying genius and taste, and leading men to the pure fountains of divine science, to transfer them from the heathen to the Christian side of the conflict. For this she levies no armies, except those bearing the weapons of a spiritual warfare. She sends out no fleets, save those under commission from the great King. She lays no siege but for the bombardment of the strongholds of principalities and powers, and to pour forth the "junipers of hot conviction" into the ancient battlements of spiritual wickedness in high places. She has no gaudy trappings, no glittering pageantry, no bewitching mysticism for the vain-glorious and imaginative. She comes to us with the Gospel of Jesus. The hopes of the race are suspended on the simple but powerful *doctrine of the cross, rendered effectual by the Holy Spirit.*

See now its *operation.* It lays its account directly with the *heart,* and in the attire of simple truth, seizes the conscience, piercing the innermost soul with the conviction of sin, and pointing the guilt-stricken sinner to the cross of Christ. Subduing the heart, its first conquest gives the pledge of victory in all its subsequent encounters. It unites the believer through a living faith to a divine Redeemer, by whom he is borne up into the dazzling visions of the spiritual world, and permitted to look upon glories that eclipse the brightness of all earthly splendor. It presents to him the great overmastering truth, that "God is love," and illustrates it to him by the cross. "Herein is love."

"God so loved the world, that he gave his only begotten Son, that whosoever believeth in him should not perish, but have everlasting life." "What words are those you read? What sounds are those I heard? Let me hear those words again," exclaims a poor South Sea islander, as the missionary Nott is reading this passage from the gospel of John. "Is that true? Can that be true? God loved the world when the world did not love him! *Can* that be true?" And when assured that it is true, with a heart too full for utterance, he retires to meditate on the amazing love of God, which has reached and subdued his soul. A wretched pilgrim on the coast of Malabar inquires of his priests how he can make atonement for his sins, and is directed to drive iron spikes through his sandals, and walk four hundred and eighty miles. While he reposes under a shady tree, and waits for healing and strength, as from the loss of blood he is often compelled to do, the herald of the gospel comes forth, and preaches to him from the words, "The blood of Jesus Christ cleanseth us from all sin." The victim of Pagan delusion rises from the ground, throws off his torturing sandals, and crying out, "This is what I want," becomes a living witness of the power of the truth to which he listened. "That is what I want, that is what I *want*," exclaimed a poor Hindoo, on hearing that "the Son of man came to seek and to save that which was lost." And this *is* what the heathen want—what all men want. It is light in darkness, hope in despair, life in death.

And this is just the instrumentality which heaven has provided. To the polluted, the gospel opens a fountain of cleansing waters. To the condemned, it presents a forgiving God. To the thirsty, it is a river of life. To the hungry, it is the bread of heaven. The weary it lays in sweet repose on the bosom of a loving Saviour. The fallen heir of glory it makes a king and a priest unto God. It illumines the darkened understanding. It rouses the slumbering conscience. It subdues the rebellious will. It descends into the affections, and like the angel-visitant at Bethesda, imparts a purifying and healing power, and recovers the whole man.

See, too, the *harmony* in the operations of this instrumentality, by principles seemingly paradoxical. The doctrine of man's apostasy is most impressively taught by the means appointed for his recovery. The soul is impressed with a sense of its ruin by that which takes from it the deep gloom of despair. Provision is made for the pardon of sin in a way which demonstrates that it cannot be palliated. The gospel provides for moral purity by a transaction which deepens the sense of moral pollution, and dispels the terrors of guilt by a fact that proclaims the turpitude of transgression. It awakens the keenest sensibility to the claims of duty by that which makes propitiation for the sin of neglected duty. It rectifies reason and subdues the will by a process which elevates the moral sentiments. It nurtures zeal without making zealots, and leads to the contemplation of mysteries, yet has no tendency to make mystics. It fosters alike reflection and action, joins faith and charity, teaches dependence and responsibility, harmonizes the discordant elements of our nature, and turns all our energies into the channel of sweet obedience and love. It unites sublimity with simplicity, gives high moral dignity to the smallest act of obedience, and chronicles for the admiration of the world the donation of "two mites" as the testimonial of love. Prudent, it is neither temporizing nor timid; cautious, it is nevertheless decisive and energetic; "sorrowful, yet always rejoicing; as having nothing, yet possessing all things." Thus radically and thoroughly, and almost paradoxically, does the gospel work in the heart of *the individual*, preparing its way to permeate and pervade society.

Going forth into the *world*, the gospel knows no truce with error, no compromise with sin, no compact with artifice, no resort to stratagem. Openly and boldly it lays the axe at the root of every evil tree, and destroys its fruit, not by clipping off the twigs, but by hewing down the trunk. It dries up the streams of human woe, not by artificial processes of heating the air, but by closing up the fountains. And it gives good guarantee of its effectual working by the class among whom it begins. "To the poor the gospel is preached;" and from this class it works upward through all the intermediate strata of society to the highest.

The gospel comes to man as a benefactor in his *social* relations. Prescribing his duties, it utters its severest anathemas against those who rudely trench upon the rights and privileges, or overleap the boundaries of the social state. It raises woman from servile, almost soulless barbarism, to civilized and Chris tian refinement, and leads her, as among the Caffres, to regard the missionary as "the shield of woman," and to consider his approach, as the female savages of New England did that of Eliot, the "advent of an angel." It nurses feeble infancy, and trains the opening mind to virtue and happiness. It extends its protecting arm to infirm old age, and administers rebuke to the "child" that demeaneth himself "proudly against the ancients." All "the lesser charities that soothe, and cheer, and bless," the domestic virtues, the sacred endearments which constitute the bliss and charm of social life, all find their source in the gospel of Christ.

With equal efficiency and success, does the Christian religion operate upon the *civil* condition of man. By creating a sense of individual responsibility, it awakens a desire for personal freedom; and through the restraint which it imposes, by motives drawn from higher than human enactments, it makes that freedom safe and salutary. It presents the Bible as the great statute-book of heaven for men, and creates loyal subjects, by securing just rulers and the enactment of just laws. It maintains incessant warfare with pride and ambition and false honor, the three grand procurers of barbarism, brutality, and bloodshed. It sets forth the law of equity, humility, and love as the rule of international commerce, and binds kings as well as subjects by the principles of individual responsibility and honesty. Under the influence of the gospel, oppression shall cease from the earth. The clarion of war shall no more call hostile armies to the field of sanguinary conflict. The hero shall be stripped of the guise of false glory, in which men

> "Smile assent at giant crime,
> And call the darkest deeds sublime;"

and he only whose works of love and mercy procure for him the approval of heaven, shall receive the applause of men. A new standard of glory will Christianity present to the nations of the earth, and challenge kings and potentates to a new style of achievement. To do good and not evil, to *save* man and not destroy him, will characterize that day when love shall smile in every eye, and peace shall dwell in every bosom, and earth shall become a type and foretaste of heaven.

The auspicious dawn of such a day already gilds the eastern horizon. What has swept idolatry with its diabolical abominations from the Tahitian, Sandwich, and Society Islands, and from nearly a hundred adjacent and other islands of the sea, and is leading to its downfall in India? The Gospel. What has brought nearly half a million of the worshippers of stocks and stones to the knowledge of the true God, and gathered half as many more youthful and adult pupils into schools in the process of intellectual and moral improvement? The Gospel. Behold a New Zealand chieftain, the veteran warrior of many battles, rising in the midst of a group of New Zealand children assembled by their native teachers for examination in the presence of their parents. Hear him exclaim with irrepressible emotion, "Let me speak; I *must* speak. O that I had known that the gospel was coming! O that I had known that these blessings were in store for us! Then I should have saved my children, and they would have been among this happy group, repeating these precious truths; but alas, I destroyed them all, and now I have not one left." Then bursting into tears, and cursing the gods which they had formerly worshipped, he continues, "It was you that infused this savage disposition into us; and now I shall die childless, although I have been the father of nineteen children. O that some one had seized my murderous hand, and told me the Gospel is coming to our shores." What has wrought this change? The Gospel. What has enabled the missionary to exclaim of two hundred thousand converts gathered into more than a thousand Christian churches, as Paul did of the Ephesians, "Ye were sometime darkness, but now are ye light in the Lord?" The Gospel. What has borne up before the throne that bright throng of ransomed ones, "out of all nations and kindreds and people and tongues," from South Africa, from Eastern Asia, from Greenland, from the savage tribes of North America, and from the islands of the sea; and has put a new song into their mouth, "Salvation to our God which sitteth upon the throne, and unto the Lamb?" The Gospel proclaimed by the missionary. Oh, it is this precious doctrine, *Christ and him crucified*, that shall be the instrument of bringing down out of heaven the new Jerusalem from God, "which shall have no need of the sun, neither of the moon to shine in it; for the glory of God shall lighten it, and the Lamb shall be the light thereof." It is by this only, that guilt is cancelled and sin taken away, the polluted cleansed, the outcast called home, and the miserable filled with "the peace of God" and "the comfort of love." Who can compute the results of such an instrumentality? They are measureless as the bliss of heaven, endless as the duration of God. Who can estimate the importance of such instrumentality? It is wise as the councils of heaven, "precious as the blood of Christ," necessary as the salvation of the soul, and commensurate with the most wide-spread and disastrous consequences of sin.

But can this instrumental agency prevail over all the mighty and malignant foes which set themselves against it? The trial has been met, the experiment made. Benevolence has prevailed over selfishness, love over hate, God over man. The church has survived, and not only so, but she has flourished in her bitterest persecutions. Fire cannot burn her, water cannot drown her, nor the "wild beasts out of the wood" devour her. Two converts are born, for every one that is burnt. "The blood of the martyrs is the seed of the church." The fires burnish her, and the waters purify her. Dangers enlarge her, and the rack emancipates her. Her opposers help her on, and her foes build her up. The fulminations of kings and cardinals against her hasten the accomplishment of the purposes of the King of kings in her favor. From temporary defeat, she rises with renewed energy for permanent triumph. Every external pressure she throws off by the operation of an internal divine power. Decrees and bolts and bars and fire and faggots hinder not her progress. Bonds and tortures and terrors and death prevent not her increase. Yea, in all these, and by means of these, she triumphs. What would destroy other things, developes the mighty power of the gospel. What would put back other causes, advances this. Under those circumstances in which other organizations would perish, the church prevails.

Do you ask how these wonders are to be accounted for? By the inherent divine power, by the elements of increase and of immortality residing in the Gospel of Jesus. The covenant of the church, in carrying out its grand beneficent work of converting the world, is with her almighty Head, who sits above the storms, and infuses his own insuppressible and indestructible spirit of energy into the hearts of all his followers. "The Lord her God in the midst of her is mighty." "The Lord hath made bare his holy arm in the eyes of all nations," therefore, "all the ends of the earth shall see the salvation of our God." Is not this an instrumentality *adequate* to the most sublime and comprehensive benevolence of the church? Is it not adapted to every want of man, in every clime and every condition? It is the "power of God." What can resist it? It is "the wisdom of God." What can counterwork it? It involves the highest moral energies, the purest moral influences, and the wisest adaptation of moral means to their ends. It is heaven's matchless instrumentality for accomplishing heaven's own most gigantic purposes of love.

See now, how this instrumentality harmonizes with the *ends* sought in beneficence. Are they vast? It is commensurate in its achieving power with their mightiest and most far-reaching aspirations. Are they important? It is equal in efficiency to the accomplishment of their weightiest results. The immortal soul, with its expanding capacities for happiness or misery, may be safely trusted to its redeeming efficacy. It has borne millions of such souls from the pollutions and miseries of earth, to bask in the sunlight and bliss of heaven, clothing them in robes of spotless purity, and placing on their heads crowns of fadeless glory. Millions more, now on the earth, it is bearing on to the same glorious consummation. And of the countless spirits yet to pass through this world of sin and sorrow, not one, to whom its mighty power may be applied, shall fail to reach that "better land," where faith passes into bright fruition, and hope melts away into the fulness of inexpressible bliss, and love achieves her seraphic heights and burns with more than seraphic fire.

"Rise, kindling with the orient beam;
Let Calvary's hill inspire the theme!
Unfold the garments rolled in blood.
O touch the soul, touch all her chords
With all the omnipotence of words,
And point the way to heaven—to God."

## THIRD GENERAL PROPOSITION.

EVERY MAN'S CHARITABLE CONTRIBUTIONS SHOULD BE PROPORTIONATE TO HIS PECUNIARY MEANS AND FACILITIES FOR APPLYING THE INSTRUMENTALITY.

This is the divinely established rule of proportion. "According to the *ability* that God giveth." "As God hath prospered you." "Every man according to his several ability." In these and similar passages of the word of God, it is implied that every one is able to do something, and it is affirmed that each one should do according to that ability. The only question on which there can be doubt or difficulty is,

What is each man's ability? In determining this question, we shall be assisted by the three following references.

1. By reference to *the beneficence of the Jewish church.* There is a tendency to make the beneficent economy of the former dispensation a directory in the Christian dispensation; and most men feel that by employing a *tenth* of their income for charitable purposes, they are meeting the requirement of the Mosaic law, and consequently fully discharging their duty. But there are two errors in such an hypothesis. One is in supposing the proportion required by the Jewish system to be only a tenth; and the other in assuming that the measure of liberality which answered the law of Moses, equally harmonizes with the law of Christ.

After their deliverance from Egypt, the first-born of every creature was required to be consecrated to the Lord, in memory of that signal event. The first-born child belonged to the Lord, and was to be redeemed at the age of one month, by a price paid to the priest. Such beasts as it was not lawful to offer in sacrifice, as horses and camels, might be redeemed or exchanged for such as were lawful to be offered, as sheep or oxen. The first-born of all clean beasts were to be sacrificed, and their flesh given to the priest. At the harvest and vintage, the first-fruits of the fields, the corn and wine and oil, were to be brought to the priest, and the gleanings and the corners of the fields were to be left for the poor. Also the first-fruits of the wool when the sheep were shorn, of the wheat when threshed, of the dough when kneaded, and of the bread when baked, were to be offered before the Lord. Of fruit-trees, they were allowed to gather nothing for themselves, until after the fourth bearing year. All fruit till this period was considered sacred to the Lord, and was given to the poor, as was also the spontaneous fruit of the fields every seventh year. In addition to these, one tenth was paid to the Levites, as a remuneration for their services to the church and nation; and after this, what remained was again assessed, and another tenth was expended in the feasts and sacrifices of the temple, and for the poor. At their feasts, besides the Levites, widows, orphans, strangers, and the poor of every description, were to be invited. And at the close of every third year, that there might be no evasion of the law, all were required to make solemn asseveration before the Lord, that the whole of this second tithe had been applied to the prescribed objects. Lev. 27 : 30–34; Deut. 12 : 17, 18; 14 : 22–29; 26 : 12–15.

And what was the chief point of instruction which Jehovah designed to impress upon his people by such an admirably arranged system of beneficence? That he was the proprietor of their fields, their flocks, and their herds, and that they were dependent on him for sunshine and rain, for seed-time and harvest

How expressively, then, does the patriarchal and Mosaic doctrine of *tithes* carry along with it the Christian idea of *stewardship*. How suited to meet and to counteract the tendencies of the human heart to covetousness. It should also be remembered, that this proportion, large as it is, was the minimum measure of Jewish liberality, the *least* which their system allowed; while the attractive and exciting circumstances under which they presented their tithes and offerings, and the influence of the temple service, especially of their public festivals, led them often greatly to exceed the rule.

But there were peculiar exigencies in the history of the Jewish church, which illustrate the spirit of their beneficence even better than the annual imposts levied upon them by the law of Moses. The liberality of the Jews in the construction of the tabernacle, and the erection of the temple, has seldom been equalled in the Christian church, and perhaps never surpassed. Just emerging from the oppressive bondage in Egypt, and destined to be wanderers for forty years in the wilderness, we should hardly have expected them to be called on to make large offerings for any purpose. Yet scarcely were they free from their pursuers, ere the word of the Lord came to Moses, saying, "Speak unto the children of Israel, that they bring me an offering: of every man that giveth it willingly with his heart, ye shall take my offering. And this is the offering that ye shall take of them; gold, and silver, and brass, and blue, and purple, and scarlet, and fine linen, and goats' hair, and rams' skins dyed red, and badgers' skins, and shittim-wood, oil for the light, spices for anointing oil and for sweet incense, onyx stones, and stones to be set in the ephod, and in the breastplate." Out of these, the tabernacle and its utensils and appurtenances were to be constructed, the ark of testimony, the mercy-seat, the altar, and laver and candlesticks, all wrought of the most precious materials, and overlaid with pure gold. See now this people, just from their degrading servitude, with comparatively small possessions, and little means of adding to them. When religion is to be promoted at the call of God, they withhold nothing, until the end is accomplished. All give with a willing mind, not a certain portion of their income, but a large part of their possessions. They devote it freely and joyfully to the service of the church. And they thus give an example of liberality which it has pleased the Almighty to transmit to all following generations, as an incentive to the same devotion, and a proof that inauspicious circumstances are not always an excuse for refusing the calls of benevolence.

Pass now to the reign of David. It was not for him to build the temple, although it was in his heart so to do. Yet, before the affairs of his kingdom were settled, and he was quietly seated on the throne, he began the work of gathering materials for the magnificent structure. "Behold," says he to his son, "in my trouble I have prepared for the house of the Lord a hundred thousand talents of gold, and a thousand thousand talents of silver; and of brass and iron without weight, for it is in abundance; timber also and stone have I prepared; and thou mayest add thereto." "Of the gold, and the silver, and the brass, and the iron, there is no number." With these immense and other additional materials, the vast and splendid edifice was reared, at an expenditure estimated by some at *three thousand millions of dollars.* How did they respond to this extraordinary call? Reluctantly? No. Did they allege pleas of poverty, or of concurrent claims for other objects? Not one. The people rejoiced, for they offered willingly, and more than was needed. And David blessed the Lord before all the congregation, and said, "Who am I, and what is my people, that we should be able to offer so willingly after this sort?"

Now, what is the principle upon which is made this voluntary consecration of treasure unto the Lord? This happy monarch's eucharistical prayer contains its announcement: "O Lord our God, all this store that we have prepared to build thee a house for thine holy Name, cometh of thine hand, and is all thine own;" "for all things come of thee, and of thine own have we given thee." It is the Christian principle of stewardship, which inheres as an essential element of every dispensation from Genesis to Revelation. It is the doctrine, that "the silver and the gold are the Lord's;" that he has an indisputable right to all that his creatures possess; that there are higher uses to which it may be applied, yielding purer and more elevated and permanent enjoyment than personal aggrandizement or selfish gratification; and that when God calls, whatever may be the proportion or amount, man's cheerful response always secures the divine favor.

When Christians refer to the tithing system of the Jews, as a guide in adjusting the proportion of their income which should be devoted to objects of beneficence, it is important to take into account the *free-will offerings* which accompanied the working of the system, as well as the regular imposts laid upon the people. The deep, underflowing *spirit* of the economy should be understood, as well as the simple letter of its statutory enactments. Yet, the careful collation of these laws will be sufficient to explode the popular idea, that the devotement of a tenth of our income brings our beneficence into agreement with the divine rule given to the Jews. The Old Testament doctrine upon the subject of beneficence cannot be fully exemplified by a less proportion, as we have said, than one fourth of a man's income

And this proportion was required of the Jews, under circumstances, in some respects, widely different from those under which Christians are called to live. It was simply for charity, and the maintenance of religion at home. The Jewish church had received no commission to diffuse her religion abroad. The difference in this particular, between the dispensations of Moses and of Christ, is great. The former was simply conservative and defensive. The latter is essentially reformatory and aggressive. The one was a system of special rules and of a cumbersome ritual service. The other is a system of religious principles, and of spiritual worship. One was for the twelve tribes; the other is for the world. In the one, THE TRUTH dwelt in gorgeous symbols and attractive ceremonies; in the other, He manifested himself in "the fulness of the Godhead, bodily," and still is present by his spiritual and subduing power.

Can those living under dispensations so diverse, with blessings so unequal, have devolved upon them only an equal measure of duty and effort? Can we make the rule of Jewish beneficence in a conservative system, the measure of our own in a diffusive and an aggressive one? Can the Christian conscience be satisfied with a scale of liberality, for both domestic and foreign beneficence, less than half as large as that which the claims of one of these objects made upon the Jewish conscience?

An opulent man deducts one tenth from his income for charity. Half of the remainder may be required for his necessary family expenditures. After this he adds four times as much to his stock in trade, or capital at interest, as he allows for charity. He reserves for himself nine parts of all that with which he has been blessed, and allows one part to God for the salvation of the world. Is he benevolent?

There are circumstances, it is true, in which a tenth of a man's income, would be a large proportion. But there are other circumstances, in which it would be a small proportion. In some, it would cost self-denial. In others, it would not be felt. Three fourths of a large income might be a less proportion than one tenth, or even one fiftieth of a small one. So that he who gave least would, in an important sense, give most, for he would do it at the greatest sacrifice. Such is the inequality which would result from adopting any fixed proportion as applicable in all cases.

2. A reference to *the beneficent spirit of the early Christian church.* It will be admitted, that the early Christians were in a condition, as favorable at least, for forming a correct judgment in the matter of beneficence, as any who have come after them. Some of them were called by the Saviour himself. They received instructions from his own lips. The sweet and elevating influence of his personal presence and conversation, embalmed in their memory the recollection of all that he did and said and suffered. Under this influence, they went forth to the world, bright examples of Christian beneficence. They "sold their possessions and goods, and parted them to all men as every man had need." They

felt that they were made the executors of their Saviour's last will and testament to a lost world, and that whatsoever of their possessions could subserve the accomplishment of the sacred trust, should be freely laid upon the altar of sacrifice. Nothing short of the dedication of their entire substance and lives to the cause of such a Master, in the execution of such a testament, met their ideas of duty, or expressed their sense of gratitude and love. Their renunciation of the world in its pride and pomp and power, was actual and entire. They lived in it only to do good. The glad tidings which they had received, it was their great object to communicate. They had contemplated the infinite riches of the grace of God, and had lost the desire for all other riches. Honor, power, wealth, learning, eloquence, were valued by them only as they contributed to diffuse the blessings of the cross, or constituted the means of a more costly sacrifice to Him who died upon it. The cross! For this, they could relinquish all, and endure all. In this, they gloried. And in the ardor of love, inspired by this, they "took joyfully the spoiling of their goods," and the crown of martyrdom. Selfishness was nearly annihilated by the antagonist power of the cross. Covetousness was quite dead, from the withholding of all that whereby it lives. A parsimonious Christian would speedily have obtained among them the unenviable notoriety of an Achan, or a Judas In giving themselves to Christ, they gave all, and were made rich by what they gave. More than this they could not do; less, their love would not allow. And to make more sure to themselves the blessings of such liberality, and as a safeguard against the growth of a penurious spirit, "On the first day of the week, they laid by in store as God had prospered them." Of the Macedonian churches the apostle says, "In a great trial of affliction, the abundance of their joy, and their deep poverty, abounded unto the riches of their liberality. For to their power, I bear record, yea, and beyond their power, they were willing of themselves; praying us with much entreaty, that we would receive the gift, and take upon us the fellowship of the ministering to the saints."

The test and the fruit of discipleship among these early Christians, was a spirit of *entire devotion.* But were their obligations more imperative than ours? Was the command "to do good and to communicate," more binding then, than now? Were the blessings promised to the liberal soul, more rich or full, or the danger and evils of covetousness less, or the calls of sorrow and of want more urgent? Were souls in greater peril then than now, or was the Gospel more effectual? No; the difference is not in the gospel, but in the spirit of the men receiving it. They understood Christianity; they felt its beneficent power, and they exemplified it. Taking their divine Master as their model, they "pressed towards the mark for the prize of their high calling." "Our blessed Lord," says one of the early fathers of the Christian church, "ate his food from a common dish. He sat upon the ground, and washed his disciples' feet without a silver basin. Nay, he quenched his thirst from the earthen pitcher of a poor Samaritan woman. And are we better than he? Will not a table contain our food, unless its legs be ivory? Certain it is, that a lamp made by a potter will give light as well as if it were the work of a silversmith."

The spirit of beneficence among these primitive Christians, led them to make no provision for the flesh. They counted self-denial better for themselves, as well as more honorable to their Master, than self-indulgence. They were Christians, and they gloried in maintaining their consistency, despite the sword and the stake. Says another of them, "We say we are Christians, and we say it to the whole world, under the hand of the executioner. In the midst of all the tortures you can heap upon us to make us recant, torn and mangled and covered with our own blood, we still cry out as loud as we are able, we are Christians. Call us by what names you please. Fill our flesh with fagots to set us on fire, yet let me tell you that when we are thus begirt and dressed about with fire, we are in our most illustrious apparel. These are our victorious palms and robes of glory; and, mounted on our funeral pile, we feel ourselves as in a triumphal chariot. We conquer when we die, and the spoils of that victory is eternal life." "What you reproach us with as stubbornness, is the best means of proselyting the world. For who has not been struck with the sight of such fortitude, and from thence pushed on to look into the reason of it? And who ever looked well into our religion, but embraced it? And who ever embraced it, but was willing to die for it?"

Does any one now ask what proportion of their possessions such men devoted to beneficence? They gave the *whole*, and themselves with it. Does he ask how much they were *able* to do for the diffusion of Christianity? They were able to live for it—to *die* for it. Their ability was measured only by the extent of their possessions, the length of their lives, and their capacity to labor and to suffer. They stopped not a whit short of this. But was their lot cast in a different dispensation from ours? No, it was the same dispensation. What then constitutes the difference? Ah, we repeat, it is in the spirit of the men. The early Christians were wholly devoted to their Master. The hearts of later ones are divided between him and the world. Covetousness has crept into the church, and like the strong man armed, has bound its members and spoiled their goods. This is the difference. We of the nineteenth century sow sparingly and reap also sparingly. The early Christians sowed plentifully, and they reaped also plentifully. We say, charity costs too much, and yield only a pittance. They said, it *cannot* cost too much, and laid down their lives.

3. A reference to *the Scripture declarations* relating to *property*, and to the duty of *liberality*. "To the law, and to the testimony; if we speak not according to this word, it is because there is no light in us." What then saith the Scripture? Does it prescribe the exact proportion of his income which should be devoted to charitable purposes? No. It is a book of facts, of doctrines, of principles and precepts. It proceeds on the assumption that inquiry, reflection, and prayer are essential to the development of the Christian character. It leaves men to a sense of responsibility in employing the facts, and applying the principles to the question of individual duty. Does a man wish to know what proportion of his property should be consecrated to beneficence? He will not find it stated in so many words, whether one tenth, or one fourth, or more, or less, ought to be thus employed. But by a careful consideration of the scripture doctrine contained in the following passages concerning property and the duty of liberality, he may be led to conclusions as safe and as certain, as if the amount were determined in every case by specific divine command.

(1.) Riches are *from the Lord, and belong to him.* "Both riches and honor come of thee." "The silver is mine, and the gold is mine, saith the Lord of hosts." "Every beast of the forest is mine, and the cattle upon a thousand hills." "The earth is the Lord's, and the fulness thereof; the world and they that dwell therein." "The Lord maketh rich." "The Lord thy God, it is he that giveth thee power to get wealth."

(2.) Riches are in themselves *a transient, unsatisfying, and disquieting* possession. "Nor trust in uncertain riches." "Riches are not for ever." "Riches make themselves wings and fly away." "Lay not up for yourselves treasures upon earth, where moth and rust doth corrupt, and where thieves break through and steal." "There is that maketh himself rich, yet hath nothing." "He that loveth silver, shall not be satisfied with silver; neither he that loveth abundance, with increase." "There is one alone, and there is not a second; yea, he hath neither child nor brother; yet there is no end of his labor, neither is his eye satisfied with riches; neither saith he, For whom do I labor and bereave my soul of good? This is also vanity, yea, it is a sore travail." "He that is greedy of gain, troubleth his own house." "In the revenues of the wicked is trouble." "The abundance of the rich will not suffer him to sleep" "Then I looked on all the works that my hands had wrought, and behold, all was vanity and vexation of spirit; and there was no profit under the sun." "For what hath man of all his labor, and of the vexation of his spirit wherein he hath labored? For all his days are sorrows, and his travail, grief; yea, his heart taketh not rest in the night."

(3.) They bring *no relief in man's greatest distress.* "Riches profit not in the day of wrath." "Their silver and their gold shall not be able to deliver them in the day of the wrath of the Lord." "Because there is wrath, beware lest he take thee away with his stroke: then a great ransom cannot deliver thee. Will he esteem thy riches? No, not gold, nor all the forces of strength." "There was a certain rich man which was clothed in purple and fine linen, and fared sumptuously every day. The rich man also died, and was buried. And in hell, he lifted up his eyes, being in torments."

(4.) It is *unlawful and dangerous to trust in and to hoard them.* "If I have made gold my hope, or have said to the fine gold, Thou art my confidence; if I rejoiced because my wealth was great, and because mine hand had gotten much; I should have denied the God that is above." "If riches increase, set not your heart upon them." "Lay not up for yourselves treasures upon earth." "Labor not to be rich." "Beware, lest when thou hast eaten and art full, and when thy herds and thy flocks are multiplied, and thy silver and thy gold is multiplied; then thine heart be lifted up, and thou forget the Lord thy God, and thou say in thine heart, My power, and the might of mine hand, hath gotten me this wealth." "Covetousness, let it not be once named among you, as becometh saints." "He that trusteth in his riches shall fall." "How hard is it for them that trust in riches, to enter into the kingdom of God." "The cares of this world and the deceitfulness of riches choke the word, and he becometh unfruitful." "He that hideth his eyes from the poor shall have many a curse." "Woe unto them that join house to house, that lay field to field." "They that will be rich, fall into temptation and a snare, and into many hurtful and foolish lusts, which drown men in destruction and perdition. For the love of money is the root of all evil; which, while some have coveted after, they have erred from the faith, and pierced themselves through with many sorrows. But thou, O man of God, flee these things." "I have seen riches kept for the owners thereof to their hurt." "Go to now, ye rich men, weep and howl, for your miseries that shall come upon you. Your riches are corrupted, and your garments are moth-eaten. Your gold and silver is cankered; and the rust of them shall be a witness against you, and shall eat your flesh as it were fire." "No covetous man hath any inheritance in the kingdom of Christ and of God." Balaam "loved the wages of unrighteousness, but was rebuked for his iniquity." "Achan answered Joshua, and said, Indeed, I have sinned against the Lord God of Israel. When I saw among the spoils a goodly Babylonish garment, and two hundred shekels of silver, and a wedge of gold of fifty shekels weight, then I coveted them, and took them. And Joshua said, Why hast thou troubled us? the Lord shall trouble thee this day. And all Israel stoned him with stones." To Gehazi, for coveting the Syrian's silver and the garments, the prophet said, "The leprosy therefore of Naaman shall cleave unto thee and unto thy seed for ever. And he went out from his presence a leper as white as snow." "Judas, when he saw that Jesus was condemned, repented himself, and brought again the thirty pieces of silver to the chief priests and elders. And he cast down the pieces of silver in the temple and departed, and went and hanged himself."

(5.) Liberality is *characteristic of the righteous, and is expressly commanded.* "The righteous showeth mercy and giveth." "He that honoreth his Maker, hath mercy on the poor." "The righteous considereth the cause of the poor." "Withhold not good from him to whom it is due, when it is in the power of thine hand to do it." "Say not to thy neighbor, Go, and come again; when thou hast it by thee." "Give to him that asketh thee." "Give to him that needeth." "Give alms of such things as you have." "Honor the Lord with thy substance." "To do good, and to communicate, forget not, for with such sacrifices God is well pleased." "Charge them that are rich in this world, that they be rich in good works, ready to distribute, willing to communicate; laying up in store for themselves a good foundation against the time to come, that they may lay hold on eternal life." "Whoso hath this world's good, and seeth his brother have need, and shutteth up his bowels of compassion from him, how dwelleth the love of God in him?" "Thou shalt not harden thy heart, nor shut thy hand from thy poor brother; but thou shalt open thy hand wide unto him." "As ye abound in every thing, see that ye abound in this grace also." "Freely ye have received, freely give." "Upon the first day of the week, let every one of you lay by him in store, as God hath prospered him."

(6.) *The highest and best use of riches is in beneficence*, which secures *exemption from want and the blessing of heaven.* "Make to yourselves friends of the mammon of unrighteousness." "The angel of God said unto Cornelius, Thy prayers and thine alms are come up as a memorial before God." "Remember the words of the Lord Jesus, how he said, It is more blessed to give than to receive." "And there came a certain poor widow, and she threw in two mites, which make a farthing. And he called unto him his disciples, and saith unto them, Verily I say unto you, that this poor widow hath cast more in than all they which have cast into the treasury. For all they did cast in of their abundance; but she of her want did cast in all that she had, even all her living." "For if there be first a willing mind, it is accepted according to that a man hath, and not according to that he hath not." "He that giveth unto the poor shall not lack." "Trust in the Lord and do good; so shalt thou dwell in the land, and verily thou shalt be fed." "Cast thy bread upon the waters; for thou shalt find it after many days." "He that hath pity upon the poor, lendeth to the Lord; and that which he hath given, will he pay him again." "Honor the Lord with thy substance, and with the first-fruits of all thine increase: so shall thy barns be filled with plenty, and thy presses shall burst out with new wine." "Blessed is he that considereth the poor." "He that hath a bountiful eye shall be blessed." "He that hath mercy on the poor, happy is he." "There is that scattereth, and yet increaseth." "The liberal soul shall be made fat; and he that watereth, shall be watered also himself." "Give, and it shall be given unto you; good measure, pressed down, and shaken together, and running over, shall men give into your bosom." "Do good and lend, hoping for nothing again; and your reward shall be great, and ye shall be the children of the Highest." "When thou makest a feast, call the poor, the maimed, the lame, and the blind. And thou shalt be blessed; for thou shalt be recompensed at the resurrection of the just." "If thou draw out thy soul to the hungry, and satisfy the afflicted soul; then shall thy light rise in obscurity, and thy darkness be as the noonday. And the Lord shall guide thee continually, and satisfy thy soul in drought, and make fat thy bones; and thou shalt be like a watered garden, and like a spring of water, whose waters fail not."

Now, if the word of God is admitted as an infallible guide, will it not aid an inquirer in determining his ability, to reflect upon these passages until his mind is imbued with their spirit? Will it not give the claims of benevolence a firmer hold on his conscience, and check the tendency to covetousness, to read that God regardeth it as idolatry, that the love of money is the root of all evil, leading the soul into foolish and hurtful lusts, piercing it through with many sorrows, and drowning it in perdition? Who would not feel his ability to give in charity increasing under the growing conviction that he that soweth bountifully, shall reap also bountifully? Does a wise man grudge the seed grain, when the increase depends on the amount that he scattereth? Will he garner up what he gathers, when he feels that much as he may have been blessed in receiving, he would be more blessed in giving? But alas, unbelief is the vampire that consumes the ability of the church. Men do not believe, when the mouth of the Lord hath spoken it, else they would not be so slow to lend to him. Let them study these passages in their full significancy, and imbibe their heavenly spirit, until all doubt vanishes, and the soul is raised up in liberality to the high ground of the Bible doctrine. Stand by the cross and study them there, invoking the divine Spirit to guide you into the truth. Cast yourself forward to the soul's transit into eternity, and study them there. Place yourself at the tribunal of God, amidst the throng of ransomed spirits in the heavenly glory, and study them *there*. Behold those shining ones casting their crowns at the feet of Jesus, and sweeping their harp-strings in full chorus to his praise, "Saying with a loud voice, Worthy is the Lamb that was slain to receive power, and riches, and wisdom, and strength, and honor, and glory, and blessing:" do this, and it will be easy to understand the scripture doctrine of beneficence, and to determine the *proportion* of your property which it is your duty and privilege to employ for Him on earth, who has all riches ascribed to him in heaven.

### PARTICULAR PROPOSITIONS RESPECTING PROPORTION.

If the reader has gone along with us in our reference to the liberality of the Jewish church, to the beneficent spirit of the early Christians, and to the scripture declarations relating to property and the duty of liberality, he will be prepared to consider the subject of proportion in beneficence, in the following particular propositions.

1. Every man's beneficence should be proportionate to the *sum total* of his property. It will be apparent in the outset, that we have to do with something

more than the single question of *income*. For although with a man who, from the commencement of his business life, has regulated his charities by the scripture rule, it might be only a question of income, yet as there are few who have done this, in determining each man's ability it is obvious that any inquiry would be partial, and any result defective, which should not involve a consideration of the sum total of a man's property. It may be, that, lured out of the pilgrim's path by the winning voice of Demas, you have been digging at the mine in "the little hill called lucre," and hoarding more than is meet. It may be, that overpowered by the spirit of worldliness which steals away the vigor of piety, you have been adding income to capital, that you might retire from business and live in ease and luxury and splendor, until a rate of liberality adjusted to your present ability would trench on your vested capital, or break in upon your accumulated stores. It may be, that the influence of fashion, or of increasing wealth, or of a plan of early retirement, like a subtle poison, has benumbed the moral sensibilities, and rendered you reluctant to draw, for benevolent purposes, upon your vested funds. All this is very natural and very probable. Early in life, John Wesley said that he had known but four men, whose piety had not suffered from their becoming rich. Longer observation led him to make no exception. His own case, however, may be alleged as an example of the power of grace to withstand the withering influence of increasing wealth. His income at first was thirty pounds a year. Of this, he reserved two pounds for charity. The next year, it was sixty pounds. Still using but twenty-eight for himself, he employed thirty-two pounds in charity And when his income amounted to a hundred and twenty pounds, he lent ninety-two pounds to the Lord, and lived himself on twenty-eight as at first. At his decease, his whole property was found to consist of his clothes, his books, and a carriage, although he had probably given away more than a hundred thousand dollars. Did the root of all evil find no more congenial soil in the hearts of other men, than it did in that of John Wesley, how different would be the state of the world! But alas, it strikes deep, and entwines its threads about every fibre of the soul, and "chokes the word, that it becometh unfruitful."

Are you sure that a course of constant accumulation is right? Are you never troubled with doubts in withholding your tens of thousands, and it may be hundreds of thousands, from the cause of God, merely as security for your own future ease, or for the gratification or aggrandizement of your children? Are you certain, in view of the pressing calls in our own land and from the heathen world, that such a course is consistent with your public vows as a disciple of Christ? Is it plain, that a portion of your interest money and other income, is all that you are called upon to consecrate to Christ, for the salvation of a world for which he *died?* Did you begin right? And if so, have you continued as you began? Have you, in past time, laid by in store for yourself, no more than you should have done—no more than you would have done, if your piety had been as elevated as was that of Brainerd or Martyn, or your love as glowing as that of John? Has avarice, or covetousness, or selfishness had no voice in determining the amount laid up for yourself? And if you have been influenced by such a motive in amassing more than was meet, is it from any better motive that you now withhold what has been thus accumulated? Might not a portion of your property, invested in charity for the poor, in missionary labor and in Bibles for the conversion of the world, yield you a larger revenue of happiness and enrich you more than the whole now does? By the accredited maxims of the world, and even of the church, we readily admit, that the man who devotes all his income to charity is justly reputed liberal. But are you sure, that under your circumstances, this is a rate of liberality proportionate to the "ability which God giveth?" Is it opening thy hand wide unto thy poor brother? Is it sowing plentifully—abounding in the grace of giving? Is it acting on the principle, that it is more blessed to give than to receive? Is it fulfilling the injunction, Freely ye have received, freely give?

We would not be understood as implying, that

there are no circumstances in which men may lawfully accumulate property. They may have large schemes of benevolence, in reference to which they are every day prosecuting their labors. There are also departments of business, extensive manufacturing and commercial interests, the successful conduct of which requires large capital. Under the influence of a benevolent spirit, and on the principle of doing all to the glory of God, this employment of funds need not conflict with the claims of charity. But to retain large fortunes with no such projects in view, devoting only the income to beneficence, places a disciple of Christ in a false position. His wealth is out of proportion to his necessities, and to the claims of benevolence. And nothing but the bestowment of a portion of his accumulated treasure, will restore him to his true position.

We are not unapprised of the plan whereby some endeavor to recover their consistency. They have made a testamentary bequest, a plan truly benevolent in circumstances which render an earlier disposal of property impracticable. But in many cases, a will is only an expedient of covetousness, to satisfy conscience, and atone for the sin of sending the needy away empty in our lifetime, by allowing the claims of charity to take effect when we are dead. God has made *you* his steward, and has nowhere authorized you to leave to others, that which he has required you yourself to do. The calls of benevolence will never be more urgent than now. Your property will never do so much good as now. Every day that you postpone its devotement, you by so much lessen the time in which it might be bearing fruit unto Christ. Therefore, God would have you the executor of your own will. No one can administer your charities so advantageously as yourself. By so doing, you make the most profitable investment of your money, and avoid the danger of losing, by reverse of fortune, what you had intended to bequeath to benevolent objects. God would also that your death be deplored as a loss to the church, rather than welcomed as a gain to its beneficent operations; that the world be blessed with the influence of your beneficent example while living, rather than be left in doubt concerning the motives of your testamentary charity when you are dead. He would not have you deprived of the blessedness of giving, by the intervention of a *will*, rendering it necessary for you to be cast out of your stewardship, before your Lord's money can be put to "the exchangers."

We have read of "a faithful steward," whose whole property at the commencement of his business life, besides the wilderness land on which he settled, valued at forty dollars, consisted of a horse and an axe. With this God gave him "power to get wealth." He began on the principle of honoring the Lord with his substance, and with the first-fruits of all his increase, and his barns were filled with plenty and his presses burst out with new wine. Together with the expense of rearing a large family of children, he is supposed to have contributed to benevolent objects not less than thirty-five thousand dollars. "He made two wills at an interval of twenty-eight years, but he lived to be his own executor, paying his bequests and settling his accounts to the uttermost farthing; so that, in fulfilling his last testament, nothing remained to be looked after when he was gone but his wearing apparel, the large Bible, Scott's Family Bible, a psalm-book, the case in which he had kept them, and the spectacles with which he had read them. Not a pound—no, not a penny, was found hid in the earth or laid up in a napkin."

Thence we conclude, that in adjusting each man's proportion in beneficence, the sum total of his property should be taken into the account, and that charitable bequests are an unsatisfactory substitute for living benevolence. In view of the subject, let us "charge them that are rich in this world, that they be rich in good works, ready to distribute, willing to communicate, laying up in store for themselves a good foundation against the time to come, that they may lay hold on eternal life."

"Largely thou givest, gracious Lord;
Largely thy gifts should be restored:
Freely thou givest, and thy word
Is, 'Freely give.'
He only who forgets to hoard,
Has learned to live."

2. Every man's beneficence should be proportionate to his *annual income.* As there are some with whom the adjustment of their proportion might trench on vested capital, so there are others from whom it would require only a portion of their income. We now refer to the latter class. Your income, then, is to be divided between your own personal and family necessities, and the claims of benevolence. On what principle should the division be made? You are a young man just entering on business, wishing to arrange your plans of benevolence according to the principles of the gospel. You will thence seek to be governed, in your expenditures, by Christian simplicity. In this, you will find the more difficulty, because the prevalent customs and fashions of society are so adverse to it. Yet be not conformed to the world. You can no more be a devotee of fashion, than a worshipper at the shrine of mammon.

If you would make the duty of beneficence easy and delightful, you will commence your charitable donations where your income commences, and give as the Lord prospers you. Let your maxims and motives of liberality be drawn from the word of God, and not from the practices and opinions of those around you. Let your plans and principles be fixed in the *outset*, subject only to such revision as increase of light and love may suggest. Before the love of money shall be strengthened by increase of gains, you will be more likely to judge correctly in the matter of proportion. Your liberality will then readily grow into habit, and habit will make it a delight, and both will perfect and confirm your principles of benevolence, and give symmetry and beauty and energy to your whole Christian character.

Your danger is not of a too rigid economy, but that you may practise it from wrong motives—with a desire of hoarding rather than of giving. Beware of covetousness, which is idolatry. Here will be your chief temptation, despite your firmest benevolent resolves. The present low standard of liberality among older and more experienced Christians, and the fact that covetousness scarcely militates against a reputable profession of Christianity, will enhance this danger. Necessary contact with business men, with whom a distinction between the morality of trade and the morality of the Bible involves no solecism, will add to it. The unhallowed estimate placed upon money, by which "worth means wealth, and the only wisdom, the art of acquiring it," will increase your danger. The world is not atheistic, but the god it serves is gold. "I do confess I am an atheist," says Sir Thomas Brown. "I cannot persuade myself to honor that the world adores." Fortify yourself against all such peril in the beginning, by putting on the whole armor of God. Resist the devil of cupidity, when he proposes to give you all the kingdoms of the world, and he will flee from you.

When you are deciding on the proportion of your

income to be added to your capital, or invested for future contingencies, two questions deserve particular attention: What are the *objects* for which you make this reservation; and what are the *motives* that prompt you to do it?

In reply to the first question you will probably say, "My object is to make provision for the *education and settlement and usefulness of my children.*" We admit the legitimacy of the object, and only ask your attention to the amount necessary for its accomplishment. You wish to employ your property, in respect to your children, in such a way as shall prepare them for the greatest usefulness here, and the highest happiness hereafter.

Now it is essential to this, that you should make provision for the development of their physical, intellectual, and moral powers; that they should be instructed in relation to their social, civil, and religious duties; that they should be subject to the influence of pure examples, and brought under the power of the gospel of Christ. You wish for them, under the combined influence of culture and Christianity, that mental expansion, that refinement of taste, that elevation of sentiment, and that firmness of moral principle, which will harmonize with their sphere of action, and with the highest ends of their existence. Is not this the sum total of what they require at your hands, the substance of your parental duty? But is it necessary for this, that you should lay up for them large stores of wealth? Would not these ends be better secured by such a degree of liberality on your part, as would leave them, when entering upon the responsibilities of life, dependent, under God, chiefly on their own exertions? Yea, do not facts abundantly demonstrate, that by exemption from the necessity of effort, through reliance on inherited, or expected wealth, their prospects of success in business or in professional life would be greatly darkened? On whom have the Indies bestowed their richest treasures, and to whom have the mines of Peru yielded most abundantly their shining dust? Who are the master-spirits of the age, that in the senate, at the bar, or in the pulpit, hold in their hands the secret of power, and wield most resistlessly the sceptre of influence, and sway as by a spell the councils of nations, and the destinies of men? Are they those whose paternal ancestry spent their lives in toil and parsimony that they might leave their children rich? Are they those who commenced their career cumbered by the cares of wealth, and subject to influences which prevent personal exertion, and paralyze the power of noble achievement? No; they are generally those, for whom their parents could do little except in the way of thorough mental and moral training, and the formation of industrious habits; whose chief inheritance was a healthful influence and a bright parental example; and who came forth to meet the trials of life, and to discharge its duties, trusting in Providence, and dependent on their own industry and skill.

But if you can overlook such well-attested facts, and jeopard the temporal interests of your children, by amassing for them the almost certain means of their failure, turn to another aspect of the subject. You desire above all things their usefulness, and their religious welfare. What can you do better to render them useful, than to be so yourself? You wish them to form habits of benevolence. How can your desire for them be more effectually accomplished than by the influence of your own example of benevolence? Withholding your property from objects of charity will not teach them to be charitable. Hoarding yourself large stores of wealth, will not dispose them to consecrate it to Christ. If you would teach them that the value of money consists primarily in the good which may be accomplished by it, in what way can you do it so successfully, as by showing them that this is the great end for which you are acquiring it? And if you would secure to them the blessing of heaven, how can you do it more certainly, than by demising to them your own bright example—the illustration of your full conviction that the love of money is the root of all evil? In this way, a check will be early given to the tendencies of selfishness, and their habits be formed on the principles of Christian benevolence. You will thus bring your children to the altar, not like Hannibal, to swear eternal enmity to a hostile nation, but to encourage in them, by the most sacred domestic influences, a desire to "do good unto all men, as they have opportunity."

Recur now to the second question, the *motives* which determine the proportion to be reserved for future contingencies. Write down the various objects of benevolence which solicit your attention: the claims of the poor, the ignorant, and the oppressed; the calls of Home and of Foreign missions, of the Bible, the Tract, Educational, and Seamen's associations, and other kindred humane and reformatory agencies. Against these, set down the amount which you have appropriated to them. Consider this amount as the measure of your regard for the poor, your interpretation of the law of benevolence, and the exponent of your love to Christ. Then write down on the opposite page the items of your personal and family expenditure, with the several sums applied to them. Look upon these as the index of your sense of personal and family necessities, as what you have considered due to your station in life. Then compare the balance-sheets. Carry them with you to your closet, and when you pray "after this manner," "Thy kingdom come," see how much you are in earnest, by the portion of your income appropriated to the advancement of that kingdom. And when continuing, you repeat the petition, "Give us this day our daily bread," inquire if you may not have been taking much more than you have asked from God. And when you further say, "Lead us not into temptation, but deliver us from evil," ask yourself if some of your expenditures may not have had a direct tendency to lead you into that from which you pray to be kept, and to confirm in you that from which you seek to be delivered. Write over one side of the equation, "The claims of the poor, the blind, the naked, of ignorance, misery, and sin;" and over the other, "The claims of myself and family soon to pass to our final account." Then decide whether you have consecrated of your income to charity, according to the ability that God giveth. Do this, and the result will assist you in determining the motives by which you have been governed in your current expenditures, and in your reservations for future use. Is this asking too much? Does it seem unnecessarily exacting? But why should you shrink from such a test? Is it that you are fearful of the results? If your scale of liberality is such as your own interests and the claims of beneficence require, an examination like this would only confirm your convictions of duty, and render its discharge more easy and delightful. But if it is otherwise, and you fear the necessity of retrenchment on the side of personal ease and gratification,

> "Think heaven a better bargain, than to give
> Only thy single market-money for it.
> Join hands with God, in making men to live."

Oh, it is sweet to know that we are doing the will

of God, and nowhere more so, than in dealing our bread to the hungry, lighting up the abode of sorrow with the smile of gladness, recalling the wandering prodigal, and guiding the weary pilgrim to his heavenly home.

3. Every man's beneficence should be proportionate to what he can *earn by industry*. Labor, although connected with the curse pronounced upon man in consequence of his sin, must yet be considered as a blessing. His physical, mental, and moral condition renders it necessary to his own welfare. The general law of equity also requires it. "If any man work not, neither should he eat." "Not slothful in business," holds an important place among the apostolic injunctions. Idleness is therefore an evil and a sin. It is burying our talent, and exposing ourselves to the condemnation of the slothful servant. No one, however opulent, is at liberty to be indolent. Self-interest forbids it, and the law of benevolence forbids it. To how many reputable disciples might the Saviour now say, "Why stand ye here all the day idle?" What are they accomplishing by their personal exertions, for the honor of God or the welfare of men? Nothing, absolutely *nothing*. Yet health, and time, and power of productive enterprise are talents intrusted to us, even more directly than is wealth, acquired by means of these. "It is God that giveth power to get wealth." Well-directed labor, either manual or mental, in some of the vari-

ous forms of human effort, is therefore a means of doing good, which cannot be left out of account in estimating proportion in beneficence.

By this means, many a poor man might obtain the blessing of giving, who now contents himself with that of receiving. By toiling a little longer, or a little harder, or by turning their labor into more productive channels, not a few, from being themselves objects of charity, might become its happy distributers. Instead of drawing upon the resources of the benevolent, they might help to swell their amount by the addition of their own "farthing." And if they could do this, should they not do it? Would not their temporal condition be improved by the effort, and they find by sweet experience that it is more blessed to give than to receive? We have read of a woman in very needy circumstances, who offered to subscribe a penny a week to the missionary fund. "Surely," said one, "you are too poor to afford this." She replied, "I spin so many skeins of yarn a week, for a maintenance: I will spin *one more,* and that will be a penny for the Society." How beautiful in its simplicity is this illustration! Let each poor man so employ the fragments of time, that it may be said of him as of Henry Martyn, "He is the man that never lost an hour," and he shall eat the labor of his own hands, and "have to give to him that needeth."

The rich, too, who in their ease can give of their

abundance, by diligence would be able to abound in this grace. Where is the warrant for a Christian to retire from active life while in the full enjoyment of his business powers? It is obvious, however, that men may sometimes be called to leave the sphere of labor in which they have accumulated their property, in order to superintend its beneficent expenditure. Public interests may require such a portion of their time and attention as shall be incompatible with the continuance of their more private business schemes.

But how different is this from the case of those who bring to a period their active business career at a time of life when they are most capable of continuing it with success. In the course of twenty or thirty years of prosperous enterprise, a man finds himself in possession of a competency, that is, he has become affluent. Now he is content. He will retire and give place to others. He has enough. But why does he retire? That he may enjoy the luxury of dealing his bread to the hungry, and of endowing institutions for the promotion of science and religion, or for the mitigation of human woe and the reclamation of man from the power of Satan unto God? No; but because he has *enough*. Enough for what? Enough for himself, for his idol, self—enough for his own enjoyment, for ease and elegance—enough to vie with the devotees of fashion, and to revel in splendor. So, these are the motives which have impelled him forward in his eager haste to be rich—ease, elegance, splendor. No thoughts of God enter into his purposes. No pity for the poor influences his plans. Poor man, thou art dead while thou livest. Thou hast "denied the God that is above," and disowned thy brother. No beam of heavenly light guides thee in thy dark career. No genial fire of love melts thy icy selfishness. "Lo, this is the man that made not God his strength, but trusted in the abundance of his riches." "The righteous shall see, and shall laugh at him." "Men shall clap their hands at him, and hiss him out of his place."

But it may be, that amid the smiles of Providence and your increasing stores, you have not been altogether unmindful of the fatherless and the widow. Yet you propose to retire from business. You are a professed disciple of Christ and have sympathy with suffering and sorrow, and have not forgotten "to do good and to communicate," and yet you have enough. And can you then do all that you desire for the cause of God, and of humanity? Are there no poor that will remain destitute; no benighted that will be left sitting in darkness, when you have done what you can? Is the Bible translated into every tongue? Has the missionary visited every land, and carried the gospel to every tribe, and made it the power of God in every heart? Oh, no. And yet *you have enough.* You are retiring from business, it may be, at the very maturity of your powers of business. Has Providence then smiled on your efforts and poured into your lap the fruits of the earth, or the products of commerce, that you might take your discharge from his service? "What, know you not that you are not your own," and that "none of us liveth to himself?" Have you forgotten the price with which you were bought? Does gratitude call for no more self-denial? Does the cross oppose no obstruction to your plan of ease and indulgence?

You may indeed be giving according to what you have. But are you giving according to what you *might* have? Your powers of business are no inconsiderable part of the ability that God giveth. His command is, "Go work in my vineyard." And it is also, "Work while the day lasts."

Besides, if you would give more if you had it, why cease acquiring? Is your beneficence on a large scale now? By adding to it the products of your continued labor, you would make it still larger, and would enjoy a richer blessing, both in what you bestow in charity and what you expend for yourself. And this blessing might come in the form of a better physical and mental, as well as of an improved spiritual condition. You would be preserved from wasting indolence and enervating ennui. By continued efforts to acquire, that you might abound still more in giving, you would be kept from the danger of covetousness attending undue concern respecting what you now possess. By observing the command, "Occupy till I come," you would be protected from the ensnarements accompanying a life of leisure, and procure at last that highest approval of your Master, "Well done, good and faithful servant; enter thou into the joy of thy Lord."

What if Christ had retired from his work, ere he had arrived at that period when he could say, "It is finished." What if he had ceased from his wearying toil, and ascended to his throne of glory, before he had come to that labor of soul in the garden, and that conflict of spirit on the cross—where would then have been the hope of the world? And why did he not thus retire? Ah, he was joined to his work by the invincibility of his love, and his devotion to his Father's will. Thence he toiled up to the very hour of his death, and expended the last of his human powers in completing his redeeming work. And shall his example have no influence to retain his followers in the field? O thou Son of Mary and of God, didst thou spend thy life in poverty and in toil for the miserable and the guilty, and in a world all thine own, have not where to lay thy head? And shall we who reap the fruits of thy godlike labor, seek exemption from service, and weary out our lives in ignoble sloth? Didst thou bear thy heavy cross, and wear thy thorny crown, and drink thy bitter cup that we, clothed in purple and fine linen, might recline upon our couch of ease?

"Woe worth these barren hearts of ours,
Where thou hast set celestial flowers,
And watered with the balmiest showers,
Yet naught we yield."

4. Every man's beneficence should be proportionate to what he can *save by economy*. In any adequate view of this subject, it is apparent that some limits are to be placed to the scale of expenditure. The gospel is no more explicit against covetousness, than against prodigality. Nor is the sin of the one greater than of the other, or the evil of it more afflictive to the church. These seemingly contradictory vices are sometimes found in the same person. He covets another's wealth and squanders his own. So intense sometimes is the sense of want occasioned by wasteful expenditure, that the prodigal, as the miser, not only "stoppeth his ear against the cry of the poor," but rapaciously devours widows' houses, as the means of continuing his riotous living. Thus prodigality leads to covetousness, and covetousness to rapacity. Unholy desire clamors for gratification, and gratification only increases the intensity of insatiable desire, until, in the midst of abundance, the soul finds itself in famine, flooded with waters, yet pining in thirst.

The economy induced by the spirit of beneficence, is equally remote from covetousness and from prodigality. It neither wastes nor buries the intrusted talent, but *uses* it. And the expenditure which is consistent with the claims of charity, is also in harmony with what is due to our station in life. True dignity is never found in conflict with benevolence. When the calls of the latter are responded to by an appropriation of the just proportion of our property, the residue will be found to impart the highest dignity to rank and station, and the most benign and salutary influences to character. "Whatsoever things are true, whatsoever things are honest, whatsoever things are just, whatsoever things are pure, whatsoever things are lovely, whatsoever things are of good report," are in happiest agreement with its claims. But it dissuades from enervating indulgences, from effeminate voluptuousness, from factitious and extravagant conventionalism, as being as incongruous with the spirit of the gospel, as the former virtues are becoming and accordant with it.

Nor can prodigal expenditures, coming as they do into the class of unproductive consumptions, be more easily justified by the principles of *political economy*, than by the spirit of benevolence. Consumed as they are in needless, if not hurtful self-indulgence, the use of luxuries adds less to the national wealth than do beneficent appropriations. Rightly directed, Charity touches the deep springs of the mental and moral energies, and instead of wasting them in profitless excitement, arouses them to the most healthful and productive effort. She feeds the poor and clothes the naked; she enlightens the ignorant, assists the feeble, and raises up the fallen. She discourages vice, that waster of time and money, that weakener of physical, intellectual, and moral vigor. She encourages Virtue, and leads her into the field as the most productive laborer for the weal of the race. She excites industry and rewards it, and stanches earth's flowing miseries by healing its deep wounds of sin. She turns the current of human desire from war to peace, from oppression to freedom, from idolatry, bigotry, and imposture, to the pure worship of the true God.

Such is the productive mission of charity to which we would divert the streams of wealth, now flowing in the spendthrift channels of wasteful superfluity. And for one who admits her claims as obligatory, it would not seem difficult to arbitrate between them and those of prodigality. Perceiving the difference in their nature from their different results, he will be sweetly *impelled* to economy, feeling that the nobleness of the end raises it above the suspicion of meanness, to the rank of the most generous and honorable virtues. He will reflect that what he expends in luxury and self-aggrandizement, is so much withheld from the poor, so much refused as a loan to the Lord, leaving a corresponding amount of grief unassuaged, of vice unchecked, and of eternal misery unprevented. He will reflect that such expenditures not only diminish his power, but lessen his desire to do good; that they are not only a robbery of others, but an injury to himself. He will remember that such superfluities, by placing him in the rank of eager competitors in the circle of fashion, take him out from the simplicity of the gospel, and setting him in practical contradiction to its precepts, present him as a tempter to others by his evil example.

Are you anxious to do good on a larger scale than you have felt your means would allow? Inspect your wardrobe, and see if something may not be saved by economy from the imposts which it has laid upon your resources, and your condition be as comfortable and your attire as comely. Survey your table, and see if something may not be spared from its viands and dainties, and enough remain for rich contentment and hospitable cheer. Make Conscience the steward of thy house, holding his lamp, like that in the urn of Olybius, "alive and light, although close and invisible." Let him report of all your appropriations, how much is for the gratification of the appetites, how much ministers to pride, to vanity, to ambitious rivalry with lovers of themselves. Let his inspection be minute, and deem him not an intermeddler. Accept his report, and from all upon which he writes "extravagance," turn the current of your expenditures into the channels of beneficence. Are you reluctant to do this? Reluctant to part with your superfluities, your luxuries—ministers to pride and fashion and voluptuousness—in order to obtain the means of a more enlarged beneficence!

But "my station in life is fixed, and I must conform to the circle in which I move." If you belong to a circle, the customs of which require you to waste your Lord's money, may it not be your duty to "come out from among them, and be separate?" Would not this, besides enabling you to give more, exempt you from many temptations and evils from which your character and influence are now suffering.

Are you unable to give more in charity than you now do? How can this be, when you are able to spend so much in superfluous and costly attire, in ornaments, "the chains and the bracelets, the rings and changeable suits of apparel, and mantles, and wimples, and crisping pins?" If you are too poor to appropriate more in beneficence, are you not too poor to wear such exponents of wealth, too poor to feast on such costly dainties, too poor to dwell in habitations which are the index of princely fortunes?

You can afford to give no more! Yes, if you will *economize*, you can. If you will "remember the words of the Lord Jesus, how he said, It is more blessed to give than to receive," you will feel that you are too poor to give *so little*. Has not your economy, if you have practised it, been rather in the department of beneficence, than in that of superfluous expenditures? Transfer retrenchment from the giving to the expending side, and you will be able to give more. Wear less of your wealth, and you will be able. Consume less in the Epicurean delicacies of your table, and you will be able. Dispose of that part of your plate and jewelry which subserves no higher purpose than ostentatious display, and you will be able to give more for the mitigation of human woe, and the salvation of the world. The very decision to commence such retrenchment from benevolent motives, would bring your Christian character, under God, to the period of a new development, and the recollection of such economy, for such a purpose, would be a sweet reflection mingling in your dying thoughts.

Happy was that distinguished example of Christian simplicity, economy, and beneficence, John Wesley, in the generous devotion with which he consecrated his substance to the cause of humanity and of God. Suspecting that he had more wealth than was apparent, the Accountant-general sent him the following note, with a copy of the "Excise order for the return of plate." "Reverend sir—As the commissioners cannot doubt but you have plate, for which you have hitherto neglected to make an entry," etc. To this, the following answer was returned: "Sir, I have two silver spoons at London, and two at Bristol, and I shall not buy any more while so many around me want bread."

If all Christians would devote to beneficence the fruits of a reasonable economy, from what practical inconsistency would the church be reclaimed. From what reproach would she be saved, among those who now see her bowing with the eagerness of a devotee at the shrine of Fashion, that "Juggernaut of Christian lands." Oh, how would it contribute to make her "the perfection of beauty, the joy of the whole earth."

We do not assume to prescribe any certain degree of economy or scale of retrenchment, or to interfere with the refinements and proprieties of a pure Christianity; but only to assert, that no one can be sure that he is doing what he ought in works of charity, unless he has introduced the principle of *saving by economy.* No rank or station or amount of wealth can exempt him from the obligation involved in it. And no one, from love to God, can thus bring his beneficence into harmony with his ability, without great benefit to himself. Subjected to the influence of His example who never wasted a single moment, nor squandered a single feeling, but turned every thing to the beneficent account of saving the world, his life would be more happy, his death more peaceful, and a brighter crown would wreathe his brow in the heavenly glory.

5. Every man's beneficence should be proportionate to what he can *spare by self-denial.* What is self-denial? Is it to give liberally of our income, yet withholding for ourselves the whole of the vested wealth from which it is derived? Is it to make large donations to the destitute and miserable, retain-

ing enough to live according to the fashion of this world, in luxury and splendor? Is it to cut off the extravagances and superfluities of life, reserving for ourselves all its conveniences and comforts? Is it not something more than this? Look at the spirit of devotion signalizing the conduct of some Christian philanthropists, of Mrs. Fry, of Sarah Martin, and of Howard, "the habitual passion of whose mind was a measure of feeling almost equal to the temporary extremes and paroxysms of common minds." Look at the self-sacrificing spirit of not a few modern missionaries—of a Harriet Newell, a Mrs. Judson—of a Swartz, a Cary, and a Morrison—of a Dober and a Leopold, who, that they might tell the poor negroes of a Saviour's love, offered to sell themselves into slavery, if no other means could be found of access to them. Look at the patriarchs—Abraham offering up his son, his only son, at the command of the Lord; Moses "refusing to be called the son of Pharaoh's daughter, esteeming the reproach of Christ greater riches than the treasures in Egypt." Look at the apostles, counting not their own lives dear unto them, "rejoicing that they were counted worthy to suffer shame" in their Master's cause. Look at the life of Jesus, at his humiliation, his ignominy, his agony, and learn what self-denial is. Are you poor? So was he, yet it was for your sake. Are you rich? So was he, yet "he became poor, that ye through his poverty might be rich." He "redeemed us from the curse of the law, being made a curse for us." It is in Christ crucified as a sacrifice for sin, that we are to learn the *full* significance of the term self-denial. It was not simply in his leaving the bosom of the Father, in his enduring the contradiction of sinners, that Christ's sacrifice consisted, nor yet in the infamy of being pronounced guilty, and sentenced as a malefactor at a human tribunal; but it was in the burden of sin which he assumed, and on account of which he was forsaken of his Father It was in the agony of soul—the anguish of a spirit which "knew no sin, yet was made sin for us." Here is suffering—sacrifice—here is *self-denial* in its divinest form. The subjection of our personal ease and tastes and conveniences, our comforts and time and possessions, to the will of Christ, for his glory and human good, is in us, its highest realization. It leads to the performance of whatever may contribute to Christ's glory, and to the relinquishment to his disposal of whatsoever of our possessions may subserve the advancement of his kingdom.

Self-denial is the great law of our religion. It began in Christ, our Head. It must pervade all the members. It led him to give up all for us. It should lead us to give up all for him. Whosoever therefore would become a benefactor of the race, must share the wants and woes of his fellow-men by personal sacrifice, in his efforts to relieve them. This is self-denial, the subjection of self to the principle of love, the annihilation of selfishness, and the enthronement of Christ in the soul. Away, then, with the idea of ease, of luxury, when that work of mercy, commenced with such a sacrifice, is pressing upon the church with all the urgency of the Saviour's last command. Away with the idea of convenience, of comfort, when such a motive calls us to sacrifice and self-denial. Oh, it is a shame that a work like this should be retarded by the self-indulgence of the disciples of so self-denying a Master. It is a sin that devoted co-laborers with him should be allowed to feel the necessity of retrenchment in their heaven-commissioned work, to stop their presses, disband their schools, and give back half-reclaimed territory to the barrenness and blight of Paganism; and this, because those who sent them to the work, are unwilling to deny themselves. We blush to remember, that in the progress of modern missions, laborers have been kept back from the whitening fields, and the reaper's sickle has been hung upon the bough, and the harvest has wasted because there were none to gather it, and this for want of nothing but *self-denial.* And we pray the Lord of the vineyard to forgive our apathy and self-indulgence, to blot out the record of the past, and to save his people from causing it again to be traced. Under the most pressing pecuniary embarrassments, imbued with the beneficent spirit of the gospel, and influenced by the example of Jesus and the worth of souls, the church could have doubled her contributions from what she might have spared by self-denial. Constrained by the influence of such motives, self-denial becomes a kind of self-gratification, and it is tenfold harder to *retain* what can be spared by self-denial, than to lay it at the feet of Christ. Before the cross, the sanctified soul repels the idea of restricting its offerings to that which costs it nothing. Gratitude casts all her living into the treasury of the Lord, and Love pours her most precious ointment upon the Saviour's dying head. The one feels that her *all* is too little, and the other, that her most costly tribute is too poor to express the fervor of her affection, and the entireness of her devotion.

Go, then, walk with Christ in the garden. Stand by him upon Calvary, and witness his ignominy and his agony. Remember, that "He was wounded for your transgressions," that "He was bruised for your iniquities." By the crown which he left in heaven, by the cross which he endured on earth, by the love which he bears for you, by the worth of the soul for which he died, he calls you to deny yourself. By the superior moral value of the gleanings of self-denial over the surplusage of abundance, and by the heavenly glory, the way to which is through his own sacrifice, he calls you to deny yourself. He calls you to this, as the only proof that "the same mind is in you which was also in him." He asks for your choicest treasures, your best services. Whom wilt thou deny? Him, or thyself? When, as from the cross, ye hear him say, "Freely ye have received, freely give," will ye not freely give? When, as ascending up on high, ye see him pointing to the whitening fields, will ye not deny yourselves, that the wasting harvest may be gathered in?

"Commit to Christ thine *all*, so shall thy treasure be
Secure from moth and rust, from theft, and fire, and sea;
And in the final day, transmuted to pure gold,
Thy safe investment then shall yield thee wealth untold."

We have now submitted the main principles relating to proportion in beneficence. We have endeavored to show that each man's charitable contributions should be proportionate to the *ends* sought, to the *instrumentality* to be applied, and to his pecuniary *ability*. We have examined the question of ability in the light cast upon it by the beneficence of *the Jewish church*, by the beneficent spirit of *the early Christians*, and by *the Bible doctrine*, as deduced from the express declarations of Scripture. We have also viewed the question of each man's ability, according to which his proportion should be adjusted, in its relation to the *sum total* of his property, to the amount of his *income*, to what he can *earn by industry*, to what he can *save by economy*, and to what he can *spare by self-denial*.

In concluding this part of our subject, we wish comprehensively to re-state and to enforce the leading MOTIVES which should secure the practical adoption of the principles.

1. The devotement to beneficence of a just portion of our property gives to it *its highest value* Nothing is more obvious than that the value of money is wholly relative, and that it is determined by its use. We concede the legitimate value and use of property for sustenance and comfort, for intellectual and moral improvement. And the amount thus applied should be all that the circumstances require. What is not necessary for these purposes, finds its highest value when devoted to beneficence. Compare its value, when thus consecrated, with that which it possesses when expended for selfish purposes. One man accumulates and *hoards*. His gains answer no higher an end than to inflame a sordid desire for wealth, and to feed a hidden fire that consumes all humane and generous affections. He makes "gold his hope, and says unto the fine gold, thou art my confidence." He toils for wealth, but when obtained, he will not use it. And the more he acquires, the less he is satisfied with what he has. His wants increase faster than his possessions, so that the richer he becomes, the poorer he feels. To such madness has this abuse of wealth been permitted, in judicial visitation, to carry men, that the possessor of thousands has clung to his hoarded treasures with such an insane tenacity, and been in such an agony of want for more, that he has died of actual starvation. Truly, "There is that maketh himself rich, yet hath nothing." Well does the

Scripture say of such an one, "He shall be buried with the burial of an ass." "His riches are corrupted, his garments are moth-eaten, his silver and gold are cankered, and the rust of them shall be a witness against him, and shall eat his flesh as it were fire."

Another accumulates and *squanders.* Appetite and pleasure absorb his substance. Disease is engendered, time wasted, vice nurtured, and mind imbruted. And the more he squanders in sensual gratification, the more imperious is the demand for still farther gratification, until "the floor of the wine-press shall not feed" him, and "he shall eat, but not have enough." Thus, whether wealth be hoarded or squandered, it loses its value. It is an abuse of the divine bounty—an abuse which deranges the mental and moral, as well as the physical powers, and dooms the soul to eternal penury—an abuse which has made the world an abode of paupers and prodigals, of misers and maniacs.

See, now, the value of wealth when appropriated to *charity.* It feeds the hungry, clothes the naked, is eyes to the blind, and feet is it to the lame. It "visits the fatherless and the widow," reclaims the vicious, and leads wandering, guilty man back to the fatherly mansions, and to a forgiving God. Such a use gratifies the benevolent desires, and this gratification adds to their strength and intensity, and every such increase of force imparts a greater excellence to the character, by bringing it into agreement with the character of God. In this way wealth attains its highest value. Thus applied, it harmonizes with the benevolence of the Creator, and with the compassions of the Redeemer. It is promotive of the end for which God created man, and of the objects for which Christ died. Its use is based upon the recognition of a higher than sensual principle in man, and a loftier than earthly destiny. It sets forth the cross as the grand central attraction, and proceeds on the conviction that the noblest of all influences, and the sublimest of all agencies, are those which combine to draw men unto it. It is, we repeat, precisely *here* that wealth attains its highest value—in subserving the interests of humanity, and the glory of God. This end, from its intrinsic dignity, imparts to whatsoever means it employs their greatest worth. Apart from this, nothing is truly noble or exalted. This makes *giving* the art of *gaining*—the true philosopher's stone. It turns the hoarded gold into lead, and the given mite into gold. When one sees that beneficence thus embalms his wealth in the form of its highest possible value, and gives it to him as a perpetually increasing fund, as an instrument of good, as a means of grace, and as an auxiliary of heaven, will he not labor to acquire, and acquire that he may *give?*

2. The devotement to beneficence of a just portion of our property, secures *our own highest inter-*

*ests.* It is a satisfaction to know that the proportion of our substance devoted to beneficence is in agreement with the divine will. It is an additional satisfaction to feel that our wealth is thus attaining its highest value. It is a happiness to witness the blessed influence thus exerted, in the alleviation of human woe, and the removal of human sin; in kindling immortal hopes, and adding star after star to Immanuel's diadem. To know and feel this, is to enjoy the *luxury* of doing good. "When the ear heard me, then it blessed me; and when the eye saw me, it gave witness to me: because I delivered the poor that cried, and the fatherless, and him that had none to help him. The blessing of him that was ready to perish came upon me; and I caused the widow's heart to sing for joy." Such a use of our property brings us into harmony with the attributes of God, and with the highest interests of man. It identifies our interests with the interests of Jehovah. Placing them under the protection of infinite power and the guidance of infinite wisdom, by the operation of all moral principles and the immutability of the divine purposes it secures them beyond the possibility of invasion.

The great secret, then, of advancing our own interests, is in the annihilation of selfishness, and in assimilation to God. His peculiar blessedness consists in doing good. He "giveth us richly all things to enjoy." Air and sunlight, rain and dew, are ceaselessly flowing from his hand. Our happiness will be like his, as, in beneficence, our lives resemble his. Hence, it is more blessed to give than to receive; for giving brings us into more perfect sympathy with Christ in his redeeming work, and pours into the soul the blessedness which he contemplated, when, "for the joy that was set before him, he endured the cross." What we give is given back to us again, good measure, pressed down, and running over. It is this that scattereth, and yet increaseth. This maketh rich, and addeth no sorrow therewith. We honor the Lord with our substance and our barns are filled with plenty, and our presses burst out with the new wine of joy. We sow bountifully, and we reap also bountifully of all the fruits of the Spirit. All that we thus give in charge to Providence, shall return in the elements of a greater good. All that we thus employ for Christ, will be treasure laid up in heaven to await our arrival. For all that we thus give to the poor, we "shall receive manifold more in this present time, and in the world to come life everlasting." Thus is solved that old, paradoxical epitaph, "What I kept, I *lost*; what I *gave*, I have." Truly, "There is that maketh himself poor, yet hath great riches." When we see that it is only what we give that enriches us, shall we not give? When we see that, in respect to property, we are worth just the amount of good which we do with it, shall we not do good? When we see that beneficence is the chief work of God, that we live in a world of which the fittest description is, it "is full of his goodness;" when we see that our happiness can be like his, only as our character and conduct resemble his, shall we not be beneficent?

3. The devotement to beneficence of a just portion of our property, promotes *the glory of God.* This is the highest motive which can influence holy beings, the noblest end to which they can devote their lives. This overwhelms all conflicting influences, and, going beyond all considerations of self-interest, leads to entire consecration. It is this—its direction to the noblest end—that gives to Christian beneficence in the simplest act, its intrinsic worth and dignity. This joins the "farthing" of a grateful love to the ends for which Jehovah created and is governing the world. It brings it within that system of means, by which is to be wrought out, in the recovery of a lost world, the demonstration that "God is love." Every beneficent act ascends up high as the throne of God, and, incorporated among the redeeming agencies of the cross, stretches wide as the curse is found. It is in this connection of beneficence with the means and influences by which the Almighty is accomplishing the redemption of the world, "to the praise and glory of his grace," that we find the most urgent calls to it. Here motive reaches its highest power, and argument its most persuasive appeal. In this is the realization of man's highest

interests, by the attainment of the highest ends of his being—the ceaseless oblation of his substance and himself to God, as a living protestation against the selfishness which dishonors and would dethrone him.

Is the divine glory promoted by human obedience? Beneficence is obedience. Is God honored by the expression of a grateful sense of his goodness? Beneficence is such an expression. Does he delight in the testimonials of a fervent love? Beneficence is such a testimonial. "Inasmuch as ye have done it unto them, ye have done it unto me." Do the opposites of these *dishonor* God? Covetousness is the concentration of them all. It closes the ear to his claims in the cries of his poor, and withholds from him the heart. It denies him his crown, and places a stigma upon Christ's voluntary assumption of poverty for the redemption of the world. "Take heed, and beware of covetousness." It is among the most humiliating forms of sin—among the greatest triumphs of Satan. Shall we dishonor him whom all the angels in heaven adore? Shall we withhold from him what it should be our chief joy to lay at his feet, our wealth, our influence, our all? By the highest value of riches, by your own best interests, by the honor of the Saviour, by the glory of God, "trust not in uncertain riches." By the goodness of the Lord, by the love of Christ, by the bliss of heaven, be "rich in good works, ready to distribute, willing to communicate, laying up for yourselves a good foundation against the time to come, that ye may lay hold on eternal life."

'Thy gold's true worth, thy weal, God's glory, are agreed
Then scatter wide and free thy heaven-intrusted seed;
So shalt thou reap a golden harvest most divine,
And like the brightness of the firmament shalt shine."

## CHAPTER III.

### SYSTEM IN BENEFICENCE.

#### I. PROVISIONS OF SYSTEM.

No system can be considered as complete, as suited to develope in the church the beneficent spirit of the gospel, and secure from each of its members a just proportion of his substance in charitable contributions, which does not make provision for *proper instruction concerning the use of property, and for communicating information respecting the condi tion and wants of the world;* for *the appropriation, at stated times, by each one, of a due proportion* of his substance to beneficence; and for some *plan* on the part of every church for *collecting* the contributions of its members, and for *applying* them to the objects for which they are designed.

1. System in beneficence provides for *instruction concerning the use of property, and for communicating information respecting the condition and wants of the world.* Too much may have been presumed on the knowledge of Christians respecting the use which God requires them to make of their property, and consequently, in the prosecution of their business, they have, through ignorance, been exposed to the growth of a covetous spirit, with the increase of their possessions. From motives of delicacy, religious teachers who receive their support from the vol-

untary subscriptions of their people, may have shrunk from the same degree of explicitness upon this subject which they have felt to be necessary in respect to other Christian duties. And the difficulty which some pastors have experienced in securing the full amount of their support, or the consciousness that when received it was inadequate for this purpose, has increased the embarrassment.

And many hearers, who have been ready to applaud the clearest and fullest exposition of dogmatic truth, have sometimes evinced a remarkable sensitiveness to any direct application of the duty of beneficence. They are sound on all points of accredited orthodoxy, and lend their approval to the rebukes of all heresy, except that of believing that their money is their own, and that they may expend it as they please, without let or hinderance. That such has been the feeling of not a few hearers, and such the condition of some pastors, is quite certain; and as a natural consequence, many churches, that have been thoroughly taught in respect to other Christian doctrines and duties, have failed to receive due instruction upon the subject of Christian beneficence.

If a people feel that they are too poor to contribute to charitable objects, let the pastor ascertain whether it may not be merely a matter of feeling, occasioned by the want of more scriptural views, or by the absence of information respecting the wants of the world, for which they may justly have looked to him. Are they poorer than the widow who cast into the treasury of the Lord all her living? If not, instruct them in the doctrine, and duty, and blessedness of Christian liberality, and they will give. Spread out before them the wastes and wants of the world, and they will give. Let them give a little once, and they will wish to give again, and a little more. And what they give to other objects will not be taken from the support of him who is leading them to the luxury of doing good. The specific for a pastor to *starve* himself away from his people, is *to decline instructing them in the duty of beneficence, and to withhold from them a knowledge of the wants of a perishing world.* By such a course, he injures both them and himself, and dishonors his Master. His people are entitled to instruction. It is his duty to give it to them. This should enter, as an important element, into his plans of ministerial labor among them. If they will be covetous, let them know that no "covetous man, who is an idolater, hath any inheritance in the kingdom of Christ and of God." If they refuse to deny themselves, they should understand that self-denial is the condition of discipleship, and that they have turned away from the cross, "sorrowful," it may be—yet they HAVE turned away.

But no; those who love our Lord Jesus Christ will no more disobey him here than elsewhere, if they are rightly instructed in their duty. The church will respond to his calls, if she understands them. She did do it in the days of the apostles and primitive Christians, and she is beginning to do it in our own days. Let the spirit of beneficence, as the antidote to selfishness, be developed in the hearts of Christians, by instruction from the pulpit, in the concert of prayer, or convention. Let the claims of benevolence be freely canvassed. They are founded in principles of the most genuine philanthropy and the purest religion. They are enforced by the power of the cross. They are urged by the woes of countless millions, and by the bliss of which these millions are capable. Oh, let them be *known*, let them be *seen* by the church, and she will open her arms to receive them as the representatives of her divine Redeemer, and honor them with her most precious treasures. If we would displace covetousness from the hearts of Christians, and introduce benevolence in its stead, we must apply the power of Christian doctrine, and open before them the channels of Christian beneficence, and lure them by the attraction of Christian motives. This is God's remedy, and, if applied, it *will* be made effectual.

If the world is to be recovered by the propagation of Christianity, nothing is more evident than that the *rising generation* is to be prepared, by thorough instruction, for a more martyr-like devotedness, and a higher style of achievement than has marked the present generation. The hope of the church, in respect merely to its own perpetuity, is, under God, in the young. For any reasonable plans of successful propagation, the main preparatory work must be with them. The present generation has accomplished more in this respect than did the last. The next must go far beyond the present. But, for this, the spirit of beneficence must be *earlier* infused into it, that, through its deeper root in a richer soil, it may yield a riper and more abundant fruit. "Tell your children of this, and let your children tell their children, and their children another generation." But who shall give this instruction? We answer, first, an important duty devolves on *parents*. They should teach their children, by precept and example, to give liberally and systematically. The *shepherd* of the flock has also a responsible agency. It is his work, made incumbent by his relations to his people, and by the terms of his commission. The main reliance, under God, for the cultivation of a beneficent spirit in the church, and for making her charity a work of intelligence, of principle, and of habit, *must be upon her ministers.* And auxiliary to the ministry in securing this important result, is *the Christian press.* By religious journals, and reports of benevolent societies, by tracts and treatises upon missions and beneficence, much may be done to diffuse information, cultivate a sense of stewardship, and awaken the elevated sentiments of Christian philanthropy. In this view, the religious press is as the right arm of the Christian ministry, the circulation of a good book like a perpetually self-repeating sermon, and all beneficent organizations are as dutiful handmaids to the Christian church.

2. System in beneficence provides for the appropriation by every one, *at stated times*, of *a due proportion* of his property to charitable purposes. This provision of the system is essential in order to secure the full benefits of the former provision. Without something of this, the principles inculcated might be left inoperative, and the impressions made be soon effaced, to be revived perhaps, from the pulpit, and lost again by inaction, or the resumed reign of covetousness. There are three stated periods, the *weekly*, the *monthly*, and the *annual*, which deserve particular consideration.

(1.) The *weekly* period. "UPON THE FIRST DAY OF THE WEEK," says the apostle to the Corinthians, "LET EVERY ONE OF YOU LAY BY HIM IN STORE, AS GOD HATH PROSPERED HIM." The same direction he also gives to the Galatians. Here is a simple but comprehensive *system*. Each one is required to give something. This is *beneficence*. His charity is to be "as God hath prospered him." This is *proportion* in beneficence. It is to be laid by "*upon the first day of the week*." This is *system* in beneficence.

The chief characteristics of this apostolic plan, PROPORTION AND SYSTEM, are precisely those in respect to which the beneficence of the church is most defective. And it is a little singular, that this divine type should have been left on record for the express benefit of the church, and yet should have been so little regarded. It is simple, easy of application, and effective. That some such plan should not have obtained general adoption, may perhaps be best accounted for by the absence of that beneficent spirit which prevailed in the primitive church.

The advantages of this plan are obvious. It is the occasion of very frequent recurrence to the providence of God as the source of our prosperity, and of a recognition of our dependence upon him, and of our obligation to him for all that we receive. It is suited to mingle thoughts of him with the pursuit of all our worldly affairs, so that our religion, instead of being secularized by our business, is made to elevate and sanctify it, by leading to its prosecution upon the highest principles. By bringing us to so frequent a review of our stewardship, it deepens the feeling of responsibleness, and quickens the sensibilities to the condition of our fellow-men, and to our final account. The mind being kept thus constantly familiar with the ennobling principles and constraining motives of Christian beneficence, selfishness is restrained, and covetousness meets with constant and almost impassible barriers. Thus a more correct judgment will be formed of the proportion which duty requires, and the devotement of that proportion will be prompted by more elevated religious affections.

The most indigent can probably lay aside a cent a week for an object to which they may feel unable, at any one time, to contribute fifty-two cents. Many more can invest in this way five, ten, or twenty cents a week, who would think it impossible to subscribe two dollars and a half, or five dollars, or ten dollars at any one time in the year, and who perhaps may not, at any one time, be in possession of an amount so large. And yet, by giving it in small weekly instalments, they will defraud no one; but, doing it from gratitude to God and love to man, they will become better neighbors, better citizens, better men, and better Christians.

Some forty years ago, a worthy deacon of an infant church in Vermont adopted this plan, from a simple desire to obey the injunction of the apostle. While under the elevating influence of the Sabbath services, he consecrated to beneficence such a portion of his income as would meet the measure of his prosperity. From this deposit the various calls of charity were answered, and the poor and needy were never allowed to go empty away, unless it had been previously much overdrawn. In this practice he continued until his death, greatly to his own temporal and spiritual advantage; for "his root was spread out by the waters, and the dew lay all night on his branch." There are those who still remember the small tin trunk to which he committed these weekly instalments, and who, receiving the rich legacy of his example, bear testimony to its happy influence upon themselves, the prosperity of the little church, and the destitute around.

The only plausible objection to this plan may arise from the difficulty which some might experience in estimating the profits of their business, so as to adjust their weekly proportion. With day-laborers, and multitudes of others, this objection could have little weight. With not a few it might be removed by a different mode of conducting their affairs, and the change might make them safer and more prosperous business men. But those whose vocations are of such a nature that this plan could not be fully carried out, might still lay by something, and refer the full adjustment of their proportion to the monthly or annual estimate, as the Jews were allowed to close the appropriation of their tithes for feasts and sacrifices at the expiration of every third year, if not done before.

(2.) *The monthly period.* Those who cannot decide on their degree of prosperity week by week, may be able to do it once a month, and to "lay by in store" accordingly. But for those who adopt the monthly system, the temptation to withhold may be increased by their being under the necessity of consecrating a sum four times as large as the weekly adjustment would require. And there may be less tendency to create a sense of *constant* dependence upon God, and to form as perfectly the habit of associating his glory with the prosecution of all their worldly affairs. Still, as a substitute, in the case of those who cannot do it oftener, let them adopt the *spirit* of the apostolic direction, and "lay by in store" every month, "as God hath prospered them." This has been found to possess important financial as well as religious advantages. Says a prosperous merchant who has adopted this plan, "This system has saved me from commercial dangers, by leading me to simplify business and avoid extensive credits. It has made me a better merchant; for the monthly pecuniary observations which I have been wont to take, though often quite laborious, have brought me to a better knowledge of the state of my affairs, and led me to be more cautious and prudent than I otherwise should have been. Since adopting this plan, I have been no longer perplexed with doubts about giving, and there is no one I meet with more cheerfulness than a servant of Christ calling for aid."

(3.) *The annual period.* To an *annual* survey of one's business affairs, and an apportionment of profits to beneficence, there can be no objection from its impracticability. It accords with the principles and habits of the best business men, to take an annual account of stock, and estimate profits and losses. The reputation and success of any one as a business man require this. Men who do nothing of it evince so little practical wisdom, that not much can be expected from them on the score of systematic beneficence. If they give largely at one time, their generosity may be at the expense of their justice, and they cannot be counted upon as having any thing to give when the call is repeated. But he who annually casts up his accounts will know what are his profits, and what the whole amount of his property. Then let him apply the rule of proportion, and set apart for the cause of his Master, the amount which that rule requires, and let the consecrated sum be considered as sacred to charity. Only let him be sure that the amount does not fall *below* the claims of duty, and of well regulated self-interest. And if he should act upon his *right* to go a little *beyond* mere duty, transcending the stern mandates of conscience, and borne on by the higher sentiments of gratitude and love, he would neither do himself wrong, nor his neighbor harm.

We cannot withhold a joint letter, written in 1822, to the treasurer of one of our foreign missionary societies, by two individuals who had adopted a plan similar to that which it has been our object to recommend.

"When, a few years since, we commenced housekeeping, God in his providence saw fit to commit to our care a small farm in a country town, for which we owed about one-quarter of its value. We had read the various accounts of the benevolent exertions of the day, and were anxious to join with our fellow-Christians in their acts of charity. But how could we obtain the means? Our family must be supported, and we must pay our debts, or we should wrong one man while giving to another.

"After deliberating upon the subject, and reflecting that what we owed would not probably all be wanted for several years, we concluded, in the first place, to attend diligently to business, as God should give us health and strength, and to expend nothing for the support of ourselves and family but what was absolutely necessary for our health and comfort We then fixed upon a certain proportion of our debts, which we would endeavor to pay annually, and so much only, unless more was wanted; but if wanted, we would pay to the last of our ability. After paying the proportion of our debts agreed upon, the remainder of our income, whether more or less, was to be expended, according to the best of our judgment, in doing good.

"When we adopted this plan, we concluded that it was best to review it at stated periods, and if we conscientiously thought it our duty, to alter it; but not otherwise. After several years' experiment, we are more and more convinced that it is our duty strictly to adhere to it. God has blessed our labors in a remarkable degree. We can almost say that he has fulfilled to us his promise to Israel, that he would bless them in all that which they should put their hands unto."

How striking is this illustration of the ease with which systematic arrangements may be introduced into our beneficent operations, even in difficult circumstances. Let every disciple of Jesus go and do likewise, and the days of retrenchment and penury and mourning to the cause of benevolence would be ended, and "Israel would blossom and bud, and fill the face of the world with fruit."

(4.) There is yet one other plan, which has been adopted by some with advantage. It is that of setting apart *a certain portion of each gain in every enterprise*, and devoting it to beneficence. This perhaps approaches nearer to the Jewish system than either of the others. Of all their several gains, the Jews were required to give a portion to the Lord, in the form of first-fruits and tithes. This brought them almost constantly under the influence of some sacred claim upon their substance. Everywhere they were reminded of their dependence upon their Maker, and of their obligations to him. Everywhere they were taught that they were constant receivers, by being called to be constant givers. And why was this but to prevent and destroy covetousness, and to induce habits of beneficence? And what could be more admirably adjusted as means to the end, everywhere meeting a divine claim, or the most animating motives to liberality? How must such a system bring one into an all-surrounding atmosphere of beneficence.

Its advantages are nearly allied to those of the first-named plan. And the near resemblance of the system proposed by the Jewish lawgiver to that presented by the Christian apostle, is easily accounted for by the fact, that both the lawgiver and the apostle were under divine guidance. It was in both cases the all-creative Mind propounding to man principles of beneficence most suited to his character and condition, and most conducive to his highest interests and the glory of God.

The operation of these principles is beautifully illustrated in the following epistle, written in 1823, and addressed to the secretary of one of our benevolent societies.

"I have long been desirous of rendering some aid to your society. My circumstances, however, have been such that I knew not how to contribute money. But having recently commenced business, with very moderate prospects, it occurred to me that I had a *right*, if it were not clearly my *duty*, to set apart a certain portion of the Lord's gifts, for his cause in the earth. I have therefore taken a certain part of every gain, small or great, and devoted it to the service of God. I would not trouble you with this communication, were it not to tell you of the *satisfaction* I have derived from this plan. The money laid aside is not considered mine. The only inquiry, when an application is made, is, 'Have I any thing in the treasury, and how can I dispose of it to the best advantage?' I feel as though I were putting my hand into the Lord's treasury and acting for him. I have no doubt, sir, *that the deductions made on every gain have been saved in carefulness and economy.*"

Who can resist the conviction of the superior excellence of such principles as this letter and the preceding illustrations exhibit? Who can doubt the utility of reducing them, as these Christians did, to systematic operation? Were they not better for their beneficence; richer in all that which constitutes true worth—richer in the means and the desire of doing good—richer in all the elements of rational enjoyment here, and in the immortal hopes of blessedness hereafter?

3. System in beneficence provides for *some plan in every church for collecting its charitable contributions, and for applying them to the objects for which they are designed.* It is obvious that this is essential to the completion of a perfect system.

There are some objects to which the donors themselves should be the distributers of their own bounty, as the poor, the sick, and the afflicted, within the sphere of their immediate action. The benign and salutary influence of bestowing private charities is too precious to be lost by making another the almoner of our bounties, when we are in circumstances to apply them ourselves.

It is mainly with respect to the prominent and accredited institutions of benevolence, whether relating to the claims of our own or of other countries, that this part of our system is to be arranged. For these various objects, collections are sometimes taken at the close of public service, at the time when the objects are presented. It is an objection to this method, that it leaves out of account those who may on such occasions be absent, and secures a smaller sum from those who are present, than a different plan might elicit. Cards are sometimes placed in the slips of the church, upon which each one is requested to write his name, with the sum which he wishes to give. In addition to the above-named objection, which is equally applicable to this mode, many who would otherwise contribute a little, disliking to place their names to a small sum, subscribe nothing. We believe that by some wise system, a larger amount may be secured, and with greater advantage to the donor. The minutiæ of a plan for charitable collections must be determined by the peculiar circumstances of the case. Little more can here be done than to draw the outline of one, which can be filled up by those who may carry it into operation.

Let provision be made by the church, at the opening of the year, for *the presentation of the claims* of the various benevolent objects *at stated times*, and let one or more suitable persons be appointed for each different object, to *solicit donations* in its behalf.

When these stated periods arrive, it will be in harmony with the provision for systematic instruction, for the pastor, either himself or by an agent, to present such *facts* and *principles* as will increase the religious intelligence of the people, elevate in their minds the great work of Christian beneficence, and bring them more under the influence of appropriate motives to liberality, in behalf of the particular object presented.

Let the solicitors appointed follow the presentation of these claims by *calling from house to house*, giving an opportunity to each individual, children as well as parents, to contribute what they may have appropriated for the object, answering any inquiries, and imparting such additional information as they way be able to give.

Let each one of these solicitors make *a list of the names* of those upon whom he calls, with the several sums contributed by each, to be given to the pastor when the collection is completed. Of the sum total of his collections let him also make a return to a treasurer chosen for the purpose, or to the pastor, by whom the money will be transmitted as soon as practicable to the treasurer of the society for which it is designed.

From the lists returned for the several objects during the year, let the pastor *make an annual report* to the church and congregation, with such instructions and remarks as the facts in the case may suggest.

Such are the provisions which seem essential to a complete system in beneficence, whether viewed in relation to the wants of the church, or the condition of the world. A system like this imposes a duty upon pastors, upon individual Christians, and upon the church. It secures *instruction and religious information*, thus touching most effectively the springs of beneficent action. It provides for *a stated time*, at which each one shall *apply the rule of proportion*, and lay by in store according to the ability that God giveth. It includes a simple but comprehensive plan for charitable *collections*, and for applying funds to the objects for which they are designed. It is in harmony with the means appointed by the Redeemer for the sanctification of his people, and through them for the salvation of the world. And it may be regarded as a recommendation to this plan, that while it recognizes the instrumentality of the general benevolent organizations, as the applying agents of the church, their influence comes in to confirm, rather than disturb the relations of the pastor to his people, and to impress upon the church its responsibility in regard to its beneficent mission as the great divinely instituted body for the world's conversion.

II. TENDENCIES AND ADVANTAGES OF SYSTEM.

1. System in beneficence *diminishes the expenditure* of benevolent societies for agencies. It is one of the evils resulting from the present unsystematized beneficence of the church, that so much expenditure is necessary for the support of agents for collecting funds. There can be no doubt, that in regard to the principal benevolent organizations, some expenditure of this kind in the past state of things has been necessary. But any considerable appropriation for this purpose has come to be felt by all to be a serious drawback, not only in respect to the funds thus expended, but also from its tendency to occasion distrust in the minds of the less informed and less interested. And it is also felt that the time has come when, by means of system, nearly the whole of this expenditure might be saved. The secretaries and officers could communicate intelligence to the pastors and churches through reports and periodicals. The pastors could diffuse information by the circulation of these publications, and by their own preaching impart such instruction as might secure systematic contributions, and regular remittances to the treasurers of the several societies. This plan *carried out* would be found effective, and would save to the cause of beneficence thousands of dollars.

But would it be *safe* to discontinue all agencies for the collection of funds? This question will find an answer in the reply to another question. Will the pastors and churches adopt the plan? Will they reduce their beneficence to system, and *carry out* the system? If they will do this, it will be safe. Indeed, there seems scarcely an alternative. The business of raising funds belongs to the churches. The tendency, in the progress of benevolent operations, especially for the last few years, has been to devolve it upon them. It should not be a matter of expense to those organizations whose appropriate work is to apply these charities. This expense is not allowed in other corporate institutions. The stockholders pay in their assessments at their own expense. And thus it should be in furnishing supplies for our benevolent associations; and thus it might be, if Christians would conduct their beneficence as other men do their business, on principles of economy and by system, not allowing "the children of this world" to be "wiser than the children of light."

2. System in beneficence tends to secure a *larger number of contributors*. It has been ascertained, that of the professed Christians who regard one of our oldest and most efficient boards as the organ of their appropriations for foreign missions, but little more than one half contribute any thing to promote the object. Can it be that they feel no interest in a work so plainly enjoined by the Head of the church? Is not the reason rather to be found in the want of instruction respecting their duty, of information con-

cerning the condition of the world, and of a systematic *plan* for securing their coöperation?

The churches which include the largest number of regular contributors, are those on which most preparatory labor has been expended. Let the same labor be bestowed upon other churches, and according to their ability will their members become interested and uniform coworkers with other laborers in the vineyard of the Lord. Let them have arrangement, system, *plan* in beneficence, and they will bring forth fruit in this department of duty as certainly, as by similar means they do in other departments. He who performs one religious duty from the right principle, may be led by proper influences to perform any other.

Thus does system in beneficence tend to secure to charitable enterprises a larger number of contributors, and to make their coöperation more regular and effective. It opens fountains of benevolence "in a dry and thirsty land, where no water is," and turns intermittent springs into the sources of perennial streams, which shall fertilize the barren wastes, and "make glad the city of our God."

3. System in beneficence tends to secure from each contributor an amount *more proportionate to his ability*. Men sometimes do less than duty requires, for no other reason than that they do not know how *little* they are doing. System would tend to remove this difficulty, and to raise the standard of

their liberality. Those who give at random, and from impulse, frequently imagine that the amount of their charities is greater than it really is. This misapprehension leads them to withhold more than they would otherwise feel at liberty to withhold. System would correct this mistake, and enlarge their donations. Many, also, give little, because they have no plan for giving any thing. The thing wanting is a *purpose.* There may be the elements of beneficence, but they are chaotic. What is needed is development and direction. Temporary ebullitions are not sufficient. Fitful, meteoric bursts of feeling are followed by a darker day of apathy and inaction. Extraordinary, spasmodic exertion, occasioned by the galvanism of large assemblies and exciting speeches, is not the kind of effort which the objects of beneficence demand. There may be excitement awakened—enthusiasm. No vast and noble achievements are secured without this. But how unlike to an elevated moral state are those flashes of benevolent feeling, which for a moment astonish the beholders by their glare, and in a moment more leave them in equal amazement at the darkness which follows.

The excitement which the church needs to bring its beneficence into agreement with its ability, is occasioned by deeply pondering the principles of the gospel, and considering the miseries and the guilt of mankind; by constant contemplation of the character of Jesus, and communion and sympathy with him. It is enthusiasm generated by the spirit of God in the deep well-springs of the soul, which bears the whole man right on, over all obstacles, in the steady prosecution of the great work of beneficence. It is excitement and enthusiasm which come from the union of the heart and the head, the blending of feeling and intellect in a uniform, growing desire to do good. Where this is, there is little danger that a man's charities will be disproportionate to his means. Every one in whose heart this healthful excitement has been produced, will give "to his power," and be willing even "beyond his power." Yet this is no hot-bed process of forcing unnaturally the benevolent sympathies. Nothing is done that, in seasons of serenest reflection, could occasion a moment's regret. All is calm, quiet, Christian deliberation. Reason approves it, conscience approves it, and the word of God approves it.

But alas, for want of this, how comparatively lean is the charity of the church. She grazes in barren fields. Caprice, accident, self-indulgence, or apathy, often determines the objects and time and amount of charitable contributions. Multitudes of the poor remain still unrelieved, of the ignorant unenlightened, and of the vicious unreclaimed. The field ripens faster than the reapers are ready to gather in the harvest. To millions who need the gospel, and to many who *ask* for it, the church does not give it. The demand vastly outruns the supply. And so it will be, until the church comes to act, in her beneficence, upon principle and by system. Till then, in her means of fulfilling her high mission, and executing the last charge of her Lord and Master, she will be poor, while her individual members, for all other purposes, may be rich.

4. System in beneficence tends to give to charitable contributions the more scriptural form of *free-will offerings*, and thus to render them more acceptable to the Lord, and a means of greater good to men. The scriptural idea of charity is love, good-will; and when donations to the poor are called charity, it is by metaphor, wherein the action or the gift receives the name of the feeling supposed to have prompted it. But it is often a misnomer to apply such a word to the donations of those esteemed charitable. It is true, that funds which are *relinquished* to the cause of beneficence may be attended with good to the recipients. God may employ them for such a result on the ground of his own right in them. But his ordinary mode of procedure leads to the conviction, that less good can be expected from such donations than from the free-will offerings of affection, while to such reluctant releasers of their property we find no promised reward. And although, in respect to the condition of the poor and the wants of the world, this is a better disposition of their wealth than to hoard or squander it, still they lose the blessing which follows the free-will offering, because, in what they

do, "they sacrifice to their own net, and burn incense to their own drag."

There are others who have principle and feeling, which are called into action in other departments of duty, but not here. They pray from principle, but *give* grudgingly or of necessity; or they contribute to sustain the gospel at home from love to that gospel, but have made its *diffusion* a subject of so little inquiry and prayer, that the same feeling hardly prompts them to do any thing for extending its blessings. So that often what they are constrained to yield to this object approaches, in their mind, to a kind of religious extortion. Such a man gives as little as he can, consistently with the generally received opinion that all professing Christians should give something. When he can plead inability without incurring the odium of penuriousness, he does it; and when he gives, it is reluctantly, and without faith or charity.

Now, what such a man needs, in order to change his views and his habits of giving, is, together with a larger measure of the divine Spirit, *system*, instruction respecting his duty, and a plan for doing it. Let him be taught whose is the silver and the gold, and why it is intrusted to him; that the great business of a disciple, so far as his property is concerned, is to *give as freely* as he has received. Let his thoughts dwell on the import of that petition which he so often repeats, "Thy kingdom come," until he feels that by his agency its advent may be hastened. Let him go to the cross and view his possessions *there*, and he will attain a moral elevation unreached before; his eye will catch visions new and strange to him, and he will begin to feel that wealth is power, and that it is a blessed thing to wield that power for the good of his fellow-men. He is now predisposed to look with favor on some *plan* for beneficence which may be submitted to his inspection. He has a new object to live for. New enlargement is given to his mind. New thoughts take possession of him. A new spirit inspires him. His donations, now prompted by love, are set apart as sacred to charity, and this gives to them the form and spirit of free-will offerings. And what is thus offered is accepted; for,

> "Where love is, the offering evermore is blest."

This is the spirit of true beneficence, which leads to the voluntary consecration of one's *entire self*, body, soul, and spirit, "a living sacrifice, holy and acceptable unto the Lord." It puts charitable donations into the most acceptable and pleasing form. It writes "holiness to the Lord" upon every thing, and converts human instrumentality into divine appliances for the recovery of lost man. How great would be the addition of moral power to the beneficent agencies of the church, if all her bounty came regularly and systematically as *free-will offerings* to the Lord.

5. System in beneficence tends to make free-will offerings the fruit of a more *cheerful* spirit, and renders beneficence a *delight*, as it is a duty. "The Lord loveth a cheerful giver," and he who gives cheerfully finds delight in giving. But seldom does one experience much pleasure in beneficence, who has left it to the contingencies of accident or circumstance. The call may come when he is "unprepared," because his bounty has not been "made up beforehand;" or he may have some sense of duty, but not be sufficiently influenced by the motives for doing good to make it a pleasure.

In order that doing good may be a cheerful and happy work, it should be, in principle at least, a *business*. And in this, as in other things, practice leads to perfection. Exercise gives strength to the benevolent as well as to the social affections. Giving once is seed sown, of which the fruit is a disposition to give still more. Scattering to the poor increases both the desire and joy of scattering. And these will be still more increased by the adoption of a regular, systematic plan for doing it.

By system, preliminaries are arranged, resources provided, and the proportion adjusted and consecrated to the Lord. Nothing remains but to make the appropriation. Such a man has no conflict with covetousness. The battle has been fought, and the victory won. He is impeded by no doubts respecting the worthiness and importance of the object.

He is hindered by no pleas of human imperfection in the workings of accredited disbursing agencies. Nothing causes hesitancy or misgiving. He lays his offering upon the altar with a cheerfulness and delight which he has experienced in no other mode of employing his property, and his only regret is, that it is no larger. This is the pleasure of beneficence, the luxury of doing good—to see joy lighted up in the abodes of poverty and distress, to hear of blessings conferred through Bibles and books distributed, and the gospel proclaimed. It is a pure and permanent delight. When it has passed away as a present consciousness, it continues as a joyful reflection, and a sweetly impelling force to still more enlarged plans of beneficence.

One who thus regulates his charities by plan, is always ready to give when he is called upon, and always cheerful in giving, because he is ready. Far from looking upon the solicitors for benevolent objects as religious mendicants, whom he sends from his door with only a covetous "Be ye warmed and filled," yet "giveth not those things which are needful," he deals to them liberally of what he has "laid by him in store," and to this adds his grateful God-speed to them in so noble a mission. Yea, his benevolence waits not to be asked, but impelling him by a spirit which "seeketh not her own," he goes forth unurged, unsolicited, to minister to the objects of want and of woe. He cannot keep his Lord's money long hid in a napkin. He puts it speedily to the exchangers, that it may gain more for his Master's use. To do good with his property has become his habit. It is his business, his pleasure, his *life*. He has experienced the blessedness of doing good, and now nothing can prevent him from continuing his enjoyment of it. He has discovered the true value of wealth in discovering the right way of using it. He is happiest himself when he does most to make others happy.

Here is the great secret of happiness, the panacea for half of earth's afflictive ills—"to do good, and to communicate." It is the intenseness of desires concentrated upon self which makes the soul a prey to itself, and multiplies its artificial wants and its corroding cares, and deprives it of the joys of life. Let men do good, and they will find happiness. To many of a constitutionally morbid temperament, who are almost strangers to the sweet sunlight of life, or to those over whose spirits the blight of hope has cast a cloud, let it be said,

"Whoso would sun himself in peace, may be seen of her in deeds of mercy,
When the pale, lean cheek of the destitute is wet with grateful tears."

Where can the afflicted find consolation so readily as in assuaging the griefs of others? In their missions of mercy, they shall find a blessed ministration made to themselves by the great Comforter.

"Wouldst thou from sorrow find a sweet relief?
Or is thy heart oppressed with woes untold?
Balm wouldst thou gather for corroding grief?
Pour blessings round thee like a shower of gold.
* * * * * *
The seed that in these few and fleeting hours
Thy hands unsparing and unwearied sow,
Shall deck thy grave with amaranthine flowers,
And yield thee fruits divine in heaven's immortal bowers."

6. System in beneficence tends to give *consistency and efficiency* to the character of Christians, by bringing *their life into harmony with their doctrines and professions.* The piety of the church needs consistency and symmetry. And this because it needs system to bring its practice into harmony with its doctrines and professions. There is a glaring contrariety between the standards of the church and its beneficent action. This is observed by the infidel, and is used as a reproach. It is perceived by the pagan as soon as he understands our professed belief and our practical disbelief. "If you Christians have known all these things," said an inquisitive heathen to the first missionary at Bombay, "and really thought that we heathens must perish unless we believe in your Jesus Christ, how could you leave so great a part of the world for so many generations to go down to perdition, without coming sooner to tell us of this only way in which we can be saved?" How can such most natural questions be answered, except by the admission of great *inconsistency?*

We recognize the justness of the comparison in our Saviour's declaration, that it shall profit a man nothing to "gain the whole world and lose his own soul," and yet we seem almost to have reversed the comparison in our systematic exertions, seeking the world as the infinite good, and passing by the soul as of little worth. We admit that "the cares of the world, and the deceitfulness of riches, choke the word, and render it unfruitful," and yet we cultivate these cares and riches, as if they would make our hearts a more fertile soil for the good seed. We profess to give up all for Christ, and yet live much as if we admitted his claim to nothing. We admire the spirit of the martyrs, but have little idea of witnessing for the cause in which they died by the surrender of any considerable amount of our property for its advancement. We profess to have laid up our treasure in heaven, but from all visible appearances, far the greater portion of it is still on the earth. In our creeds, we renounce "the world, the flesh, and the devil;" and in our lives practically renounce our creeds, which contain such a renunciation. We pledge ourselves, in our profession, to entire consecration, and seal our vows in "the cup of blessing," and yet evince by our practical reservations that we do not feel obligated by these vows. Doctrinally, the church admits self-denial as the condition of discipleship; practically, as a body, she construes the condition as consistent with the denial of almost every thing rather than self. The practical significancy of the golden rule with many, is the surfeiting of self from the table of abundance, and the bestowment upon our poor neighbor of the crumbs that fall therefrom. Our great Exemplar was self-denying, and we admit ourselves bound to be like him, yet our course of life is eminently self-indulgent. The church is organized for aggressive movement, but as a body remains stationary. As she strives for more extended empire, she strengthens, and yet she strives not. Inaction enfeebles her, and yet she is comparatively inactive. It is by scattering that she increases, and yet she scatters little. Exporting her treasures enriches her, and yet, for the greater part, she consumes them at home. Keeping her goods is her bane, and yet she keeps them. Hiding her Lord's money, it shall be taken away, and yet she hides it.

Is this consistency? Is there not a sea of apathy lying between our creeds and our conduct, between our doctrines and our deeds? The Saviour and the perishing world are on one side; the body of the church, with its wealth, is on the other. The voice says, "Come over and help us;" but there is no answering movement. There is indeed some stir in the camp of the Lord's hosts, some feeble attempts at crossing—a few bold leaders have seized the ark, and borne it over. But what are these from so many? And these are left to fight almost alone.

What are two or three thousand missionaries for six hundred millions of benighted souls?

What, now, is needed? We answer, *consistency.* Nothing but consistency in the life of the church. The fault is not in her creeds. Her organization is in harmony with the letter and spirit of her commission. Her professions and admissions are explicit and full. The fault is in her *practice*—the *life of her members.* In this, she virtually disowns her creeds, repudiates her organization, and contradicts her admissions and professions. Without plan in beneficence, *this contrariety is reduced to system.* Men pursue their various schemes for self-indulgence or self-aggrandizement most systematically. When we contemplate the grandeur of the objects proposed to her, and the comparative pittance which she relinquishes for their accomplishment, we are constrained to say, that she is systematic in *the diversion* of her energies and her possessions from the great end to which her doctrines and her professions direct them—*systematic in self-contradiction.*

Now, let this order of things be reversed—let the system be extended from schemes of selfishness to those of benevolence—let plans be formed for harmonizing the practice of the church with its doctrines and professions—let her charitable contributions be made from an elevated Christian devotion, and be proportionate to the legitimate objects of beneficence, and regularly applied; and how changed will be the whole aspect and condition of the church. As she joins with Christ in his great work, he will join with her in a visible success, that will animate her hopes and strengthen her courage for renewed effort and fresh victories. What symmetry and beauty would such a change impart to her—to cease planning for self-indulgence, and to begin to plan for the glory of God. How would she put on her beautiful garments, the fragrance whereof is like the smell of "myrrh and of cassia." "No weapon that is formed against her shall prosper, and every tongue that shall rise against her in judgment, she shall condemn." "She shall break forth on the right hand, and on the left; and her seed shall inherit the Gentiles, and make the desolate cities to be inhabited."

7. System in beneficence tends to raise the church, in her charitable contributions, to a more *elevated Christian devotion.* Whatever shall lead the church to a greater simplicity of purpose, and give her a more single eye to the glory of Christ—whatever shall kindle in her the spirit of entire consecration—whatever shall train her to a higher standard of faith and a more ardent love, and a purer and more constant zeal—whatever shall give an elevated Christian basis to her benevolent efforts, and excite a more intense longing after the coming of Christ's kingdom, will directly augment her moral power, and give increased efficiency even to the present rate of charitable contributions. God requires the pecuniary resources

of the church, not because he cannot accomplish his plans of redemption without them, but because he sees that it will be for her advantage to do it by means of those resources. His object is to perfect in his people their estrangement from the world and their devotion to him, while he employs this devotion as the means of accomplishing his scheme of redeeming love towards the race.

And in proportion as this spirit of obedience and self-denial and love is increased, however small the amount of charitable donations which it yields, the work of beneficence will be found advancing. If the resources of the church are only as a "handful of meal in a barrel, and a little oil in a cruise," with the devotement of these in the spirit of entire consecration, "the barrel of meal shall not waste, neither shall the cruise of oil fail," until the whole work be accomplished. He who could feed five thousand with "five loaves and two fishes," can convert the world through the generous, self-denying sacrifices of his people, be they ever so small. On the other hand, the absence of this spirit leaves the church to declension, and the world to perish, although the richest mines in the bosom of the earth be dug up and cast into her treasury. Though we "bestow all our goods to feed the poor, and have not love, it profiteth nothing." Who have accomplished so much for modern missions, in proportion to their means, as the Moravians? When their whole number did not exceed six hundred persons, a large part of whom were exiles, they began the beneficent work of Christian missions. At the expiration of ten years, they had carried the light of truth to Lapland, Greenland, St. Croix, Surinam, and to the Indians of North America; to Algiers, the cape of Good Hope, Ceylon, and Tartary. Whatsoever they possessed which could subserve so sublime an end, they laid upon the altar with a noble and self-denying devotion to Christ; and their success was according to their faith and love. So it was in the first propagation of Christianity. It was not their numbers, nor was it their wealth which gave such signal triumphs to the primitive followers of Christ, but it was their invincible moral courage, their ardent love, their untiring zeal, their pure Christian devotion.

It is the spirit of *entire* consecration which makes the soul rich in all the elements of liberality. It is a simple, confiding trust in Providence, a warm and glowing love to Christ, which, withholding all sacrifices to pride and fashion, and pervading the whole business and arrangements of life with the spirit of supreme devotion to God, produces a degree of beneficence which men who live unto themselves deem extravagant and ruinous. This entire subjection of the soul to Christ forms a style of philanthropists who, in the esteem of many even in the church, are so far beyond the requirements of reason and Scripture, that their influence is lost as examples, and they are considered as fit only for ridicule or admiration. And this, because the spirit of the world has crept into and corrupted the church. Her beneficence is meagre, and upon low and earthly principles. Her light is dim. Her strength is weakness. Her enemies exult over her. Feebly does she fulfil her mission to the poor, the ignorant, and the vicious at home. Still more feebly does she execute her commission to the Pagan, the Mohammedan, and the Jew abroad. Nothing but supreme devotion to Christ will restore her beneficent power, and open fountains of benevolence, and send forth streams, "to satisfy the desolate and waste ground, and cause the bud of the tender herb to spring forth."

Urgent as are the calls for funds from the waste-places of our own country and from heathen lands, there is a greater urgency that the whole subject of beneficence be canvassed and systematized, and placed on a higher and broader ground of Christian principle and Christian devotion. This done, the requisite amount of contributions will be made sure, and the condition of their greatest efficacy will be complied with.

The very attempt to form a system will give a new impulse and elevation to all the beneficent movements of the church. And the incorporating in a *plan*, of such influences as led to its formation, will give them permanency as causes, of which still other advantages will be the legitimate effects. The plan has given these influences prominence, as elements of a man's daily life. They interweave themselves in all his thoughts and business. What was low in the church would thus be raised up; what was weak, would be made strong; what was wavering, would be confirmed, and her beneficent career become like the rising light, "shining more and more unto the perfect day."

> "Oh, then, let her scatter broadcast of her seed,
> Rich in prayer, and in alms, and in every good deed,
> Till her seed-grain is garnered in ripe golden sheaves,
> And her guerdon of glory from Christ she receives."

8. System in beneficence tends to promote *union among Christians of different denominations*, and thus to increase the moral power of the whole church for the good of the world. The ground of hope that the adoption of system in beneficence would increase the spirit of union among the several denominations is, that it presents a common *object* to be accomplished, and a common *plan* for accomplishing it. How might all distinctions of name and sect be blended in the great work of blessing the world, like the primary colors in the beams of light, that gladden the earth and make it fruitful. Or, at least, how might they be so harmonized, like these same colors set in the resplendent arch of glory which spans the darkened heaven, as to betoken that the wrathful storms are past, and to give promise of perpetual peace. And this hope is the greater, in-

asmuch as the main object is, not to unite the church, but by new conquests to *enlarge* it—not to form a new association, but to perpetuate and make universal an old one. It is not so much to harmonize creeds, as to give system and consistency and efficiency to *practice*. However much may be gained in the work of uniting the church by discussions and conferences and alliances, it will readily be admitted that much more may be done by leading the followers of Christ to a self-denying, systematic effort for the conversion of the world.

It is to *action*, rather than discussion, that we look with most sanguine expectations for the union of the church. By the former, good men will work themselves, in a common cause, into greater doctrinal or ecclesiastical proximity, while, by the latter, they may reason and resolve themselves into a wider separation. The one places them upon their points of difference. Passion and self-interest, always irrelevant in the search after truth, creep in and blind the eye, and inflame the zeal for fortifying and defending those points. The other sets them upon their points of agreement, and all their ardor of engagement deepens their sense of the absolute and relative importance of these points. Each will rejoice in the fruits of the labor of all, as ripened by the same divine influence, and gathered from the same common field. "Ephraim shall not envy Judah, and Judah shall not vex Ephraim. But they shall fly upon the shoulders of the Philistines toward the west; they shall spoil them of the east together." A common cause gives them common sympathies and bonds of attachment. By engaging in earnest, and upon system, in the great work of doing good, the whole church is pervaded by one spirit, the spirit of Christian beneficence, influenced by one motive, elevated by one sentiment, the tendency of all which is to overpower sectarian peculiarities, and melt the whole company of disciples into one mass, and mould them after one divine likeness. Instead of repelling the world by her frowning battlements reared for intestine warfare, the church, united in her separate sections, like the several tribes of Israel in one common phalanx, and moving at the sound of the same "silver trumpet," towards the same land of promise, would attract and subdue the world.

By what name soever you may call yourself, if you are a child of God, the points on which you differ from your brethren are probably fewer, and certainly less important, than those in which you agree with them. The views and feelings which characterize both you and them, as the friends of God and of man, are the *catholic* views and feelings—the only bond of a common fellowship among all the regenerate and holy on earth and in heaven. These constitute precisely that character which qualifies all Christians to engage in the work of beneficence with the highest degree of success, and which, the more earnestly and systematically that work be prosecuted, assumes more and more the ascendency over all dividing lines and enfeebling agencies. This would give to the church a union, and a power and stability from union, to which she is now a stranger. The preponderating force would be a *centripetal* force. The attraction would be to a common centre, by a common law of affinity. With what deep grief did the devoted Martyn, an attached member of the church of England, hear, while at Aldeen, of an order of the British government, to prevent his Baptist brethren from preaching and distributing tracts. "So perplexed and excited was he by the intelligence," says his biographer, "that it even deprived him of sleep. And he spoke afterwards with so much vehemence against the measures of government, as upon reflection, to afford him matter of self-condemnation." "How small and unimportant," exclaims this heroic servant of God, in view of the combined powers of evil that oppose the progress of the church in heathen lands—"*how small and unimportant are the hair-splitting disputes of the blessed people at home, compared with the formidable agents of the devil, with whom we have to combat here.*"

We would not affirm, that all differences of opinion and denominational distinctions would necessarily disappear, even in the most systematic and successful prosecution of the work of beneficence. We only say, that the elements of system are the elements of success, and that these, combining a rule that is safe with motives that are sufficient, are common to all the followers of Christ. We say, "the field is the world," the harvest is already ripe, the command is, "Go, work in my vineyard." The world is to be saved by the inculcation of those essential doctrines on which the disciples of Christ are *agreed*. Christianity is, therefore, incomparably better than the peculiarities of any *sect* of Christians. Let it be remembered, that our Saviour's last command to the church is, "Go ye into all the world, and preach the gospel to every creature," and let her begin this work in earnest and upon system, and strifes will cease. Discordant tempers and conflicting interests will be harmonized in hearts fused into one common constraining love, by the ardor of their zeal in the accomplishment of one common, sublime end. Let the church task herself to minister to the poor and distressed, to give the word of God free course in every language and dialect under heaven, to place Bunyan's Dream in the hand of every pilgrim to the "celestial city," and to make Doddridge and Baxter as living preachers in the tent of the Arab, the hovel of the Hindoo, the hut of the Hottentot, the wigwam of the Indian—in every human habitation setting forth the simple power of the cross—grace, in its beginning and continuance in the soul, the same in every age and every clime, and its consummation in "the saints' everlasting rest." Let the church begin and continue this work systematically till it is completed, and in the symmetry and consistency and beauty and power acquired in such a work, let those who together have achieved such victories, return and strive and dispute with and malign each other, *if they can.* Their differences would all disappear in their love and labor for the common cause, or, by general consent, would be allowed to cause no unhallowed division among brethren on earth, and would be left to be lost in the harmonies of heaven.

We have now contemplated beneficence in its most prominent aspects, as Christian, proportionate, and systematic. We have analyzed it in relation to its *distinguishing spirit*, in the elements or *motives* which give to it its moral character. We have considered it in the *degree of effort* which each one is called upon to make, as indicated by the *wants of the world*, the *instrumentality* for supplying those wants, and the *ability* of each one to aid in applying that instrumentality. We have surveyed it in respect to the *presentation* of its appropriate motives, and the *plan* for carrying its principles into most *effective* operation. We have seen the tendency of system in beneficence to *diminish the expenditures* of benevolent societies, and enable them to prosecute their work on more *effective plans;* to *enlarge the number* of contributors to benevolent objects; to give to their contributions greater *regularity;* to make them more *proportionate* to each man's ability; to impart to them the more acceptable form of *free-will offerings*, thus increasing their moral value; to render beneficence a *delight*, by causing it to flow from a more *cheerful spirit;* to give increased *consistency* to Christian character; to raise the benevolent action of the church to a more *elevated Christian devotion;* and to promote *union among Christian denominations*, thus bringing the *whole united church* into active coöperation with Jehovah in the redemption of the world.

---

## CONCLUSION.

We hardly need say, that in the work of reducing beneficence to system in the church, and prosecuting it vigorously, more, under God, depends upon *pastors*, than upon any other class. They are the regularly constituted leaders of the flock. Their ordination is to this end. Their calling is to explain and enforce the doctrines of the gospel, and to develope and illustrate the spirit of that gospel, in its beneficent bearings upon the church and the world. Christianity is a mine of the richest ore. Who shall enter it as explorers, bring out its precious treasures, and apply them for the enriching of the church, for the good of the world, and for the glory of God, if they do not? "It depends upon us," says a distinguished pastor to his brethren, with respect to the great work of beneficence—"it depends upon us mainly, under God, whether the blessing shall ooze and trickle upon the world in scanty or occasional drops, or whether it shall flow in mighty streams. We are icebergs to the cause, or central fires in the midst of our population."

All things conspire at the present period to call out the beneficent power of the gospel, and to awaken its benevolent spirit in the hearts of God's people, for the salvation of the world. The prophecies and promises and providence of God bear directly and powerfully on the church, to arouse it to its appropriate work of doing good. Who shall interpret these to her, if her ministers do not? Who stand on such vantage ground as they, for bringing her to feel her obligations, and discern her privileges? The benevolent habits of her members need to be formed upon higher principles, and their beneficent action to be called forth by purer and more elevated motives. Who can be instrumental in accomplishing this, if they cannot? Who will lead the disciples to walk in the garden with their divine Master, and teach them to view their possessions there; or take them to the sacred mount, where all selfish considerations are lost in the love of the cross: who will do this, if they do not?

And if it is the duty of the shepherd to lead, is it

not the duty of the *flock* to follow? If he must inculcate the doctrine of beneficence, should they not cherish and exemplify its spirit? It is the spirit of Christ, and it flows out from him to the hearts of all his followers. And from them it should go forth, in ministries of love to the ignorant and suffering and guilty of earth's teeming population. For the diffusion of this spirit, the extension of Christ's kingdom, the church was constituted, and in this it is "the light of the world," "the salt of the earth." But it is only as ye Christians who compose this church, are like your divine Exemplar—only as the mind that was in him is also in you—only as ye commune with him in the garden, and have sympathy with him on the cross, that these his declarations can be verified. "Let your light so shine before men, that they may see your good works, and glorify your Father which is in heaven." "Remember the words of the Lord Jesus, how he said, It is more blessed to give than to receive." "Freely ye have received, freely give." "Inasmuch as ye have done it unto them, *ye have done it unto me.*"

"A poor wayfaring man of grief
Hath often met me on my way,
Who sued so humbly for relief,
That I could never say him nay:
I had not power to ask his name,
Whither he went, or whence he came;
Yet there was something in his eye
That won my love—I know not why.

"Once, when my scanty meal was spread,
He entered—not a word he spake—
Just perishing for want of bread.
I gave him all; he blessed it, brake,
And ate, but gave me part again.
Mine was an angel's portion then,
And while I fed with eager haste,
The crust was manna to my taste.

"I spied him where a fountain burst
Clear from the rock; his strength was gone:
The heedless water mocked his thirst;
He heard it, saw it hurrying on.
I ran and raised the sufferer up—
Thrice from the stream he drained my cup,
Dipt and returned it running o'er;
I drank, and never thirsted more.

"'Twas night, the floods were out, it blew
A winter hurricane aloof;
I heard his voice abroad, and flew
To bid him welcome to my roof:
I warmed, I clothed, I cheered my guest,
I laid him on my couch to rest,
Then made the earth my bed, and seemed
In Eden's garden, while I dreamed.

"Stript, wounded, beaten nigh to death,
I found him by the highway side;
I roused his pulse, brought back his breath,
Revived his spirit, and supplied
Wine, oil, refreshment: he was healed.
I had myself a wound concealed,
But from that hour forgot the smart,
And peace bound up my broken heart.

"In prison I saw him next; condemned
    To meet a traitor's doom at morn:
The tide of lying tongues I stemmed,
    And honored him 'midst shame and scorn.
My friendship's utmost zeal to try,
He asked if I for him would die;
The flesh was weak, my blood ran chill,
But the free spirit cried, 'I will'—

"Then in a moment to my view,
    The stranger darted from disguise,
The tokens in his hands I knew—
    My *Saviour* stood before mine eyes.
He spoke, and my poor name he named.
'Of me thou hast not been ashamed,
*These deeds shall thy memorial be;*
*Fear not, thou didst them unto me.*'"

MONTGOMERY.

1

# PUBLICATIONS

OF THE

# AMERICAN TRACT SOCIETY.

These works are not exceeded in high evangelical character, spiritual power, and practical worth, by any spiritual collection in any language. They have been carefully selected for the great body of intelligent readers throughout the country, and the most watchful parent may supply them to his family or to others, not only with safety to their best and eternal interests, but with hope of the richest spiritual blessings.

D'AUBIGNE'S HISTORY OF THE REFORMATION. A new translation, revised by the author, in four volumes 12mo, with portraits. Price $1 75 extra cloth.

BAXTER'S SAINTS' EVERLASTING REST, 12mo, in large type; also 18mo.

BUNYAN'S PILGRIM'S PROGRESS, 12mo, in large type, and 18mo. Both editions neatly illustrated.

JAY'S MORNING EXERCISES.

MASON'S SPIRITUAL TREASURY, *for every day in the year*. Terse, pithy, and evangelical.

FLAVEL'S FOUNTAIN OF LIFE, or Redemption *provided*.

FLAVEL'S METHOD OF GRACE, or Redemption *applied* to the Souls of Men.

BISHOP HALL'S SCRIPTURE HISTORY, or Contemplations on the Historical Passages of the Old and New Testaments.

BISHOP HOPKINS ON THE TEN COMMANDMENTS. Two standard works of the times of Baxter.

PRESIDENT EDWARDS' THOUGHTS ON REVIVALS.

VENN'S COMPLETE DUTY OF MAN.

OWEN ON FORGIVENESS, OR PSALM CXXX.

GREGORY'S (OLINTHUS, LL.D.) EVIDENCES OF CHRISTIANITY.

PALEY'S NATURAL THEOLOGY.

DR. SPRING'S BIBLE NOT OF MAN, *or the Argument for the Divine Origin of the Scriptures drawn from the Scriptures themselves.*

NELSON'S CAUSE AND CURE OF INFIDELITY.

MEMOIR OF MRS. ISABELLA GRAHAM. A new and standard edition.

MEMOIR OF MRS. SARAH L. HUNTINGTON SMITH.

SACRED SONGS FOR FAMILY AND SOCIAL WORSHIP. Hymns and Tunes—with a separate edition in patent notes. Also, the Hymns separately.

DODDRIDGE'S RISE AND PROGRESS OF RELIGION IN THE SOUL.

EDWARDS' HISTORY OF REDEMPTION.

VOLUME ON INFIDELITY, comprising five standard treatises: Soame Jenyns on the Internal Evidence; Leslie's Method with Deists; Littleton's Conversion of Paul; Watson's Reply to Gibbon and Paine.

PIKE'S PERSUASIVES TO EARLY PIETY.

PIKE'S GUIDE TO YOUNG DISCIPLES.

ANECDOTES FOR THE FAMILY AND THE SOCIAL CIRCLE.

UNIVERSALISM NOT OF GOD.

DIBBLE'S THOUGHTS ON MISSIONS

## ELEGANT PRACTICAL WORKS.

Wilberforce's Practical View.
Hannah More's Practical Piety.
James' Anxious Inquirer.
Jay's Christian Contemplated.
Elijah the Tishbite.
Nevins' Practical Thoughts.
Melvill's Bible Thoughts, selected by late Rev. Dr. Milnor.
Harris' Mammon.
Gurney's Love to God.
Foster's Appeal to the Young
Abbott's Young Christian
Abbott's Mother at Home
Abbott's Child at Home.
James' Young Man from Home.

## CHRISTIAN MEMOIRS

Rev. Claudius Buchanan, LL.D., including his Christian Researches in Asia.
Rev. John Newton.
Rev. Henry Martyn.
Rev. David Brainerd.
Rev. Edward Payson, D. D.
Harriet L. Winslow, Missionary in India.
James Brainerd Taylor.
Harlan Page.
Normand Smith.
Richard Baxter.
Archbishop Leighton.
Matthew Henry.
Rev. C. F. Schwartz, Missionary to India.
Rev. Samuel Pearce.
Rev. Samuel Kilpin.
Hannah Hobbie.

## OTHER SPIRITUAL WORKS.

Edwards on the Affections.
Baxter's Call to the Unconverted.
Alleine's Alarm to the Unconverted.
Flavel's Touchstone.
Flavel on Keeping the Heart.
Helffenstein's Self-Deception.
Pike's Relig. and Eternal Life.
Sherman's Guide to an Acquaintance with God.
Baxter's Dying Thoughts.
Matthew Henry on Meekness.
Andrew Fuller's Backslider.
Scudder's Redeemer's Last Command.
Scudder's Appeal to Mothers.
Burder's Sermons to the Aged.

## MISCELLANEOUS WORKS.

Bogue's Evidences of Christ'y.
Keith's Evidence of Prophecy.
Morison's Counsels to Young Men.
The Reformation in Europe.
Nevins' Thoughts on Popery.
Spirit of Popery, [with 12 engs.]
The Colporteur and Roman Catholic.
Mason on Self-Knowledge.
Beecher on Intemperance.
Raising of Lazarus from the Dead.
Hymns for Social Worship.

## POCKET MANUALS.

Clarke's Scripture Promises.
The Book of Psalms.
The Book of Proverbs.
Daily Scripture Expositor.
Gems of Sacred Poetry.
Bean and Venn's Advice to a Married Couple.
Reasons of Repose.
Daily Food for Christians
Heavenly Manna.
Cecil and Flavel's Gift for Mourners.
Daily Texts.
Diary, [Daily Texts interleaved.]
Crumbs from the Master's Table.
Milk for Babes.
Dew-Drops.

MANY OF THEM BEAUTIFULLY ILLUSTRATED WITH ENGRAVINGS

GALLAUDET'S SCRIPT. BIOGRAPHY, 7 vols., from Adam to David.
GALLAUDET'S YOUTH'S BOOK OF NATURAL THEOLOGY.
CHILD'S BOOK ON REPENTANCE.
PEEP OF DAY.
LINE UPON LINE.
PRECEPT UPON PRECEPT.
AMELIA, THE PASTOR'S DAUGHTER.
TREES, FRUITS, AND FLOWERS OF THE BIBLE, [9 cuts.]
ELIZABETH BALES. By John Angell James.
EMILY MARIA.
NEWTON'S LETTERS TO AN ADOPTED DAUGHTER.
CHILD'S BOOK ON THE SABBATH.
NATHAN W. DICKERMAN.
MARY LOTHROP.
JOHN MOONEY MEAD.
HENRY OBOOKIAH.
CAROLINE HYDE.
GALLAUDET'S LIFE OF JOSIAH.
THE DAIRYMAN'S DAUGHTER, etc
CHARLES L. WINSLOW.
WITHERED BRANCH REVIVED.
PEET'S SCRIPTURE LESSONS.
CHILD'S BOOK OF BIBLE STORIES
CHILDREN OF THE BIBLE.
AMOS ARMFIELD, or the Leather covered Bible.
THE CHILD'S HYMN-BOOK. Selected by Miss Caulkins.
SCRIPTURE ANIMALS, [16 cuts.]
LETTERS TO LITTLE CHILDREN [13 cuts.]
PICTORIAL TRACT PRIMER.
WATTS' DIVINE AND MORAL SONGS
With numerous similar works.

ALSO—

DR. EDWARDS' SABBATH MANUAL, Parts 1, 2, 3, and 4.
DR. EDWARDS' TEMPERANCE MANUAL.
IN GERMAN—31 vols. various sizes.
IN FRENCH—12 volumes.
IN WELSH—Pilgrim's Progress and Baxter's Saints' Rest and Call.

ALSO, upwards of 1,000 Tracts and Children's Tracts, separate, bound, or *in packets*, adapted for convenient sale by merchants and traders, many of them with beautiful engravings—in English, German, French, Spanish, Portuguese, Italian, Dutch, Danish, Swedish, and Welsh.

☞ It is the design of the Society to issue all its publications in good type, for the poor as well as the rich; and to sell them, as nearly as may be, at cost, that the Society may neither sustain loss nor make a profit by all its sales.

www.ingramcontent.com/pod-product-compliance
Lightning Source LLC
LaVergne TN
LVHW010150110826
845151LV00002B/475

* 9 7 8 1 4 2 5 5 3 7 0 9 8 *